The Team
That Changed
BASEBALL

T0307809

The Team
That Changed
BASEBALL

*Roberto Clemente and the
1971 Pittsburgh Pirates*

Bruce Markusen

WESTHOLME
Yardley

Westholme Publishing, LLC
904 Edgewood Road
Yardley, Pennsylvania 19067
Visit our Web site at www.westholmepublishing.com

ISBN: 978-1-59416-089-9
Also available as an eBook.

Printed in United States of America

Dedicated to the memory of
Dock Ellis

CONTENTS

PREFACE

With two outs and no one on in the top of the fourth inning, Mike Cuellar was in command of the most important game of the 1971 season—the seventh game of the World Series. A 20-game winner, the masterful Baltimore Oriole southpaw set down the first 11 Pittsburgh Pirates he faced with relative ease.

Roberto Clemente, the Pirates' aging superstar, was next to bat. Aside from the rivalry that had developed between the Pirates and the Orioles during the first six games of the World Series, these two baseball veterans simply didn't like each other. The previous off-season, Clemente had managed Cuellar in the Puerto Rican Winter League. Cuellar had annoyed the no-nonsense Clemente with his lack of conditioning and his refusal to follow orders in making specific pitches against certain hitters. When Clemente attempted to discipline Cuellar, he left the team in a huff, further infuriating his manager.

But Clemente's lesson was not lost on Cuellar. The Orioles' pitchers had been given a clear scouting report: *Throw Clemente breaking pitches and keep them low and away*. He would now show his manager that he knew how to pitch. Stepping into the batter's box, the Great One stretched his arms and rotated his head in his characteristic pre-swing preparation, settled in, and stared back at Cuellar. Cuellar took a deep breath and sent a looping curveball toward the outer half of the plate. But instead of breaking, this curveball hung high. For some batters, the pitch might have been impossible to hit—it was too high and too far outside. For Clemente, it felt right. Kicking his front leg toward the mound, he lunged and uncoiled a long, ferocious swing.

To Orioles outfielders Merv Rettenmund and Don Buford, the ball appeared to be catchable and they pursued it toward Memorial Stadium's warning track, but before they converged they slowed their strides. Both outfielders watched as the ball carried over their heads, and over the left-field wall. Having traveled nearly 400 feet in the air, the small white speck landed in a section of empty bleachers. The fans were stunned.

Clemente's unexpected home run delivered a crushing blow against a defiant pitcher who had showed him a lack of respect just one year earlier. More important, it gave the Pirates a 1-0 lead, putting the Pittsburgh team just six innings away from what was once considered unthinkable—a World Championship.

No one today would think there was anything unusual about these Pirates, but this was 1971, and no team in major league history had ever attempted to win the World Series with such an even mix of black, Latino, and white players. In 1971, newspapers and magazine articles still referred to black baseball players as "Negroes." There were just six black coaches employed by American and National League teams. Only one African American resided in any of the major league broadcast booths: Bill White, who had just been hired by the Yankees. There was not a single black or Latino general manager among the 24 major league teams. No team had an African-American or Latino field manager. And no team since the advent of integrated major league baseball in 1947 had ever fielded a team assembled purely on available talent with no consideration of skin color.

That last premise would finally change in 1971. The Pittsburgh Pirates, one of the most progressive organizations in the 1960s, would become responsible for a major shift in baseball orthodoxy. They assembled the best team they could, with ability being the only consideration—casting quotas and other unspoken prejudices aside. Their roster reflected this approach, and one night in September for the first time in major league baseball history the entire starting lineup happened to be made up of black and Latin American players. The Pirates' organization, from scouting through minor league development, to allotment of playing time in the majors, worked on the presumption that players would be chosen regardless of ethnic group and would get along on the field and in the clubhouse. But conventional wisdom said it could not be done, there would be too many obstacles, poor communication, and too many differences to overcome. The Pirates of 1971 would prove the "experts" wrong and in the process change baseball forever.

Chapter 1

UNWRITTEN RULES

Jackie Robinson's entrance into the National League in 1947 did not signal the end of racial bigotry in major league baseball. Nor did it spur major league general managers and owners to sign all of the best African-American and Latino talent available. Rather, the process of true racial integration in baseball—where players were judged by ability alone—took place much more slowly, over a period that spanned nearly two and a half decades.

Prior to Robinson's first game for the Brooklyn Dodgers, a number of Latin Americans—generally those viewed as light-skinned by white Americans—had played in the majors. Although some baseball historians have successfully argued that some of these Latinos were also black, and that some players presented as Cubans were actually African Americans, none of these players was credited with breaking baseball's most significant unwritten rule: the color line. Major league teams simply refused to sign black players who did not have Latino-sounding names, or who did not at least contend they were of Latin American descent. These men continued to be barred from Major League Baseball.

The ban on black major league players officially ended on April 15, 1947, when Robinson made his debut at first base for the Brooklyn Dodgers. Team president Branch Rickey had promoted Robinson from the club's top minor league affiliate, the Montreal Royals, where he had played in 1946. On July 5, Cleveland Indians owner Bill Veeck followed Rickey's lead when he signed outfielder Larry Doby, the first African-American player in the American League. That same month, the St. Louis Browns purchased the contracts of outfielder Willard Brown and infielder Hank Thompson from the Kansas City Monarchs, one of the best teams in the Negro

Leagues. In August, Dan Bankhead joined Robinson on the Dodgers' roster to become the majors' first African-American pitcher. These five players joined a handful of Latin Americans, including Mike Guerra and Jesse Flores of the Philadelphia Athletics, who already held jobs in the major leagues.

After Jackie Robinson, baseball's integration proceeded at a snail's pace for three seasons. Reflecting the feeling of some executives and players in baseball, *New York Daily News* sports editor Jimmy Powers once said "Robinson will not make the grade in the major leagues. . . . The Negro players simply don't have the brains or skills." In 1948, the Dodgers promoted former Negro Leagues star Roy Campanella, the first—and ultimately one of the few—minority catchers. Only one other black player, venerable pitcher Satchel Paige, debuted in 1948. Paige signed a contract with Veeck's Indians, drawing the wrath of such publications as *The Sporting News*, which railed against adding a forty-something hurler well past his prime. Meanwhile, the Washington Senators, one of the most progressive teams in their pursuit of Latinos, added two Cubans to their roster: shortstop Angel Fleitas and pitcher Ramon Garcia. The Senators, who employed full-time scout Joe Cambria in Cuba, had signed a number of Cuban players in 1944 and 1945, but they had disappeared from the roster. In 1948, the Indians defeated the Boston Braves four games to two in the World Series. The Indians boasted only two black performers, Hall of Famers Larry Doby and Satchel Paige, while the Braves featured not a single African American or Latin American on the roster.

Although some baseball historians have contended that racist motivation prevented a faster rate of integration in the late 1940s and early 1950s, one of the most significant writers of the time cited a completely different reason. Wendell Smith, writing for the black newspaper, the *Pittsburgh Courier*, believed that a shortage of black players in 1948 had slowed the pace of integration. "The scouts are out there snooting around like Scotland Yard detectives looking for talent," Smith wrote, "but having a difficult job uncovering it. The fact that Cleveland signed the [42-year-old Paige] indicates that there is a definite shortage of talent, both white and Negro."

Smith argued that the Negro Leagues had featured far more talent during the twenties and thirties. "It was better talent than we have today," wrote Smith in the *Courier*, "and plenty of it. That's why there won't be a large number of Negro players in the majors for some time to come." Smith believed that the major leagues would have to wait several years for young black players to graduate from American sandlots. Despite Smith's optimism, it would be more than "several years" before all players had an equal opportunity.

The Negro Leagues, a direct result of baseball's color line, flourished alongside major league baseball, and became immensely popular in the 1930s and 1940s with stars such as Cool Papa Bell, Josh Gibson, Satchel Paige, and Judy Johnson (all of whom are now Hall of Famers and all played, prophetically, for the Pittsburgh Crawfords). The leagues began a rapid decline with the integration of Major League Baseball in 1947, and before the decade was out, the Negro Leagues had essentially disappeared. Nearly all of players left in the wake, however, never had an opportunity to play in the majors, despite minor league contracts and outstanding performances.

By winning six World Series in the seven years from 1947 to 1953, the New York Yankees were the epitome of baseball excellence. The Yankees, however, did not debut their first black player until 1955, when catcher-outfielder, Elston Howard, earned a promotion from the minor leagues. In four of those World Series, the Yankees defeated the Dodgers, who had unquestionably led the way in the effort to integrate major league baseball with black players. Despite their impressive pioneering spirit, the Dodgers numbered no more than five black players on any of those National League pennant teams. And although the presence of five black athletes on a 25-man roster was progressive for the time, the Dodgers had signed very few Latino players during that span of years. Over the next few decades, the number of minority players on any given team would expand and contract, but another unwritten rule was beginning to take shape: quotas.

In addition to unstated quotas, throughout much of the 1950s, black players and white players on the same teams stayed at separate hotels. In some cases, hotel space for black players could not be obtained, necessitating that the team's minorities sleep in the homes of black families, on the team's bus, or in even less desirable locations. Black players who hoped to eat in restaurants with their white teammates often encountered segregated seating policies, or outright rejection. Under such circumstances, black and white players had little chance to spend time with each other away from ballpark or clubhouse settings.

Baseball's rate of African-American integration remained relatively steady over the balance of the decade, while the number of Latino entries increased, and then dipped. In 1955, 12 black players made their major league debuts, including a black Latino, the Pirates' own Roberto Clemente. In terms of Latino talent, three Puerto Ricans, eight Cubans, and three Panamanians joined major league clubs that season.

The 1955 Brooklyn Dodgers made several major inroads on the integration path. For the first time, a World Championship team featured four black players in the regular lineup: Jim "Junior" Gilliam at second base, Jackie Robinson at third base, Sandy Amoros in left field, and Roy Campanella behind the plate. The team's best starting pitcher, Don Newcombe (20-5, 3.19), became the first black hurler to post two 20-win seasons in the major leagues. Yet, the Dodgers, after trading pitcher Joe Black in mid-season, carried no other African-American players on their pitching staff. Similarly, there were no black players on the bench.

The class of 1958 black newcomers totaled 13, including Jim "Mudcat" Grant of the Indians (who would wind up with the 1971 Pirates) and Leon Wagner of the Giants. Joining Wagner for the Giants' first season in San Francisco were Latino standouts Felipe Alou and Orlando Cepeda, who represented the best of the eight Spanish-speaking entrants.

In 1959, major league clubs added 16 black players, most of whom joined National League teams. The Boston Red Sox became the last team to integrate when they promoted Elijah "Pumpsie" Green and later in the season, pitcher Earl Wilson. The new wave of black stars was laden with impressive talent, including future Hall of Famers Bob Gibson of the Cardinals, Willie McCovey of the Giants, and Billy Williams of the Cubs. Highlighting the class of five Latinos who debuted in 1959 were Cubans Mike Cuellar of the

Reds, who would ultimately face the Pirates in the 1971 World Series, and Puerto Rican Jose Pagan of the Giants, who would find himself a member of the Pirates championship team in 1971.

Despite the Dodgers, Giants, Reds, and other teams showing some aggressiveness in adding minorities to their roster, these additions were often accompanied by transactions that dispatched other minority players, leaving teams with a similar racial makeup year after year.

In 1959, the Dodgers won their first World Championship while in Los Angeles—debuting the postseason talents of pitchers Don Drysdale and Sandy Koufax, but the team continued to provide opportunities to only a fixed number of minorities. Jackie Robinson had already retired, and Sandy Amoros played only five games and had a mere five at-bats during the regular season, but Junior Gilliam remained, John Roseboro had replaced Roy Campanella behind the plate, and Charlie Neal was the starting second baseman. Maury Wills and Tommy Davis made their major league debuts on this team, although Davis received just one at-bat, while Wills served primarily as a utilityman. The Dodgers' opponent in the World Series, the Chicago White Sox, carried only two black veterans for part of the season, Harry Simpson and Larry Doby.

In 1960, the Yankees returned to the World Series and faced the upstart Pirates. New York, as usual, was loaded with talent, including Mickey Mantle, Yogi Berra, Roger Maris, Whitey Ford, and African-Americans Elston Howard and Jesse Gonder, and Latinos Hector Lopez and Luis Arroyo. The last four were the only minorities on the team. The Pirates also featured great talent, including stars like Dick Groat, Bill Mazeroski, Don Hoak, and Roberto Clemente in their starting lineup; in addition, the minority presence included Gene Baker, Roman Mejias (from Cuba), R. C. Stevens, and Joe Christopher (of the Virgin Islands) off the bench; and Bennie Daniels and Diomedes Olivo on the pitching staff. The Pirates were typical of major league ball clubs of the time, but they would soon move beyond the rest of baseball.

By 1961, black players had begun to stay with whites in hotels and eat with them in restaurants during the regular season.

Yet, at spring training sites in the South, particularly in Florida, segregation remained an alarming practice. As sportswriter Wendell Smith wrote in the *Chicago American*, "the Negro player who is accepted as a first-class citizen during the regular season is tired of being a second-class citizen in spring training." Smith went on to describe specific ways in which black major leaguers encountered pre-season segregation. "The Negro player resents the fact that he is not permitted to stay in the same hotels with his teammates during spring training, and is protesting the fact that he cannot eat in the same restaurants, nor enjoy other privileges."

This alarming practice affected the Pirates, as well. When the Bucs traveled to spring training sites like St. Petersburg, Florida, the white players on the team were immediately taken to one of the city's first-class hotels. Black players—whether they be journeymen like Roman Mejias, solid contributors like Donn Clendenon, or even stars like Roberto Clemente—were relegated to seedier lodgings in the poorer sections of town.

Such methods of segregation affected the morale of many black players. "We have a terrible time during spring training," one African-American player told Wendell Smith anonymously. "We played an exhibition game in one town, for example, and afterward couldn't find a decent place to eat. We couldn't eat in the same hotel with the other players and there wasn't a decent Negro restaurant in the town. We went to a store and bought a loaf of bread and some cold meat. . . So we walked around the streets and ate the bread and cold meat like a bunch of vagrants."

In response to Smith's reporting, teams like the Cubs and White Sox soon announced that they would stay only at spring training hotels that would willingly house all of their players, regardless of color. The Cubs, who based their preseason camp in Mesa, Arizona, also declared that they would not play any exhibition games in southern cities where hotels refused to permit black patrons. Yet, such open-minded responses did not occur across the board. Other teams, like the Kansas City Athletics, announced that they would continue to abide by their hotel's segregationist policy.

Baseball entered a new era in 1961, when the American League expanded by two teams. The National League followed suit with two expansion clubs in 1962. In theory, the four new teams would provide additional opportunities for talented players to make major league rosters.

The Giants of the early 1960s featured a multitude of black and Latino standouts and seemed poised to break all the unwritten rules, assembling a championship team based on talent alone. The 1962 team, which included eight minorities, won the National League pennant before bowing to the Yankees in the World Series. In 1963, the Giants maintained their minority corps of Orlando Cepeda, Jose Pagan, Willie McCovey, Willie Mays, Felipe Alou, and Juan Marichal, and added players like Jim Ray Hart, Jesus Alou, and Jose Cardenal to the mix. Yet even with such an array of talent, the Giants fell off to 88-74, 11 games behind the league-leading Dodgers. The cause, in part, may have been the San Francisco management. The front office discouraged Latino players from associating with each other. Manager Alvin Dark banned the speaking of Spanish in the clubhouse and on the field, a decision that made Latino players even less comfortable in unfamiliar environs. "Alvin Dark segregated the team," recalls Orlando Cepeda. "He [divided] the whites, the blacks, and Latins. We had to strike against that, you know, being black and being Latin." It was an unspoken legacy that stretched back to the days when the team was still in New York. Giants owner Horace Stoneham, when pressed by manager Leo Durocher to recall Willie Mays from the minor leagues in the early 1950s, delivered this rebuttal: "No, we've got too many [blacks] already."

The compositions of teams like the Dodgers, Giants, Reds, and St. Louis Cardinals throughout the 1960s displayed the National League's superiority over the American League in the quest to fully integrate baseball. These teams enjoyed substantial progress in populating their teams with high-quality Latino and African-American players, having succeeded in scouting and signing minority players, and promoting the most talented ones to the highest professional level. Yet, most of the minority players on these—and other—teams played as regulars, particularly at first base and in the outfield. For example, the 1967 World Champion Cardinals included only three minorities on their bench: Alex Johnson, Dave Ricketts, and Bobby Tolan. In general, very few African-American and Latino players made major league rosters as utility players. It was clear that most teams in the fifties and sixties were operating under another unwritten rule: an African American or Latino had to be considered a star, or at least good enough to make it as a starter, to be included on the roster—at all. The utilityman, backup, and pinch-hitting jobs would fall to the white players, unless a black athlete had shown that he was unquestionably superior.

Much like the tendency to keep black and Latino players from having bench jobs, many clubs discouraged the development of minority pitchers and catchers. Even the most progressive National League teams of the sixties had lagged behind in their development of African-American and Latino pitchers. Players like Bob Gibson, Don Newcombe, and Juan Marichal represented a minuscule percentage of teams' pitching staffs. Unfortunately, very few organizations exhibited trust in African American and Latino pitchers and catchers to be able to call games. Therefore, those teams rarely recruited minority amateurs as pitchers, but sought to convert them to the so-called "athletic" positions of center field and shortstop. Second, only the most dominant minority pitchers gained advancement to the majors. Borderline black and Latino pitchers had to compete for back-end spots in the starting rotation and roles in long relief, and often lost out to white pitchers of similar abilities. Minority players had long since proven their worth to major league teams, but only as outstanding members of a starting lineup. Yet, most major league teams had little interest in keeping African Americans and Latinos around in any other capacity. In that way, general managers and owners could maintain an acceptable quota of minority players while still keeping the overall numbers of such players low and reinforce their own misguided beliefs about the ability of black and Latin American players to act in leadership roles or to direct a team from the mound or from behind the plate.

In 1969, the major leagues expanded by four teams, and re-aligned into four divisions, with East and West factions in both the American and National leagues. The following year, the Pirates won the National League Eastern Division title. In total, 15 minorities played at some point for the Pirates during the 1970 season, alongside 21 white regulars and spot players who came and went from the minor leagues. While Manny Sanguillen, Willie Stargell, Matty Alou, and Roberto Clemente were all secure in their positions, the Pirates did not feature an African American or Latino who played the infield as a regular throughout the season. Whether this was because the talent was not available or upper management—like the rest of baseball—was still wary of having too much of a minority presence is not clear. Furthermore, the Pirates of 1970 were not a championship team in the classic sense. They won the division with a record-low 89 wins, but failed to win the National League pennant, losing in an embarrassing series to the Reds in three straight games. But when it came to putting together next season's team, Pittsburgh general manager Joe Brown was willing to make a gamble—one that would break all the unwritten rules and that would pay off handsomely.

Chapter 2

ASSEMBLING A TEAM

S ome observers of the national pastime contend that pennants are won and lost in August and September. Others believe that the early months of April and May are critical to the launching of a divisional or league championship, or nowadays at the least a wild-card berth. One might also argue that pennants are decided in November and December, when a general manager establishes his team's nucleus for the following season. As Hall of Fame manager Earl Weaver once said, "A manager's job is simple. For 162 games, you try not to screw up all that smart stuff your organization did last December"—when trades are made, free agents are signed, and expensive, fading veterans are released.

The Pittsburgh Pirates of 1971 pre-dated the era of free agency, but the composition of the team evolved through a careful blend of off-season trades and minor league promotions. As general manager Joe Brown waded through the months prior to opening day 1971, several key decisions awaited his attention. The son of famed comedic actor Joe E. Brown, the younger Brown had been the Pirates general manager since 1956 and had a reputation as being a baseball intellectual who evaluated players for their ability alone— not their color or rank in a quota system—and who listened to and trusted his scouts. He also listened to his players, and Roberto Clemente proved to be an excellent judge of talent.

The Pirates had finished the 1970 season at 89-73, good enough to claim the franchise's first postseason berth since the championship season of 1960. The 1970 Pirates followed up what some considered a mediocre divisional championship by falling to the Cincinnati Reds in a three-game playoff sweep. The loss to the Reds dictated that the Pirates needed to make tangible moves to elevate themselves to a World Series level.

Joe Brown's first concern, however, involved his manager, Danny Murtaugh, known as the "Whistling Irishman" for whistling loudly in between pitches during his playing days. Now, in his third tour of duty as Pirates' manager, he had successfully guided the Bucs into postseason play, earning Murtaugh *The Sporting News* Manager of the Year Award. Despite the Pirates' success and general acclaim for his managerial skill, Murtaugh was pondering whether he should return for another season. He had suffered numerous health problems over the past decade, and had resigned as the team's manager back in 1964 due to a serious heart condition. After working as a Pirates' scout, Murtaugh came back to manage for part of the 1967 season before again giving up the post to become the Bucs' director of player acquisition and development.

Murtaugh enjoyed a close relationship with most of his players, even though he was from a different generation and culture. The son of an Irish Catholic shipyard worker, Murtaugh had grown up in a ramshackle house in a tough, poverty-stricken city neighborhood. According to the Associated Press, the Murtaugh house featured a "hole in the floor, and in order to get to the kitchen the family had to walk across a plank." His family struggled so much to pay its bills that Murtaugh often walked the railroad tracks near his neighborhood searching for coal to heat their home. After graduating from Chester High School in Pennsylvania, Murtaugh hoped to enter professional baseball, but received no playing offers. Murtaugh settled for a job in the shipyards, performing menial work like catching rivets in a cup for 34 cents an hour.

In the years before Jackie Robinson's integration of baseball, Murtaugh received a tryout and a pro contract with the Cardinals' organization, and eventually earned a berth in the major leagues. Murtaugh played for nine seasons with the Phillies, Boston Braves, and Pirates during a lackluster career that was interrupted by infantry service in World War II. He then remained in baseball, becoming a coach with the Pirates.

When Murtaugh returned to the Pirates for his third stint as manager, he replaced Larry Shepard, whose managerial tenure had been marked by losing and in-fighting. Murtaugh succeeded in molding a fragmented, divisive clubhouse into a more familial unit.

As New York sports writer Jimmy Cannon described the Pirates: "It was a cranky team under Harry Walker and Larry Shepard. Guys didn't get along. They complained and split into grumbling factions. But Murtaugh appears to have straightened them out. The tension isn't obvious anymore. They don't talk as if they were dissatisfied."

Although Cannon did not publicly attribute clubhouse friction to racial problems, it seemed that some of the factions had separated along ethnic lines. With Murtaugh in charge, the Pirates did not suffer from racial divisiveness. "Murtaugh's a beautiful dude," pitcher Dock Ellis told *Sport* magazine in 1971. "Beautiful. Winning. That's all he cares about. Nothing else. Screw up, you hear about it. Black or white." The press seemed to agree with Ellis' assessment of Murtaugh. After the 1971 season, *New York Times* sportswriter Arthur Daley lauded Murtaugh for his fairness. "He treated all the same," wrote Daley, "never playing off one man against another. He gave the blacks a fair shake, too."

Murtaugh often handled the issue of race the way he did other concerns—with humor. One day during his playing career, in a game against the Brooklyn Dodgers, Murtaugh stepped to the plate and took a called strike. Murtaugh objected to the call by umpire Beans Reardon, who then ejected Danny with a quick jerk of his arm. "Listen, Beansy," Murtaugh announced (according to a media report), "these guys got [Don] Newcombe pitching, [Roy] Campanella [catching], and [Jackie] Robinson at second—all colored guys. They got that Italian, [Carl] Furillo, in right field. They got [Gil] Hodges at first base, and I don't even know what in the hell he is." Murtaugh continued his speech, finally making his point. "In short, Beansy," said Danny, "you and me are the only Irishmen on the field and you're proposing to throw half of us out of the game." Reardon, changing his original decision, told Murtaugh to step back into the batter's box and continue his at-bat.

Although Murtaugh hailed from an older, more conservative generation than his Pirate players, he did his best to tolerate their "radical" ways. Murtaugh did not particularly care for his players' long hair, large Afros, and "mod" clothing, but he allowed his players such forms of self-expression in the early 1970's. Murtaugh was willing to tolerate his players' fashion statements in exchange for their respect, loyalty, and dedication to the Pirate cause of playing hard and winning.

Murtaugh worried that the stresses and anxiety of managing, coupled with the strain of traveling, might prove detrimental to his physical well-being. Shortly after the Pirates' playoff loss to the Reds, Murtaugh met with Brown to discuss his future. Murtaugh put off making a commitment either way so that he would have more time to consider the pros and cons of continuing. If Murtaugh were to declare his retirement, Brown was prepared to offer the managing job to the Pirates' well-respected coach, Bill Virdon. Although Pittsburgh executives held Virdon in high regard, they had no desire to see Murtaugh leave his post.

After weeks of wrangling with the decision, Murtaugh made a formal announcement on November 12. It was what Brown and the Pirate players had hoped to hear. "I think I will be a healthier and wiser manager,"

Joe L. Brown joined the Pittsburgh Pirates' front office in 1954 and became general manager one year later, succeeding Branch Rickey. Named "Major League General Manager of the Year" by *The Sporting News* in 1958, Brown traded for third baseman Don Hoak, catcher Smoky Burgess, and pitcher Harvey Haddix as the final critical pieces to the 1960 World Championship team. Throughout the sixties, Brown pursued a plan to build another championship team by heavily recruiting minority players, giving the Pirates one of the most diverse clubhouses of the era. (*National Baseball Hall of Fame Library, Cooperstown, NY*)

the popular Murtaugh proclaimed at the press conference announcing his return. Brown and Murtaugh agreed on a one-year deal that would pay Murtaugh $50,000 for the 1971 season.

Relieved that Murtaugh was in place for another year, Brown turned his attention toward adjusting his pennant-contending roster at baseball's annual winter meetings in Los Angeles. Some writers speculated that starting center fielder Matty Alou was at the center of a proposed trade for Reggie Jackson of the Oakland A's, but that turned out to be nothing more than a rumor. In November 1970, Brown held trade talks with Kansas City Royals general manager Cedric Tallis. Brown targeted some of the young pitchers the Royals might be willing to surrender in return for the right package of position players. Finally, at the winter meetings, Brown engineered a seven-player trade with the Royals. The December 2 deal, however, did not involve Matty Alou. Instead, Brown let go of diminutive shortstop Freddie "The Flea" Patek, backup catcher Jerry May, and right-handed pitcher Bruce Dal Canton in exchange for three players: backup catcher Jim Campanis, reserve shortstop Jacinto "Jackie" Hernandez, and—the key to the deal—hard-throwing right-hander Bob Johnson.

Joe Brown was clearly captivated by a 27-year-old pitcher who could throw better than 90 miles an hour, possessed an above-average breaking ball and exhibited the versatility to start or relieve. In 1970, Johnson had finished second to Minnesota's Bert Blyleven in *The Sporting News*' rookie pitcher of the year voting. Johnson had displayed a live arm, striking out 206 batters, the most of any American League right-handed pitcher, surpassing even Jim Palmer, who was considered the league's best right-handed starter. That impressed Brown more than Johnson's unsightly won-lost record of 8-13. Brown realized that Johnson's ledger was affected by playing for a Royals' team that had entered the American League in 1969 as an expansion franchise. In their first season, the Royals finished 69-93; in 1970, they regressed to a record of 65-97, 33 games back in the Western Division. The Royals didn't exactly feature an offensive powerhouse in 1970, having trailed the American League in runs scored with a measly total of 611. Lack of run support explained Johnson's sub-.500 record more than his own pitching inefficiency.

If Brown had experienced any doubts about the trade, they were nullified when, after making the deal, he received inquiries from two American League general managers about Johnson just before the December 15 inter-league trading deadline. Another high-ranking official, Baltimore Orioles player personnel director Harry Dalton, had already expressed the opinion that Johnson could crack the O's vaunted starting rotation, which featured three 20-game winners in Mike Cuellar, Dave McNally, and Jim Palmer. Buttressed by opinions such as those, it was easy for Brown to tell other teams that Johnson would not be traded.

The qualities that Brown viewed in Johnson were apparent. The qualities that he saw in Jackie Hernandez were not. The 30-year-old Cuban shortstop possessed the look of an expansion player. In his first full season as Kansas City's shortstop, Hernandez had stolen 17 bases, totaled 40 RBIs, and exhibited deftness in the field. In 1970, Hernandez stole only one base while batting .231. Hernandez had all the makings of a good fielder, but a player's defensive skill, no matter how good, could not justify a lack of everyday offense. Even a notoriously weak hitter like the Baltimore Orioles' shortstop Mark Belanger had mixed in a few decent offensive seasons with his otherwise unproductive bat. And while Hernandez was a good defensive shortstop, he was no Mark Belanger, who was a perennial Gold Glove winner.

But the Pirate general manager realized he needed a shortstop— any shortstop—in the deal, since he was trading Patek in order to obtain Johnson and knew that Pittsburgh's regular shortstop, Gene Alley, continued to be bothered with injuries. Brown decided that Hernandez would suffice. "Hernandez was the regular Kansas City shortstop in 1969. Hernandez can't hit. But he can field," Brown explained to *The Sporting News* in a brutally honest scouting report that hardly served as a riveting endorsement. Although it was difficult for most Pirate observers to see at the time, perhaps even for Joe Brown, the little-known Hernandez would become the most important player of the seven in the deal between the Royals and Pirates.

Brown firmed up another even more important trade on January 29. He finally decided to deal center fielder Matty Alou, sending him to the St. Louis Cardinals for outfielder Vic Davalillo and popular right-handed pitcher Nelson "Nellie" Briles.

For Briles, the deal to the Pirates represented the first time in his major league career that he had been traded. At first, Briles felt somewhat traumatized by the trade. "I was obviously shocked at the time, and disappointed because I had put an awful amount of time and energy into my years with St. Louis. They were successful years with World Championships and pennants. But as I thought about it on the drive back to my house, I said, 'Wait a minute, the Pirates have just won a division in 1970, they've got a good ballclub, and it doesn't look like they're making a lot of changes. Here might be a chance to get back in the World Series again.' So that kind of softened the blow. But I think the first time you're traded, that's probably the most traumatic one."

At best, the swap of Matty Alou and Vic Davalillo seemed like a wash for the Pirates. Joe Brown had watched Alou's batting average fall off to .297 in 1970, after a torrid .331 in 1969. Yet, the five-foot, nine-inch, 160-pound Alou was regarded as the best bunter in the National League, was capable of executing the hit-and-run, and still owned enough foot speed to swipe 19 bases. His exit, along with the previous departure of Freddie Patek, left the Pirates devoid of their two best base-stealing threats. In the field, Alou possessed a ragged arm, but was still considered an above-average center fielder.

Davalillo played a similar game to Alou, but lacked his aggressiveness on the base paths. While he fit the scout's definition of a "professional hitter"—one who was capable of line drive after line drive—he had shown little inclination to use his speed to steal bases over the previous two seasons. On defense, he played left field creditably, but his arm was just as weak as Alou's. Most significantly, Davalillo's frail build and advancing age (34) prevented him from playing the outfield on an everyday basis.

Still, there was some logic to Brown's thinking. Brown felt that Alou's abilities in center field were declining and believed that he would soon have to replace him with a younger man. The Pirates also had a young outfielder in Al Oliver, who had shown the ability to hit for both average and power, with a splash of speed thrown into the all-purpose mix. A regular player for the Pirates, Oliver had played 151 games in 1970, but had split his time between first base—his best position—and both left and right field, where he felt far less comfortable. With star players like Roberto Clemente and Willie Stargell firmly entrenched in right and left field, respectively, and with the youthfully powerful Bob Robertson beginning to stake claim to first base, Brown began considering other ways of getting the 24-year-old Oliver into the lineup. Furthermore, Brown worried that the

Al "Scoop" Oliver (left) was signed by the Pirates as an amateur free agent in 1964. A seven-time All-Star selection over his 18-year career, Oliver was a productive batsman and capable fielder for Pittsburgh, but had more celebrated seasons later in his career with Texas and Montreal. Signed by Cincinnati as an amateur free agent in 1958, Vic Davalillo (right) played for Cleveland, California, and St. Louis before being traded to the Pirates in 1971. Davalillo proved to be one of the most productive and versatile bench players on the '71 championship team. (*National Baseball Hall of Fame Library, Cooperstown, NY*)

constant shifting from one defensive position to another had affected Oliver's hitting ability. He had enjoyed a fairly productive second season in 1970, but both his batting average and home run total had fallen off from the level of his rookie year. In order to achieve his potential, Oliver needed a stable place in the Pirates' lineup.

In considering other possibilities—and there were few given that Oliver was a left-handed thrower—Brown regarded center field as the best available option. By way of the media, Oliver had already sent Brown a public message indicating that he could handle the stressful demands of the position. "I played center field in the instructional league two years ago," Oliver told Charley Feeney, corresponding for *The Sporting News*. "I think I can play it. One thing I'd like for next year. I'd like to have one regular position. . . I'll play center field if they want me." Still, Brown needed more input before making a final decision. He sought out the opinion of Pirates coach Bill Virdon, who had been a fine defensive outfielder during his major league career and had played regularly in center field for Pittsburgh's 1960 World Championship team. Virdon agreed with the general consensus that Roberto Clemente was Pittsburgh's premier defensive outfielder, but he regarded Oliver as second best on the team, despite his lack of everyday experience.

Although others in the Pirate organization felt Oliver might be lacking in center field, Brown decided to take heed to Virdon's advice. During the off-season, Oliver played center field for the San Juan Senadores (Senators), the winter league team that was managed (not so coincidentally) by Clemente. The great right fielder offered a favorable opinion of Oliver's defensive play. "He plays too shallow with men on base," Clemente explained in an interview with *The Sporting News.* "[But] it is a fault that will be corrected the more he plays the position." Now that he had been awarded the center field job, the Pirates believed Oliver would better his .270 average and 12 home runs.

Although the Bucs appeared to have plenty of starters—what with Steve Blass, Dock Ellis, Luke Walker, Bob Moose, and the newly acquired Bob Johnson and Nellie Briles—Joe Brown was fully aware the Pirates would need the pitching insurance he had supplied. Staff ace Steve Blass had been hit by a line drive in 1970 and had failed to win a game from the Fourth of July through mid-August. Dock Ellis' elbow injury had landed him on the disabled list from August 10 through September 17. The versatile Bob Moose had struggled through a bout with tendonitis, while veteran left-hander Bob Veale had been bothered by a chronically sore shoulder. These pitchers comprised nearly 50 percent of the Pirate pitching staff—hardly the physical condition Murtaugh and Brown desired of a pennant-contender.

In the bullpen, closer Dave Giusti, who had enjoyed a career year in 1970, and well-traveled veteran Jim "Mudcat" Grant, recently acquired from the A's, appeared to form a devastating late-inning tandem. That left only two spots open on the 10-man staff. Of the potential candidates, the Pirates considered promising young right-hander John Lamb—who happened to be Steve Blass' brother-in-law—a favorite to latch onto one of the long relief roles.

If there was a weakness to be found on this pitching staff—other than the brittle condition of several starting pitchers—it was the lack of depth from the left side in the bullpen. Brown and Murtaugh would have to choose from 35-year-old Bob Veale, non-roster journeyman southpaw Ramon Hernandez, and minor league veterans Ray Cordeiro and Lou Marone. Veale had enjoyed success as a starter but had little experience as a reliever and was suffering from a sore back and advancing age. Hernandez and the other contenders were relatively unproven. If none of the left-handers panned out, Brown might be forced to make yet another trade to bolster his pitching staff. Otherwise, Murtaugh would have to ask Dave Giusti and Mudcat Grant to face tough left-handed hitters like Matty Alou and Lou Brock of the Cardinals, Chicago's Joe Pepitone and Billy Williams, and San Francisco's Willie McCovey in critical late-inning situations.

Trades brought in key help, but the success of the team hinged on the core veteran Pirates. Roberto Clemente had already reached superstar status, Manny Sanguillen had emerged as one of the best catchers in the National League, and Dave Giusti had become one of the league's most reliable closers. Second baseman Bill Mazeroski, although approaching the end of his career, remained an excellent defensive player. Yet, left fielder Wilver Dornel Stargell was a major league disappointment. He had not driven in 100 runs since the 1966 season, when he came closest to superstardom, finishing that year with 33 home runs, 102 RBIs, and a tidy .315 batting average. In 1970, he had slumped to a .264 average. To make matters worse, a torn tendon in Stargell's heel had limited him to 136 games and only 85 RBIs. Yes, Stargell had established himself as a very good player with his mammoth power and strong outfield throwing arm, but he had yet to experience the breakout season that the Pirates had envisioned.

Stargell vowed to have a better season in '71. "It will be different this time," Stargell promised Charley Feeney of the *Pittsburgh Post-Gazette*. "I want to concentrate on avoiding injuries. You know, those muscle pulls that slow you down." Stargell set a goal of playing in at least 152 out of 162 games.

Skeptics would have been excused if they had dismissed Stargell's remarks as so much talk. Stargell was no longer a young prospect who could be expected to improve greatly from one season to the next. After all, Stargell would turn 31 in 1971. (Most players reach their physical peak between the ages of 26 and 29, according to baseball writer Bill James, who has has studied players' performance by age. Thirty is an age when many players embark upon a gradual decline that will continue for the rest of their baseball careers, not when they are likely to show sudden improvement.) Stargell also carried too much weight on his six-foot, two-inch frame, a fact that was often pointed out by critics of the slugger. In the past, Stargell had used spring training as a time to lose weight that he had gained during the winter. Stargell planned a different kind of spring training regimen in 1971. "For the first time, I am going to spring training to work and not to think of my weight," Stargell told Feeney. "I am going to work harder than I ever did in my life. But it isn't going to be a weight-reducing practice." A healthier and more confident Stargell would give the Bucs a legitimate cleanup hitter against right-handed pitching, and provide ample protection for Roberto Clemente, the all-important No. 3 hitter in the Pirate lineup.

The Pirates featured another player of potential, but questionable production, in lefty-swinging third baseman Richie Hebner. Although scouts applauded the 23-year-old Hebner's ability to adeptly field topped grounders and slow choppers, critics claimed that he lacked the sure hands, fielding range, and strong arm required of playing the hot corner on the new artificial playing surface of Three Rivers Stadium. Offensively, in his first two full major league seasons, Hebner had batted .301 and .290, respectively, but seemed to lack the power that the Pirates ideally wanted from their regular third baseman. Hebner had totaled only 19 home runs in his first 880 major league at-bats. Joe Brown and the Pittsburgh media made it clear that they wanted Hebner to improve his defense and power production to give the Bucs another left-handed threat to complement the home run swing of Willie Stargell.

According to one of baseball's oldest clichés, a ballclub must be strong up the middle. Playoff-bound teams usually have quality

Selected by the Pirates in the first round of the 1966 amateur draft, Richie Hebner (left) had seemed destined for a career swinging a hockey stick, not a baseball bat. As a standout hockey player in high school, Hebner was scouted heavily by several National Hockey League teams. In 1966, the Boston Bruins used their first draft pick to select Hebner, whom they projected as a big, high-scoring winger at the NHL level. To Boston's disappointment, Hebner rejected a $10,000 bonus from the Bruins, and opted for a $40,000 bonus from the Pirates. "I'm no money grubber," Hebner contended in an interview with the *New York Times*. "It's just that I liked baseball better." By 1971, Manny Sanguillen (right) had emerged as one of the best catchers in the National League. Signed by Pittsburgh in 1964 after a short career as an amateur boxer, "Sangy" would play 12 years for the Pirates, including both of their World Championship seasons of the 1970s. (*National Baseball Hall of Fame Library, Cooperstown, NY*)

players at catcher, second base, shortstop, center field, and on the pitching mound. At most of these positions, the Pirates seemed dubious, at best—with one exception. The Pirates' catching situation was one of the strongest in the majors. Manny Sanguillen had emerged as the National League's second-best catcher behind Johnny Bench of the Cincinnati Reds. Sanguillen's live bat, strong throwing arm, and smiling clubhouse personality made him one of the league's most desired backstops.

Sanguillen had not started playing baseball until the age of 18, when he had enrolled in Bible school in Panama. When Pirate scouts Howie Haak and Herb Raybourn (who eventually signed

Sanguillen) had first observed the energetic Panamanian, they witnessed a raw talent, a youngster who was playing out of position as an infielder-outfielder. "You look like a catcher," Haak told Sanguillen, according to an article that appeared in the March 1971 issue of *Sport* magazine. When Sanguillen disagreed, Haak replied, "You will be a catcher!" But not without a struggle. Sanguillen recalled the first time that he chased a foul pop-up as a catcher, while playing a game in Panama City. "I run and I run, and all of a sudden, the ball hit me on the head. Then I hear the fans boo," Sanguillen told *Sport*. "I can laugh about it now. It wasn't funny when it happened. I run back, back and I don't see ball. Then my head. . . oh, how it hurt. The people... they don't think it was funny. . . They called me crazy when I got hit on the head with the foul pop-up." Sanguillen had struggled with other basic aspects of defensive play behind the plate. "I did not really understand this game when I first started," he told Charley Feeney, corresponding for *The Sporting News*. "I made many mistakes. I didn't know how to shift my feet when I was catching. I didn't know how to call for certain pitches." Haak, impressed by Sanguillen's quickness, agility, and strength, as well as his bat speed, believed that he would soon make it to the major leagues as a catcher. By 1971, a polished Sanguillen had confirmed Haak's beliefs—and justified Raybourn's decision to sign him—by becoming one of the game's best receivers, and also one of its hardest-hitting catchers.

In case Sanguillen went down, the Pirates featured a potentially fine backup receiver in Milt May, who had played in the International League the previous season. In 1970, he batted .280 with 21 homers and 86 RBIs for Columbus and was voted the International League's top prospect. Indeed, May's combination of strength *at* the plate and quickness *behind* the plate made him one of baseball's best minor league prospects.

D espite the Pirates' first-place finish of 1970 and the additions of Johnson and Briles to the pitching staff, media experts refused to brand the Bucs as pre-season favorites in the National League East. In fact, most pre-season publications tabbed the Pirates for either second or third place in the improved division.

Numerous questions about the team's personnel dogged the front office as the Pirates headed into the new season. Most experts recognized the ability of the Pirates' offense: Roberto Clemente, Willie Stargell, Manny Sanguillen, Richie Hebner, Al Oliver, and Bob Robertson formed the nucleus of arguably the best eight-man line-up in the major leagues. The Pirates did not lack for power, or .300 hitters, or good baserunners. Yet, their regulars lacked patience at the plate. In 1970, the Pirates had drawn only 444 bases on balls, or about 2.7 per game, figures that represented the lowest totals of any major league team. At times, the Pirates' unwillingness to take walks had prematurely ended potentially large scoring rallies.

As spring training in Bradenton, Florida, approached, Joe Brown expressed optimism over the potential of his team. And he was clearly proud of his fruitful offseason transactions. "I feel we are the only contender in the [National League] East who has made any significant improvements," Brown told Charley Feeney of the *Pittsburgh Post-Gazette*. Brown, who had been with the organization for 17 seasons, including the World Championship team of 1960, told *The Sporting News* without hesitation: "This Pirate team is the best rounded, most talented club since I've been in Pittsburgh."

Those words might have been considered sacrilege by supporters of the 1960 Bucs, who featured a young Roberto Clemente, the terrific double-play combination of Bill Mazeroski and National League Most Valuable Player Dick Groat, solid veterans in Don Hoak and Bob Skinner, and pitching mainstays like Vern Law, Bob Friend, Vinegar Bend Mizell, Harvey Haddix, and ElRoy Face. Some of the older observers of baseball in Pittsburgh probably rolled their eyes over Brown's audacity in comparing the new Pirates to those Pirates. Little did they realize that Brown knew some things about the 1971 team that few others did.

Chapter 3

SPRING TRAINING

W ith an atmosphere of bold optimism about the upcoming season, Pirate catchers and pitchers reported to Bradenton's
McKechnie Field on February 17 and awaited the arrival of the
team's infielders and outfielders in Florida on February 21. As the
Pirates embarked on spring training, the team's double-play combination represented manager Danny Murtaugh's largest concern. The
second base position posed a special dilemma. The team's brass
deemed part-timer Dave Cash ready to battle Pirate legend Bill
Mazeroski for the starting job. Especially popular with the team's
fans, Maz had been the Pirates' starting second baseman since 1956,
when he was only 19 years old. The 15-year veteran had also
endeared himself to most mainstream baseball fans—at least those
that didn't favor the New York Yankees—with his historic ninth-
inning home run in Game Seven of the 1960 World Series.

Yet it was Mazeroski's marvelous defensive play that thrilled the
game's purists. His resume included eight Gold Gloves in the brief
14-year history of the award. In his prime, Maz had been blessed
with good range and soft hands. He owned a lightning-quick trigger
on the double play pivot, so fast that he was given the nickname of
"No-Touch," for he barely held the ball in his glove before making
an instantaneous transfer to his bare hand and throwing on to first
base.

Defensive abilities aside, the Pirates had to face certain negative
realities regarding their longtime pivotman. Maz was now in his
mid-thirties and coming off one of his worst offensive seasons in the
majors: a .229 average with only seven home runs and 39 RBIs. To
make matters worse, he had not won a Gold Glove since 1967, a
product of his diminishing range afield. As one scout so brutally
summarized, Maz still had great hands, but his legs were gone.

By contrast, Dave Cash had batted .314 in a reserve role in 1970, and had displayed the kind of speed, range, and hitting ability that Maz no longer possessed. The biggest concern the Pirates had about Cash revolved around consistency—specifically on defense. They knew he possessed the tools to become a fine major league middle infielder, but pondered the same questions that any team might have regarding a young second baseman: whether he could make the routine plays game after game and execute the double play pivot skillfully. The Pirates were defending National League East champions and they needed a reliable second baseman who could handle ground balls in the late innings and who could work in tandem with a veteran shortstop like Gene Alley.

Although Mazeroski supported Cash and took time to tutor him on the finer points of defensive play, he was not yet ready to relinquish his second base throne. "I think I have a couple of more good years in front of me," Mazeroski told Charley Feeney, corresponding for *The Sporting News*. "People have asked me about retiring. I'm not thinking about it right now."

The battle between Cash and Mazeroski for the starting second base position provided enough intrigue that it drew attention from baseball writers and observers outside of the Pittsburgh area. As award-winning baseball scribe Bud Saidt wrote in the Trenton (New Jersey) *Evening Times* that spring: "A major part of the daily drama here is watching 22-year-old Dave Cash easing 34-year-old Bill Mazeroski out of the Pirates' lineup and into the rocking chair. It hasn't happened completely, but it will."

In the article, Cash credited Mazeroski with helping to educate him about the subtleties of playing second base, a position that required both finesse and efficiency. For example, Mazeroski taught Cash to keep his feet planted while turning the pivot at second base, and emphasized that foot quickness, rather than hand quickness, was essential in turning the double play. "Everything I know about playing second base I've learned from Maz," Cash told Saidt. "He has helped me in so many ways it would be impossible to list them. From the moment I first showed up here, representing a threat to his job, he has gone out of his way to work with me."

The relationship between Cash, a young black man who was relatively new to the big leagues, and Mazeroski, an established white
veteran, typified the Pirates' unity—racial and otherwise. As Saidt
described, veteran major leaguers of previous generations rarely
made an effort to help out younger, up-and-coming players. In fact,
older players often went out of their way not to speak to rookies. Yet,
in 1971, Cash was not subjected to such harsh treatment. "Never
happened to me," Cash said in the article. "I doubt it happens to too
many others nowadays. Times have changed in baseball." Then, as
Saidt wrote, Cash "pointed to the color of his face." Mazeroski, the
fading white incumbent in jeopardy of losing his job, had willingly
offered his own expertise and guidance to Cash, the younger, more
talented black prospect. Cash, in turn, had gracefully accepted the
advice and wisdom of Mazeroski, without the skepticism or hesitan-
cy often seen in a young player.

Such relationships had been mostly foreign to baseball in previous decades—with one notable exception. In the late 1940s,
Brooklyn Dodger teammates Jackie Robinson and Harold "Pee Wee"
Reese had forged a special friendship. Robinson had initially experienced resistance from both white opponents and teammates.
Reese, a Southerner from Kentucky, later came to Robinson's
defense, essentially sending players and fans the message to lay off.
Reese, who would eventually become Robinson's full-time double
play partner, befriended his young teammate at a time when it was
not considered fashionable for white players to fraternize with black
players, even those who wore the same uniform.

Cash's own strength of character played a key role in his ability
to deftly handle the competition with the well-liked Mazeroski.
Pittsburgh writers described Cash as articulate, intelligent, hard-
working, and disciplined, the kind of qualities that would help
Pittsburgh fans and media accept Cash more readily if he were to
secure the second base job during the coming season. And what if
Mazeroski were to retain the position, rendering Cash a second-
string utilityman? Cash assured reporters that there would be no
tantrums or pouting sessions in response. While acknowledging that
he wanted to play every day, Cash emphasized the importance of
being unselfish, something that he and Mazeroski had talked about
during the spring.

Signed by the Pirates in 1954 and called up to the big leagues in 1956, Hall of Famer Bill Mazeroski (left) will forever be remembered for his game-winning home run against the New York Yankees in the bottom of the ninth inning of Game Seven of the 1960 World Series, a win that gave the Bucs their first World Championship since 1925. By 1971, "Maz" was relegated to back-up duty, but still played a key role as one of the team's leaders. Dave Cash (right) was selected by the Pirates in the fifth round of the June 1966 amateur draft. With his amiable disposition and dedication to the game and its history, Cash proved to be the ideal replacement for the aging, but popular Mazeroski at second base. (*National Baseball Hall of Fame Library, Cooperstown, NY*)

The other part of the Pirates' middle infield suffered a setback, however, during the team's first full-scale spring training workout. The team's starting shortstop, Gene Alley, suffered a broken hand while taking batting practice. Pirates team physician Dr. Albert Ferguson estimated that Alley's cast would be removed by late March, a timetable that would almost certainly prevent him from being ready for Opening Day. The Pirates would have to thrust the newly acquired Jackie Hernandez into the spotlight sooner than originally anticipated. With little hesitation, Danny Murtaugh delivered a solid endorsement of Hernandez as a starter. "Until Gene Alley gets healthy, Jackie Hernandez is my shortstop," Murtaugh told the *Pittsburgh Press*.

On February 26, the Pirates suffered another blow to their pitching staff's already suspect manpower. As promising right-hander John Lamb, one of the candidates for a long relief job, lobbed pitches to Dave Cash during a routine batting practice, the second base hopeful hit one of the pitcher's tosses particularly hard. The ball—a searing line drive up the middle—eluded the protective screen that usually shielded batting practice pitchers, striking Lamb just above the right ear. The Pirates quickly carted the young pitcher to a local hospital, where a follow-up examination revealed that Lamb had suffered a fractured skull.

Injuries were becoming the unfortunate theme of the Pirates' spring camp in Bradenton. In addition to the mishaps suffered by Lamb and Alley, third baseman Richie Hebner injured his non-throwing shoulder, landing him on the sidelines for several days. Later in the spring, the Pirates learned that utility infielder Jose Martinez would have to undergo surgery to repair damaged cartilage in his left knee.

Amidst the feelings of pessimism brought upon by the wave of injuries, the Pirates opened the exhibition season on March 5 in Sarasota against the Chicago White Sox. In a relatively uneventful game, the Pirates totaled only three hits but capitalized on defensive mistakes by infielders Bill Melton and Lee "Bee-Bee" Richard to post a 2-1 victory. The Pirates' offense lacked its usual sock, in part because of the absence of Manny Sanguillen, Richie Hebner, and Roberto Clemente. Jackie Hernandez impressed Pittsburgh's coaching staff with a 2-for-4 effort and a run scored. Defensively, Al Oliver showed his adaptability to center field by backing up a bad throw to second base. As for the pitching staff, Dock Ellis hurled three solid innings in a starting role and unveiled nearly a half-dozen effective change-ups, which he was now throwing with an altered grip at the suggestion of pitching coach Don Osborn. Luke Walker, Dave Giusti, and rookie Ray Cordeiro followed Ellis by each pitching scoreless stints of relief.

For Giusti, the exhibition opener represented the first in a series of personal tune-ups for his unquestioned role as the Pirates' relief ace. One season earlier, spring training had conjured up an entirely different scenario. Based partly on Clemente's recommendation, Joe Brown had acquired Giusti from the Cardinals on October 21, 1969. Previously, Giusti had been an effective starting pitcher for the Houston Astros, winning 37 games over a three-year stretch spanning from 1966 to 1968. Curiously, the Astros decided to leave Giusti unprotected in the expansion draft and watched him get selected by the Padres. San Diego then dealt him to St. Louis in a five-player trade. Giusti shuttled between starting and relieving jobs with the Cardinals while enduring a back injury. He struggled badly in the role, prompting the trade to the Pirates. He arrived in Pittsburgh's 1970 camp looking to make the team in a less-than-glamorous role as the staff swingman, pitching mostly in long relief, but he longed to be part of the starting rotation.

In an unplanned stroke of luck, Danny Murtaugh turned to Giusti as his closer during the 1970 season. After pitching horribly in the spring of 1970, Giusti switched to short relief, as part of Murtaugh's desperate attempt to relocate his confidence. Giusti responded by using an array of pitches that he had accumulated as a starter to set up his "out" pitch: the palmball. Giusti went on to log 66 games and 103 pressure-packed innings, while recording 26 saves, second-highest in the National League. In reward for his outstanding work, Murtaugh tabbed Giusti as the Pirates' most valuable player of the 1970 season. Giusti ranked as the league's sixth most efficient pitcher, according to the much-debated George Sisler rankings, behind Tom Seaver, Dick Selma, Ferguson Jenkins, Bill Singer, and Bob Gibson. The palmball specialist even garnered significant support in the Cy Young Award voting, finishing fourth behind heavyweight starters Gibson, Gaylord Perry, and Jenkins. At the age of 30, Giusti had found a new career for himself as one of the top closers in the major leagues.

The Pirates won their first four exhibition games, even though Roberto Clemente had yet to make an on-field appearance. There was nothing physically wrong with Clemente; Danny Murtaugh had simply decided to give his star right fielder and elder statesman some time off. Clemente finally made his spring training debut on March 9, when the Pirates traveled to St. Petersburg to face the New York Mets, another contender in the National League East. Clemente went 0-for-2 in a 3-0 loss to the pitching-rich Mets.

Although Clemente was not ailing in any way, Murtaugh had chosen a cautious approach in playing his venerable star only occasionally during the spring. During the offseason, the 36-year-old

Clemente had undergone treatment on his bad back. The problem dated back to December 31, 1954, when a drunk driver had broadsided his car at 60 miles per hour. The impact of the crash had jarred three of Clemente's spinal discs, causing him chronic back pain for the rest of his career. As a result, Clemente habitually rotated his head and neck before and during most at-bats, as part of a continual effort to loosen his back muscles.

In 1970, Clemente's back had acted up more than ever, limiting the aging outfielder to 108 games. In spite of recurrent back pain, Clemente had still marveled as a hitter; his .352 mark in 1970 represented the second highest batting average of his career. Nonetheless, doctors decided to give Clemente's back a thorough examination in late November. The check-up, followed by Clemente's rehabilitation, gave the Bucs every indication that he would be healthy in 1971.

Although Clemente's batting skills remained crisp and his back pain manageable, he had reached the stage of his career where he might not be able to play every day, especially on the unyielding artificial turf of Three Rivers Stadium. Therefore, Murtaugh had no intention of extending him during spring training, especially in games that had no bearing on the pennant. Despite his age, Clemente was still the most important player on the Pirates' roster.

Prior to the 1971 season, Clemente had made a riveting impression on the national media at the annual Baseball Writers' Association of America banquet in Houston. There he received the Tris Speaker Award for his lifelong accomplishments in baseball, and during his acceptance speech, which one awestruck writer called the best he'd ever heard from a major league player, Clemente delivered perhaps his most memorable observation:

> "If you have an opportunity to accomplish something that will make things better for someone coming behind you, and you don't do that, you are wasting your time on this earth."

He also addressed his desire for improved race relations, an issue that had affected his own relationships with teammates, opponents, the media, and fans throughout his career, imploring the audience to "live together and work together, no matter what race or nationality."

At the end of his speech, the crowd of more than 800 baseball writers and dignitaries stood and applauded. As *The Sporting News* reported, the Master of Ceremonies, Morris Frank, turned to Reverend Tom Bagby, who was about to deliver the invocation and said, "Tom, you'd better learn to play right field. This guy has taken your field."

On March 12, the Pirates opened up an unusual three-game series in Panama City, Panama. The Pirates played a team of all-stars selected from the Panamanian Professional Baseball League. The all-star team featured several current major leaguers, including Gil Garrido of the Atlanta Braves, Chico Salmon of the Baltimore Orioles, and a youngster named Renaldo "Rennie" Stennett, one of the Pirates' own minor league prospects. The Panamanian team also included another Pirate property, backup catcher Jim Campanis, whom the Bucs agreed to loan out just two hours before gametime.

After Hall of Famer Joe DiMaggio threw out the ceremonial first pitch, the Pirates lost the first game, 3-2. In the second game of the series, they were blanked by former major league hurler Pedro Ramos, 1-0. The Bucs then salvaged the finale, 8-0, thanks to the combined shutout pitching of Dock Ellis and Bob Veale, and a grand slam home run by one of the team's newcomers, Vic Davalillo. In addition, Sanguillen contributed a home run. Sangy, who went 5-for-11 in the three-game set, exhibited no signs of jitters playing in front of his mother, who had never seen her son play professionally.

One development in the Panamanian series was unexpected: the 19-year-old Stennett had impressed the team's front office by doing damage for one of the Pirates' opponents. Stennett had hardly been mentioned in the preseason publications that highlighted each team's top minor league prospects. Now the Pirates talked publicly about the possibility of promoting the teenaged prospect two full levels—from Class-A Salem to Triple-A Columbus. While at Salem, the young second baseman-outfielder had won the Carolina League batting title with a .326 clip. Stennett then followed up his regular season performance by capturing the batting championship in the fall instructional league.

After the Pirates returned from their Panamanian jaunt, they proceeded to string together another series of stateside victories. Despite the rash of injuries during spring training, the Pirates had raced out to a National League-best record of 10-3 in Grapefruit League play. The efforts of the starting pitchers, coupled with the fine batting performances of Dave Cash and Richie Hebner, had given Pittsburgh even more reason to be optimistic about the 1971 pennant race. Although there were still questions at the shortstop position, the Pirates had now even convinced the Baseball Writers' Association of America that they were the team to beat in the National League's Eastern Division. Despite receiving fewer first-place votes from the writers than the Chicago Cubs, the Pirates' vote total, bolstered by a large number of second-place predictions, put them just ahead in the overall tally.

The next order of business called for the Pirates to reduce their roster to the mandatory 25-man limit. A wave of spring cuts contained some intriguing talents. Pitchers Bruce Kison and Ramon Hernandez—who would both earn recalls to Pittsburgh later in the season—fell victims to the Pirates' pitching depth. Top outfield prospect Richie Zisk, who led the Class Double-A Eastern League with 34 home runs for Waterbury in 1970, was also included on the cutdown list. He had impressed the Pirates with his powerful spring swing, but with a starting outfield of Willie Stargell, Al Oliver, and Roberto Clemente, there was no place for Zisk on the roster. . . yet.

With the regular season only days away, the Pirates played three of their final preseason games against the same team that had swept them in last year's National League Championship Series—the Cincinnati Reds. In the first exhibition game, Bill Mazeroski batted 2-for-4 out of the leadoff spot, Richie Hebner drove in three runs, and Al Oliver slammed a game-tying ninth-inning home run against Cincinnati's relief ace, Clay "Hawk" Carroll. In spite of such individual efforts, the Pirates lost to the Reds when Tony Perez lined a game-winning single against Bob Veale in the bottom of the ninth. The Pirates found encouragement, however, in the unexpected early return of Gene Alley, who had made incredible progress in the rehabilitation of his broken hand. He started the game at shortstop before being lifted for a pinch-hitter prior to his first at-bat.

After two games against the Chicago White Sox and one against the Boston Red Sox, the Pirates readied for two more grudge matches against the Reds. In the first game, Alley played all nine innings. Al Oliver and Vic Davalillo each delivered two hits in the 5-4 victory over the National League champs, yet Mudcat Grant struggled in relief. He allowed back-to-back ninth-inning homers to Tony Perez and Johnny Bench before holding on for the victory.

In their next game, the Pirates delivered a sterner message to the Reds—and the rest of the National League. Dave Cash and backup outfielders Gene Clines and Vic Davalillo each banged out three hits, while Richie Hebner supplied the power, cracking two home runs and driving in a half-dozen runners in a 12-0 shellacking. The offensive showing overshadowed an excellent start by Nellie Briles, who thwarted the Reds' lineup on five hits and no runs through seven innings.

The wins over the Reds provided the Pirates with a dose of confidence as they prepared for the National League pennant chase. After losing to Cincinnati last October, Danny Murtaugh had sung the praises of a Reds' team that seemed on the verge of a dynasty. "They're the best club I've seen since the old Brooklyn Dodgers dominated our league," Murtaugh told Charley Feeney. Murtaugh was referring to Dodger teams that had won pennants in 1952, '53, '55, and '56 and included future Hall of Famers Jackie Robinson, Pee Wee Reese, Duke Snider, and Roy Campanella, and stalwarts like Gil Hodges, Carl Furillo, and Don Newcombe. Without question, Murtaugh had placed the Reds of the early seventies with some heavy company.

In its April 10, 1971, issue, *The Sporting News* offered capsule previews of all 24 major league teams. The Pirates' beat writer, Charley Feeney, wrote the following summary of the National League's defending Eastern Division champions:

> "Pitching—Strong point with addition of Briles and Johnson.
>
> Catching—Real strong because of Sanguillen's durability and Milt May's potential.

Infield—Alley's physical condition key to it all.

Outfield—Davalillo valuable No. 4 man behind Clemente, Stargell, and Oliver.

Summation—Best Pirate club since 1960 World Champions."

If Feeney's assessment were to be believed, Joe Brown's pre-season optimism had been founded—not in wishful thinking—but in a tangible level of talent.

Chapter 4

APRIL

The mix of injuries and unexpected developments left the Pirates with the following Opening Day roster as they broke spring training:

CATCHERS (3): Manny Sanguillen, Milt May, Charlie Sands
INFIELDERS (7): Bob Robertson, Dave Cash, Gene Alley, Richie Hebner, Jose Pagan, Bill Mazeroski, Jackie Hernandez
OUTFIELDERS (5): Willie Stargell, Al Oliver, Roberto Clemente, Gene Clines, Vic Davalillo
PITCHERS (10): Steve Blass, Dock Ellis, Luke Walker, Bob Moose, Nellie Briles, Bob Johnson, Mudcat Grant, Dave Giusti, Jim Nelson, Bob Veale

With his roster and pitching staff in place, Murtaugh was now faced with another traditional rite of spring—that of making out an Opening Day lineup. The Pirates were scheduled to open at home against the Phillies and their veteran left-hander Chris Short, so Murtaugh countered with a predominantly right-handed hitting lineup:

Bill Mazeroski, 2B
Richie Hebner, 3B
Roberto Clemente, RF
Manny Sanguillen, C
Bob Robertson, 1B
Willie Stargell, LF
Al Oliver, CF
Jackie Hernandez, SS
Dock Ellis, P

In a surprising move, Murtaugh bypassed the impressive spring phenom Dave Cash and selected old reliable Bill Mazeroski, not only as his second baseman but also as his leadoff man. Mazeroski, not known as a prolific hitter or base-stealing threat, had served as a leadoff man very briefly about 10 years earlier, and only because of an injury to the team's regular leadoff hitter, Bill Virdon.

While Murtaugh's decision to employ Mazeroski as his leadoff man for the opener seemed to make little practical baseball sense, it may have reflected the manager's respect for one of the senior members of his team. Perhaps Murtaugh wanted Maz to enjoy one last hurrah as a starting second baseman on Opening Day. Or maybe Murtaugh sought to ease the pressure on a relative novice like Cash. Whatever the rationale, Cash reacted to the decision with class. "I know I'm going to get plenty of chances to play this year," Cash told Charley Feeney. "Our main concern is winning. You have to be unselfish in this game."

The Opening Day game against the Phillies would offer evidence that the routines and practices of the spring, criticized as boring and inconsequential by some, can reap dividends during the regular season. Pirates batting coach Bill Virdon had spent each day of spring training working with two or three pitchers to sharpen their bunting skills. The repetition seemed to have a lasting effect on Dock Ellis, who was called upon to bunt three times in the opener and succeeded each time. Two of the bunts moved runners up a base and set up scoring rallies. The other, a successful squeeze bunt, scored a run directly from third base. Ellis' bunting ability overshadowed his own stellar pitching—nine innings of two-run, eight-hit baseball, with eight strikeouts thrown in for good measure in a 4-2 win.

The Bucs resumed their schedule on April 8. Another left-hander, Woodie Fryman, took to the hill for the Phillies. As a result, Danny Murtaugh used the same lineup, and tabbed his own left-hander and his most effective starting pitcher in 1970, Luke Walker, as his starter. Walker and Fryman shackled opposing batters through the first five innings, before the Pirates finally broke through against Fryman in the bottom of the sixth inning.

In the past, Willie Stargell had often heard criticism that he did not fare well against left-handers, despite a .273 mark against them

The 1971 Pittsburgh Pirates. Front Row, seated, left to right: Nelson Briles, Jose Pagan, Vic Davalillo, Ramon Hernandez, Coach Bill Virdon, Coach Don Osborn, Manager Danny Murtaugh, Coach Don Leppert, Coach Frank Oceak, Coach Dave Ricketts, Dock Ellis, Manny Sanguillen, and Charlie Sands. Middle Row, standing, left to right: Equipment Manager John Hallahan, Gene Alley, Bob Miller, Jack Hernandez, Dave Cash, Bill Mazeroski, Rennie Stennett, Roberto Clemente, Willie Stargell, Al Oliver, Milt May, Trainer Tony Bartirome, Team Physician Dr. Joseph Finegold, Traveling Secretary John Fitzpatrick. Top Row, standing, left to right: Luke Walker, Carl Taylor, Dave Giusti, Bob Veale, Bob Moose, Bob Johnson, Bruce Kison, Steve Blass, Bob Robertson, Gene Clines, and Rich Hebner. (*National Baseball Hall of Fame Library, Cooperstown, NY*)

in 1970. In his second start of the new season, Stargell belted a two-run double against Fryman, who had earned a reputation for being especially nasty against southpaw hitters. Although Stargell was subsequently left stranded by Al Oliver, the two runs would prove sufficient for Walker. The left-hander, in a start reminiscent of his success the previous September, held the Phils to five hits and cruised to a complete-game 2-0 shutout. The Pirates had played two games—both wins—and Murtaugh had still not signaled to the bullpen.

The Pirates moved their pitching show to the road the next night in Atlanta. Braves skipper Lum Harris selected right-hander Pat Jarvis as his starter, which forced Murtaugh to make some refinements with his lineup. Murtaugh promoted Stargell and Oliver to the fourth and fifth positions, while dropping Bob Robertson and Manny Sanguillen to sixth and seventh, respectively.

Stargell responded ably to the demands of the cleanup position, playing a part in five of the Bucs' runs during an 8-2 destruction of the Braves. His three hits included his first home run of the season, a two-run blast in the sixth inning off reliever Ron Herbel. The following night, taking advantage of the warm, humid air of Atlanta, Stargell tormented Braves knuckleballer Phil Niekro to the tune of two home runs, and hit a third against Atlanta left-hander George Stone. The occasion marked the third time in his career that "Big Willie" had clouted three home runs in a single game. The trio of longballs accounted for four runs, but was not sufficient to prevent an extra inning loss to the Braves. Hank Aaron's two-run ninth inning homer against Steve Blass squared the game at 4-4. Three innings later, a single by Hal "The Horse" King against reliever Nellie Briles scored Ralph Garr with the game-winning run. Briles, in his debut as a Pirate, surrendered a leadoff triple to Garr, then walked Aaron and Orlando Cepeda to intentionally load the bases before yielding the hit to King. Although no player wanted to make a bad first impression on his new team, Briles had done just that.

The loss to Atlanta highlighted concerns about the top of the batting order. Leadoff man Bill Mazeroski and second-place hitter Richie Hebner failed to reach base in 12 plate appearances, minimizing the impact of Stargell's multiple home runs. The Pirates needed better overall tablesetting, and more speed, from the first two slots in the order. Sooner or later, Murtaugh would have to turn the offense's ignition role over to a younger and faster player.

To no one's surprise, Dave Cash earned his first start of the season the following afternoon. Murtaugh installed his swift second baseman into the leadoff role, but the adjustment did not forestall a 3-1 loss. Cash delivered a hit that scored Jackie Hernandez in the fifth inning, but the Pirate offense was stymied by the pitching of "Jumbo" Jim Nash, who scattered seven hits in a complete-game victory. Dock Ellis—the complete-game loser—pitched well, but fell to 1-1 after tiring in his final two innings.

On April 13, the Pirates scored a 9-3 win in the second game of a series against the Phillies. Five different Pirates, including Willie Stargell and reliever Nellie Briles, slammed home runs during an 11-hit assault against three Phillies hurlers. Stargell, with five home runs in seven games, had accounted for half of the Pirates' season total of 10 home runs.

Playing on April 16, a Friday night, Dock Ellis and the Pirates faced one of the National League's best pitchers, the Mets' Tom Seaver. The Mets won the Shea Stadium duel, 1-0, on a fourth inning home run by former Pirate slugger Donn Clendenon. Seaver derailed the Pirates' offense, limiting Pittsburgh to a scarce three hits.

The Pirates bounced back the next day with a 2-0 shutout of the Mets, thanks in large part to Steve Blass' complete-game performance and Willie Stargell's sixth roundtripper in the seventh inning. On Sunday, the Mets and Bucs split a doubleheader, dividing the four game series at two wins apiece. In the nightcap, Gene Alley made his first start of the season at short, playing nine errorless innings in the field and belting a solo home run at the plate. The return of Alley provided Murtaugh with another option at the all-important shortstop position.

Still, the Pirates had to be more than a bit concerned after watching the dominant pitching of Tom Seaver. Man for man, the Pirates appeared to be the deeper and better team than the Mets, but they did not possess a franchise pitcher who could match the likes of a Seaver. If the pennant race were to come down to one series in

September—perhaps even one game—and Seaver were on the mound, the Bucs' offense might be hard-pressed to mount many substantial rallies against the future Hall of Famer. In general, despite Stargell's long balls, the Pirates were experiencing difficulty scoring runs. Other teams, like the Mets and Cardinals, could succeed without scoring bushels of runs per game. If the Pirates were to win the National League East, they would need to be an outstanding offensive team, not just a good one.

After a shutout at the hands—and knuckles—of Phil Niekro, the Bucs rebounded with a 10-run outburst in a victory over the Braves on April 21. Stargell hit three home runs, duplicating his feat earlier in the season in Atlanta. This time, the trio of home runs took place in front of the Three Rivers Stadium faithful, a small contingent of 7,992 fans. Stargell's first, fourth, and sixth inning moonshots accounted for six runs in a 10-2 victory, the kind of win that Danny Murtaugh had been expecting to see more often. Now with four career three-home-run games, Stargell joined the only three other major leaguers—all future Hall of Famers—who had accumulated as many three-homer games: Johnny Mize, who held the record with six, and Ernie Banks and Ralph Kiner, who did it four times apiece.

Stargell's hitting was aided by the Pirates' new ballpark. In 1970, the Bucs had started out the season in old Forbes Field, before moving into the newly built Three Rivers Stadium on July 16. "Modern," reinforced concrete, antiseptic stadiums featuring the synthetic turf, like Three Rivers, were the latest thing. Cincinnati had brand-new Riverfront Stadium, and another of these "cookie-cutter" stadiums was about to open up in Philadelphia, where Veterans Stadium would replace the decrepit Connie Mack Stadium, which like Forbes and Crosley, had fallen victim to old age and the wrecking ball. Forbes Field had featured deeper, more spacious power alleys that were not as inviting as the dimensions of Three Rivers. The right field power alley at Forbes Field measured 408 feet, while the left field power alley stretched out to 406 feet. At its deepest point, just to the left of straightaway center field, the distance measured 457 feet. As a result, no Pirate team had ever led the National League in home runs while playing at Forbes Field.

In contrast, the power alleys at Three Rivers measured a more reasonable 385 feet to both right-center and left-center field, and 410 feet to its deepest point in center field. Given those dimensions, it came as no surprise that the Pirates had hit 30 home runs in 40 games at Three Rivers during the second half of the 1970 season, as opposed to only 14 home runs at Forbes Field over the first 42 home games of the season.

Stargell achieved another significant bit of baseball history the following night when he collected his 10th home run in a 7-4 decision over the Braves. The solo blast matched the major league record for most home runs in the month of April, the shortest month of the regular season (excluding the few days played in October). In 1969, Baltimore's Frank Robinson had clubbed 10 homers in April, a feat that was equaled the following season by the Reds' Tony Perez. The humble Stargell appeared unmoved by the sharing of such a record. "The record is the last thing in my mind now," Stargell told *The Sporting News*. I'm just happy to be swinging so good, so early." In spite of his modesty, Stargell seemed primed for the breakout season that Pittsburgh critics had been clamoring for throughout his Pirate career.

Stargell's early-season power spree had prompted some writers to place him in the same category as the game's established stars, players like Aaron, Clemente, Mays, and Yastrzemski. The hot-hitting Stargell intimidated opposing pitchers with his massive size and uppercut swing; he also unnerved some of them with his ritualistic "wind-milling" of the bat. As he awaited each pitch, Stargell rocked back and forth in the batter's box, motioning his bat forward, pointing it for a moment toward center field, and then bringing the bat backward for another swirl. The wind-milling seemed to relax Stargell and aid his timing at the plate. At the same time, the constant motioning of the bat appeared to wear down the concentration of opposing pitchers, as if they envisioned serving up another pitch for Stargell to knock out of the park's confines.

One night after the barrage led by Stargell, the Pirates' offense again disappeared, this time against the San Francisco Giants. With Stargell held out of the lineup with a virus, rookie right-hander Steve Stone—who in 1980 would win the American League Cy

Young Award for the Baltimore Orioles—stymied the Bucs on five hits and earned his first major league victory, a 2-0 shutout.

The Pirates' frustration continued the next day. With a weakened Stargell sitting out again, young left-hander Ron Bryant—a reliever who was pitching only because of an injury to scheduled starter Frank Reberger—limited the Pirates to three hits in a 2-0 Giants win. For the second straight game, the Bucs had allowed a young, unproven pitcher to spin his first major league shutout. And without Stargell in the lineup, the Bucs badly lacked his middle-of-the-order presence. The Pirates, the team with arguably the best eight-man lineup in the National League, had now been held without a run for 20 consecutive innings and had been shut out four times.

Stargell returned to the lineup for the finale against the Giants, picking up one hit in four at-bats, as the Bucs' offense lifted the club to a 6-2 victory over San Francisco's ace, Juan Marichal. Danny Murtaugh made several lineup changes in response to the Pirates' persistent slump, benching Richie Hebner in favor of Jose Pagan at third base and inserting Vic Davalillo at first base in place of Bob Robertson. Davalillo, a strange sight at first base because of his five-foot, seven-inch frame, made two errors at the unaccustomed position, but also lined out three hits and three RBIs. Davalillo's singles in the sixth and eighth innings padded the Pirates' lead and provided Nellie Briles with a comfortable margin. Making his first start of the season after pitching in long relief, Briles survived eight and two-thirds innings of 11-hit baseball to earn the win.

As the month drew to a close, it seemed possible that Stargell would break the record for most home runs in the month of April. On April 27, in front of 6,518 fans at Three Rivers Stadium, the Dodgers trailed 3-0 heading into the seventh, but crushed Dock Ellis and Bob Veale for seven runs in the seventh and eighth innings. Now trailing 7-3, Stargell batted in the ninth inning against former Pirate Pete Mikkelsen, pitching in relief. Stargell promptly connected against the sinkerballing right-hander, launching a 430-foot line drive over the center field wall, for his record 11th home run. Stargell earned personal congratulations from Pirates owner John Galbreath, who attended the game, and later received a football in the mail from Pittsburgh Steelers owner Art Rooney.

The new record of 11 homeruns provided the signature to an incredible month of power and also provided Stargell with a forum to sound off on the issue of racism in baseball. Stargell had grown up in a governmental project in Alameda, California, where he had experienced very little prejudice or discrimination. Once he signed his first professional baseball contract in 1959 and reported to the Pirates' minor league affiliate in the Class-D Sophomore League, he discovered a different, more antagonistic world. "When I first entered baseball in New Mexico and Texas," Stargell said in an interview that appeared in the *Syracuse Herald American*, "they separated the black players. They emphasized that blacks were less superior than whites." Since many hotels did not permit black guests, Stargell often slept in cots on the back porches of residential homes. "Black people would put us up in private houses," Stargell explained to Arnold Hano of *Sport* magazine. "Except the blacks didn't have anything." Restaurants also discriminated against black patrons. Stargell often had to sit in the kitchen, where he was handed small scraps of food. At other times, Stargell had to wait on the team bus while the white players ate comfortably in roadside diners.

Other aspects of segregation were just as demeaning. "We had to drink from different fountains," Stargell recalled. "There was always a constant reminder that we were less superior." Stargell found little solace at the ballpark, where fans treated him and other black players cruelly. "I'd get to the ballpark," Stargell told *Sport*, "and the fans would be name-calling me—'Nigger,' 'Pork Chop.' They'd threaten to shoot me if I beat their ballclub. It scared the hell out of me. I would go home and cry." The racial hostilities that Stargell and other black players experienced left the slugger feeling understandably bitter—at least early in his career. "I couldn't understand how the color of my skin could make people hate me for something I had never done."

In 1961, the situation improved somewhat when the Pirates assigned Stargell to Asheville, North Carolina, their affiliate in the Sally League. "The people of Asheville gave us a warm welcome," Stargell revealed to Arnold Hano in the *Sport* magazine story. "We were still segregated, but at least there were five blacks on the team." Stargell felt a greater sense of safety among African-American teammates.

By 1971, Stargell's bitterness had given way to a feeling of hope-fulness for better race relations in the future. "I realize I can't go around hating the system, hating what happened to me," he said in the article that appeared in the *Syracuse Herald American*. "I just can't wait to get in the position where my son doesn't have to get into that." Stargell felt it incumbent for prominent black athletes to reach out to the black population while providing solid examples of behavior for African-American youngsters. "I think the black ballplayer should be responsible to the black community," Stargell explained to Lacy Banks of *Black Sports* magazine. "The people, in many ways, helped to put him where he is. He should be visible to the kids in the ghetto. Sometimes just a smile and a word of con-cern from him can help change the life of a young brother toward the better."

Although open segregation no longer plagued baseball, Stargell raised another important racial issue—the salaries of comparable white and black stars. Stargell pointed to what he considered a dis-turbing discrepancy. "When I see someone like Carl Yastrzemski making what, $175,000. . . " Stargell said, his voice trailing off in an interview with the Associated Press. "Usually a ballplayer gets paid on what he has done, his ability as an outstanding ballplayer. But if you take his statistics and put them with [Willie] Mays or [Hank] Aaron, why they have double and triple the statistics he has." Stargell explained that he didn't want to see Yastrzemski get a pay cut, but preferred black stars to be paid at a similar or higher level. "I'm not saying he doesn't deserve everything he's getting," Stargell said of the Boston Red Sox' star. "I'm just saying that Mays, Aaron, and Clemente should be paid double or triple what he is getting."

Stargell said that a lack of endorsements for minority players had exacerbated the problem. He had never received an endorsement opportunity, while older black stars like Clemente and Frank Robinson had received very few offers. "We have a long way to go in endorsements," Stargell observed to *Black Sports* magazine. "You see a few blacks, but that's tokenism. Clemente has been shaving for years, I eat cereal every morning, and Robinson drives cars." The absence of televised promotional opportunities for black stars also disturbed Stargell. "The first time I ever saw Clemente on TV, outside baseball," Stargell revealed, "was on the Mike Douglas Show, a year ago. For one of baseball's time-honored superstars, that's a shame."

The spring of 1971 represented the maturation of Stargell as a complete hitter. His power numbers, impressive enough, told only a small portion of the story. Stargell's batting average at the end of the month rested at .347, including an average of nearly .300 against left-handed pitching, putting to rest the notion that he should be moved in the batting order, or flat-out benched against southpaws. In an April 28 game against the Dodgers, one night after Stargell had broken the home run record, and with the score tied at 5-5, the Bucs batted in the bottom of the seventh inning. Gene Clines, pinch-hitting for Steve Blass, reached first on a walk, and then moved up to second base on a balk by Dodgers left-hander Dan O'Brien. Dodger skipper Walter Alston, in one of the less cogent moments of an otherwise brilliant managing career, elected to walk Roberto Clemente, so that his southpaw could face Stargell. The big man crushed a double, scoring both Clines and Clemente, for a 7-5 victory. By the end of April, Stargell was batting cleanup regularly, regardless of the opposing pitcher.

The Pirates needed Willie Stargell's breakthrough performance in April because of the unanticipated problems of other key hitters. Richie Hebner had suffered through a 0-for-20 slump. Roberto Clemente, too, had struggled badly. He had entered the season with a lifetime batting average of .316, but in April of 1971, Clemente's average hovered around the .250 mark. His inability to drive in runs was an even more glaring concern. During a 16-game stretch in April, Clemente had stranded 25 men on base, an unacceptable figure for a hitter of his ability. Some writers pointed to Clemente's age as the cause; he was 36 years old and perhaps on an inevitable and irreversible career decline. Clemente, however, blamed his winter occupation, managing in the Puerto Rican Winter League. In Puerto Rico, teams traveled by bus, trips which placed additional strain on Clemente's back. The possibility of Clemente missing more than a few games did not portend well for the Pirates. Simply, put, Pittsburgh needed a healthy Clemente to win the National League East.

Clemente was the ultimate Pirate, having played his entire major league career in Pittsburgh. He had actually begun his professional career in another organization, however. As a teenager in Puerto Rico, Clemente had played a variety of positions: the outfield, the infield, and even catcher. Brooklyn Dodger scout Al Campanis, the father of Pirate minor leaguer Jim Campanis, had viewed Clemente during an amateur tryout and asked him to make some throws from the outfield. "Campanis put me in the outfield about 400 feet from home plate," Clemente told *The Sporting News*. "He had me make some throws to the plate, and when I was through, Campanis said, 'Forget any of those other positions, kid. You're an outfielder.'" Campanis appreciated what more than a few scouts would come to call the greatest throwing arm they had ever seen.

The Dodgers eventually signed Clemente, only to lose him in a special postseason draft because of their failure to place him on the major league roster. In 1954, other teams had the option of drafting players who had been given substantial bonuses and had not been protected on a 40-man major league roster. Since Clemente had received a bonus well over the $4,000 limit, he fell into the category of unprotected players. Buzzie Bavasi, who was the Dodgers' vice president at the time, claimed that Brooklyn's motivation in signing the Puerto Rican prodigy was simple: they wanted to prevent the rival New York Giants from placing Clemente and Willie Mays in the same outfield.

Others disagreed with Bavasi's contention, claiming that he was simply trying to explain away a monumental mistake by the Dodgers' front office. Those skeptics observed that the Dodgers could have held on to Clemente if they had put him in Brooklyn right away instead of assigning him to their Triple-A affiliate in Montreal. The Dodgers argued that they already had three terrific starting outfielders in 1953: Jackie Robinson in left, Duke Snider in center, and Carl Furillo in right field. If they had brought Clemente to Brooklyn in 1954, he would have wasted away on the bench.

Born in Carolina, Puerto Rico, on August 18, 1934, and drafted from the Brooklyn Dodgers by the Pirates after the 1954 season, Roberto Clemente combined athleticism, intelligence, and charisma in becoming a baseball superstar. His determination and effort to achieve excellence made him an inspiration to teammates and those fans who followed his exploits at stadiums, through the newspapers, on the radio, and occasionally on television. Despite performing in an era that preceded 24-hour media saturation, "The Great One" achieved notoriety beyond the world of professional sports, particularly through his humanitarian efforts to address social inequalities. During his career, he earned 12 Gold Glove awards, 12 All-Star selections, four National League batting titles, two World Series championships, and numerous other milestones. (*National Baseball Hall of Fame Library, Cooperstown, NY*)

The skeptics had a different theory. According to those of a more cynical mind, the Dodgers had reached their unstated quota of black players on the major league roster: Robinson, Roy Campanella, Junior Gilliam, and Joe Black had played for the Dodgers in 1953. Don Newcombe, about to return from military service, would give the Dodgers another African American. The addition of Clemente would give the Dodgers too many black players.

Coincidentally, a former Dodger employee played a major role in the Pirates' discovery of Clemente. Clyde Sukeforth had earned a reputation as one of the game's color-blind thinkers. In 1945, while working as a scout with the Dodgers, Sukeforth had received a special assignment from team president Branch Rickey, who told him to observe a Negro Leagues prospect named Jackie Robinson. The young shortstop was drawing rave reviews playing for the Kansas City Monarchs, one of the Negro Leagues' most formidable teams. Although an injured shoulder prevented Robinson from playing that day, Sukeforth interviewed the infielder for two hours after the game, and came away impressed with the young man's character and intelligence. Perhaps encouraged by Sukeforth's findings, Rickey signed Robinson to a minor league contract within three days.

After the 1951 season, Sukeforth left the Dodgers and rejoined Rickey in the Pirates' organization, where "The Mahatma" had become the president and general manager. In 1954, Rickey instructed Sukeforth to scout pitcher Joe Black, who had been demoted to the Dodgers' affiliate at Montreal. Rickey was considering making a trade for Black, but wanted to know about the condition of the right-hander's arm. Sukeforth stayed to watch an International League series between Montreal and Richmond, but Black did not pitch.

The trip did not, however, turn out to be a waste of time. Prior to one of the games, Sukeforth observed outfield practice and noticed the powerful throwing arm displayed by Montreal's right fielder. In the seventh inning of the game, the right fielder came up as a pinch-hitter. "He hit a routine ground ball at the shortstop," Sukeforth recalled in an interview with *Sports Collectors Digest*, "and the play at first base was just bang-bang. I mean, they just did get him. So he's showed me he could throw and run right then." The player was a young prospect named Roberto Clemente.

Since the Pirates were heading toward a last-place finish in 1954, the front office felt confident that the team would have the first pick in the special draft of unprotected players. Sukeforth recommended that Rickey select Clemente.

Intrigued by Sukeforth's enthusiasm, Rickey sought a second opinion from a top scout. Howie Haak received the assignment to follow up on Clemente. "I went to Rochester to see him play and the strangest thing happened," Haak told the Associated Press in 1971. "Clemente got two triples and a double, and when they removed the southpaw pitcher. . . Clemente was taken out for a pinch-hitter. The Dodgers were trying to hide Clemente."

Although claims that the Dodgers organization intentionally tried to conceal Clemente have been disputed in recent years, the lack of regular playing time clearly frustrated the young Clemente, who didn't understand how the bonus rules and the draft might have resulted in his diminishing role with the team. Clemente became so unhappy that he sought out Al Campanis, whom he knew spoke Spanish. When Clemente told him that he wanted to leave the team and return to Puerto Rico, Campanis explained why he believed that Montreal manager Max Macon had been keeping him tied to the bench. (For his part, Macon repeatedly denied that he tried to hide Clemente; he says he received no such orders from the Dodgers to do so.) Campanis assured Clemente that there would be a resolution to his problem—beginning in 1955.

Even though Clemente came to bat only 148 times for Montreal, with a paltry average of .257, the Pirates were not fooled. On November 22, 1954, Rickey drafted Clemente for the grand sum of $4,000.

Clemente struggled in his rookie season with the Pirates, batting only .255 with a mere five home runs and 47 RBIs. In his first five seasons in Pittsburgh, Clemente batted as high as .300 only once, and reached a high of only seven home runs. Finally, in 1960, the find uncovered by Haak and Sukeforth blossomed into stardom. Clemente set personal marks by batting .314 with 16 home runs and

94 runs batted in. Clemente followed that performance in 1961 by leading the National League with a .351 average while crushing 24 home runs. Once raw and unrefined, Clemente would evolve into legitimate National League stardom during the early 1960s.

The criticism of Clemente early in 1971 typified the general reaction of the media during the times that he struggled, especially because of professed injuries. Although Clemente had suffered a serious bout with malaria, and had once developed painful bone chips in his elbow, it seemed that many sportswriters did not believe his claims about being sick or hurt.

In a common refrain, some Pittsburgh writers labeled Clemente a hypochondriac. Even the most praiseworthy of articles made a point of underlining Clemente's repeated injuries and his alleged unwillingness to play with pain. The unending criticism, especially the doubts that lingered over Clemente's effort and work ethic, irritated not only the veteran right fielder but also several of his teammates. "Before I came over to this ballclub," Dave Giusti revealed in an interview with United Press International, "I heard how Clemente is always ailing and wanting to sit out games, but everything I heard was strictly bull. He goes full blast all the time."

Clemente believed that some of the criticism stemmed from racist motivation. In an April 25 interview with Milton Richman of United Press International, Clemente spoke at length about the issue of race relations in major league baseball. Clemente remembered that when he had first joined the Pirates in the mid-1950s, the organization had very few minority players. At the time, most players, black or white, hesitated to speak out against what they considered unjust treatment. Players did not want to upset the team's management, which held most of the leverage in contract negotiations. Clemente, however, represented one of the exceptions. "Anytime I feel something is wrong," Clemente told Richman. "I'm gonna say something. Baseball has changed in many ways since I first came to the big leagues. Ballplayers feel they can speak up much more now than they did then. I spoke up even then."

In 1955, Clemente had sounded off loudly on the game's race problem. At the time, Pittsburgh had only two other Latinos, pitcher Lino Donoso and outfielder Roman Mejias, and only one black

American, a second baseman named Curt Roberts, the first African-American player in the history of the Pirates' franchise. Fuming at the way some of his teammates treated Roberts, Clemente couldn't let such behavior pass without a protest. "I didn't like some of the things the white players said to Roberts," Clemente recalled in his interview with Richman, "so I said some things to them they didn't like."

Although racial relations between Pirate players had improved considerably since Roberts' difficult days in Pittsburgh, Clemente was not completely satisfied with the ways that black and white major leaguers, especially on other teams, related to each other. "Baseball has come a long way in this regard, but there is still room for improvement," Clemente informed Richman. "When I came here you very seldom saw a black player get together with a white player and go someplace together after a ballgame. Now it is more common. Yes, there has been some improvement but some things still remain the way they were."

In the coming months, things would not "remain the way they were" as more and more white and black players on the Pirates interacted with each other freely at the ballpark, both before and after games. Black, white, and Latino players often gathered at bars, restaurants, or each others' homes, helping to build team unity while breaking down any potential racial barriers. "After the games, we would go out together and do different things," explains Bob Robertson. "I think that's what made us a winning ballclub, that we had the respect and admiration [for all of the players], whoever it may be. If somebody on the ballclub had a problem, or if we had seen something that wasn't right, we would approach that and fix it. And that's just the type of people that I was so glad to be surrounded with." What had not been achieved with other teams was becoming a reality in the Pittsburgh clubhouse.

Chapter 5

MAY

A s the Pirates completed a weekend series with San Diego on May 2, their overall record stood a mediocre 14-10. Yet, they had won three games in a row, putting them just one-half game off the pace set by the Mets in the National League East. As for the other two preseason favorites, the Cardinals' record of 14-11 placed them just one-half game back of the Pirates, while the Cubs' tally of 10-13 had them a full four games out of first place. Chicago's slow start had prompted a series of trade rumors and a general feeling that major changes might be taking place in the Windy City, in addition to the annual gloom that descended on Cub fans.

Of greater concern to the Pirates than the Cubs, Cardinals, or Mets were injuries, which had tormented the Bucs throughout spring training and were beginning to surface again in early May. The first injury involved the valuable Vic Davalillo, who tore a muscle near his left elbow. Although Davalillo could still swing a bat, the pain prevented him from making throws, from either first base or the outfield. Reserve outfielder Gene Clines had to substitute for the ailing Roberto Clemente in right field, but the Pirates expected Clemente to miss games on occasion due to back pain. Another ailment posed the greatest worry for the Pirates. Dock Ellis complained of soreness in his right arm after toiling in cold, rainy weather against the Padres on May 2. It was the same elbow that had bothered the right-hander during the 1970 season. Ellis was critical to the ballclub's chances and if he ended up on the disabled list, it would be difficult for the Pirates to keep pace with their division rivals. The next day, the Bucs' team physician, Dr. Albert Ferguson, examined Ellis' arm. Ferguson reported no physical damage to the muscles, tendons, or ligaments in the right arm. The favorable medical report distracted the Pirates from any worries they might have had over their middling record, but the Pirates would now find their depth tested.

It was a healthy clubhouse atmosphere that kept the team from faltering. While teams in the past composed of a diverse group of nationalities and backgrounds had difficulty keeping tempers from flaring and arguments from spinning out of control, particularly during moments of stress, the Pirates found ways to remain positive and unified. The "kangaroo court," a mock trial that would soon become a common practice in major league clubhouses, became an important mechanism in breaking down any racial barriers while strengthening relationships in a semi-social setting. According to Dave Giusti, Steve Blass organized one of the earliest examples of a kangaroo court: "Whether it was on the field or off-the-field antics—if somebody made a mental error or if somebody screwed up off the field—Steve would take it upon himself to have court sessions and would describe exactly how things happened. Steve was probably the funniest man on the ballclub. He would have these sessions and come out with a verdict. If you were guilty, you still had to sit there and take it. . . . You had a gathering of past histories, a lot of blacks, and a lot of Latins," points out Giusti. "We just found some way to relate to each other, and because of this kangaroo court type thing, it was a good way to release tension."

Bob Robertson says white players felt free to joke with black players, Latinos tossed barbs at African Americans, and black players kidded whites, all without repercussions. "That's exactly what took place," Robertson says. "We could tell jokes to one another. We could call each other different names in different situations and it was all in fun. We never thought twice about it. It was just a tremendous atmosphere."

As one of the prominent players on the team, Al Oliver concurs that the racial jousting on the Pirates was always good-natured. "I totally agree with that," exclaims Oliver. "There's no question that we had a great cross-section of people on that ballclub. I've always said that sports and entertainment can bridge gaps. And that '71 team proved that. Right, we did a lot of joking with one another. We never had any problems as far as race on that ballclub. We were professionals. We were ballplayers. We had a lot of confidence in one another. And I think the reason why we did was because most of us played along with one another in the minor leagues. I think we got to know each other as people, and when you get to know each other as people, then you don't have problems."

"That's the problem with the world today," Oliver continues. "That's why racism is going on in this world today. People don't take time to sit down and learn and get to know people. After all, hey, we're all God's children. That's the way that we approached it in 1971."

Giusti says irreverent exchanges between the races made the '71 Pirates distinct from the Houston and St. Louis teams that he had played for in his early major league career. "I think it was more sacred with these other clubs." The Colt .45s, Astros, and Cardinals steered clear of any interactions about race. "I mean you just didn't try anything. It was just understood that if anything popped up in a racial environment, nobody said anything about it. [Such talk] was kept by themselves and to themselves." On other teams, racial kidding and jousting might have led to outright warfare in the clubhouse. With leaders like Roberto Clemente and Willie Stargell around to keep things in perspective, few such problems arose between Pirate teammates.

Having pounded the cellar-resting Padres, and with Dock Ellis' injury scare fresh in their minds, the Pirates moved on to a stiffer challenge, one traditionally posed by the schedule maker: the first of two dreaded trips to the West Coast. Because of their length and the changes in time zones, such trips have often unraveled even the best of Eastern Division teams, especially since the addition of San Diego meant that East Coast teams now had to play three series out west, instead of two. The early-season games on the coast posed an even more difficult first-stop obstacle for the Pirates: the Western Division-leading Giants, who also possessed the league's best overall record.

In the first of a two-game set, the Bucs posted one of their most impressive efforts of the season, a 10-2 shellacking of the Giants. Manny Sanguillen fueled the assault with four hits in five at-bats, while Richie Hebner, Roberto Clemente, and Willie Stargell each

A frequent occurrence in 1971. Willie Stargell (No. 8) touches home plate after hitting his 12th home run of the season during the eighth inning of a May 4th game at Candlestick Park. The blast scored three runs, including Roberto Clemente (No. 21), who greets him at home plate during the Pirates' 10-2 thrashing of the Giants. On-deck hitter Al Oliver (No. 16) also congratulates Stargell, who had set a major league record for the most home runs in April. (*National Baseball Hall of Fame Library, Cooperstown, NY*)

netted two hits. Steve Blass, Bob Moose, and the suddenly impressive Mudcat Grant—who hurled three shutout innings—contained the power-hitting Giants on eight hits and two runs.

Grant had seen his baseball career evolve along the same lines as his bullpen partner, Dave Giusti. Like Giusti (and, in later years, like Dennis Eckersley), Grant had undergone a mid-career transition from starting pitcher to bullpen fireman. In his younger days, Grant had been an effective starter for the Minnesota Twins. In 1965, he won a career-high 21 games and might have won the Cy Young Award if not for the dominating presence of Los Angeles Dodgers' ace Sandy Koufax. (At that time the writers handed out one award for both leagues, a practice that would come to an end two years later.) Grant also became the first black pitcher in

American League history to win at least 20 games in a season, contributing to Minnesota's World Series berth against Koufax and the Dodgers. After a 13-13 season in 1966, the Twins moved Grant to the bullpen on a part-time basis.

On November 28, 1967, the Twins traded Grant to Los Angeles, where he became a full-time reliever. After brief pitstops in Montreal and St. Louis, Grant flourished in the role of bullpen ace for his new team, the Oakland A's. In 1970, he forged a microscopic earned run average of 1.82 as Oakland's top reliever before being traded to the Pirates for the stretch run. "I'm having success at a late age," Grant told the Associated Press in 1971. "I could have folded up, after not starting and falling into the relief pitching thing. But I count it as another experience."

Yet, Grant's transition to relief stardom almost didn't happen. In the spring of 1970, Grant had pitched so poorly for the A's that Oakland owner Charlie Finley prepared to give him his unconditional release. A release at Grant's age might have ended his major league career. But A's broadcaster Harry Caray, who had known Grant from their days together with the Cardinals, cautioned Finley about Grant's annual spring training woes. "I was having my usual bad spring, and I was awaiting the word—release," Grant recalled in an interview with *The Sporting News*. "But Caray told Finley that I never pitched well in the spring and he told him I did a good job with the Cardinals. Finley doesn't listen to many people. He listened to Caray. . .Harry Caray. . .he got Finley's ear." Grant was right. Finley didn't often listen to other people when it came to making baseball decisions. On this occasion, Finley's willingness to listen to Caray may have saved Mudcat's baseball life.

In the second game at Candlestick Park, left-hander Luke Walker pitched eight innings of two-run baseball, but the Pittsburgh offense hardly dented San Francisco starter Juan Marichal. The Dominican right-hander held the Bucs to three measly hits in a 2-1 win for the Giants. Yet a key play on defense decided the game. The Pirates, whose fielding had been stellar in the early season, failed to turn an essential double play on a routine comeback in the seventh inning. Although no error was charged on the play, the miscue allowed the game-winning run to score.

To make matters worse, the Pirates prepared to face the Dodgers for three games in Los Angeles without the services of Dave Cash and Richie Hebner, who had been summoned to the East Coast for weekend duty in the Marine Reserves. Danny Murtaugh called upon veterans Bill Mazeroski and Jose Pagan to fill in as starters at second base and third base, respectively.

The Pirates responded to the loss of manpower by sweeping the three-game weekend set. Both probable and unexpected heroes contributed to the Pirate cause. In the first game, Dodger tormentor Willie Stargell belted his 13th home run in support of starter and winner Bob Johnson. (Of Stargell's 99 career hits against the Dodgers, 16 had reached the seats.) In the next matchup, Jose Pagan, sporting an .095 batting mark, began his 1971 turnaround by slamming a two-run homer against left-hander Al Downing. Dave Giusti pitched three impeccable innings of scoreless relief to save a 5-3 victory for Nellie Briles.

Then, in the finale against the Dodgers, little-used lefty swinger Charlie Sands smashed a bases-loaded double against tough southpaw Jim Brewer. The extra-base hit highlighted an eight-run, eighth-inning rally. Appearing as a pinch-hitter, Sands was taking his first major league turn at-bat since his 1967 campaign with the Yankees.

In addition to Sands' cameo appearance, Bill Mazeroski had emerged as an offensive contributor against the Dodgers. Maz went 3-for-10 with a run scored and a run batted in. With Dave Cash and Richie Hebner continuing to fulfill their military obligations, the veteran subs would remain in the starting lineup for the balance of the road trip.

The Bucs moved on to San Diego, where they split two games with the lowly Padres, to conclude the West Coast swing at 5-2. In the first game at San Diego Stadium, Roberto Clemente managed his first home run of the season, as part of a 10-4 thrashing of the Padres. Clemente had actually shown some hopeful signs earlier on the West Coast trip. He had erupted for four hits in one game against the Dodgers and collected two hits in another game against Los Angeles, before blasting his first home run as part of a two-hit game against the Padres.

On May 14, the Pirates returned to Three Rivers Stadium to open up an important early season series against the division-leading Mets. The first game proved to be a near disaster for the Bucs, who failed to muster much of an offensive attack against southpaw Jerry Koosman in a humiliating 8-2 loss. The Pirates embarrassed themselves further the next night, stumbling to a 9-5 loss that featured three errors before a disappointed crowd of 22,042 fans.

The Pirates' frequent lapses in the field angered manager Danny Murtaugh. "You expect a bad game defensively once in awhile," Murtaugh told *The Sporting News*. "But that doesn't mean you have to forget it." Murtaugh was a firm believer in the value of a team's defensive play. He often talked to his players about not giving the opposition one or two extra outs during an inning. Murtaugh cringed when he saw his fielders make mistakes, and often reacted by hurling a few profanity-laced phrases in their direction. Although the usually amiable Murtaugh tended to support his players, he occasionally allowed his anger to show when the Pirates made what he considered unprofessional mistakes.

In the meantime, minor injuries derailed Willie Stargell for a few games. During the series against the Dodgers, Stargell had suffered soreness in his hand after checking his powerful swing. He missed the two games against San Diego before playing in the first game of the series against the Mets. Stargell later re-aggravated the injury, forcing him to the bench for a second time. In addition, a bruised right foot that had been damaged by a series of foul balls made him even more uncomfortable.

Even though Stargell wanted to play, Murtaugh elected to take a cautious approach with his slugger, especially in regard to his injured hand. Later in the season, Murtaugh discussed his conservative treatment of Stargell, which resulted in the slugger missing a total of seven starts. "I know this [sitting out] had to bug Willie," Murtaugh told *Baseball Digest*. "I know he is looking for the big year, the year that will be able to make him a real high-priced player. I called him to my office and explained that I wasn't trying to hurt his chances to earn money. I just didn't want him swinging a bat when he wasn't right." Stargell, who liked and respected Murtaugh, understood the approach that the manager had taken.

Bolstered by Dock Ellis' return from elbow soreness, the Pirates salvaged the finale of the three-game set against New York, upending the Mets, 4-2. The Bucs capitalized on six walks by Nolan Ryan.

Although the Pirates had played well prior to the Mets series, the front office had noticed the lack of fan response in Pittsburgh. One of the important weekend games against the Mets had drawn a scant crowd of 17,622 fans; on average, the Bucs were bringing in roughly 12,000 a night at Three Rivers Stadium. Perhaps the lingering cold weather was the primary reason, or so Pirate executive Tom Johnson hoped. "If weather isn't the reason for the small crowds," Johnson told *Sports Illustrated*, "then we're all in the wrong business." The low turnout would become an issue again later in the season.

In fact, attendance concerns would crop up periodically throughout the 1970s. The Pirates, who would end up drawing just over 1.5 million fans by the end of 1971, would bring in even fewer fans in subsequent seasons. Even in the championship season of 1979, Pirate attendance would total only 1.4 million fans. Such mediocre figures would lead some members of the media—and even some officials in the Pirate organization—to cite racial backlash as a possible cause. Perhaps the city of Pittsburgh, where black citizens accounted for only about 20 percent of the population in 1971, didn't want to support a team so heavily laden with minority players. As a result of such speculation, one Pirate official—scout Howie Haak—would become engulfed in major controversy several years later. There was also a perception that African Americans arriving from elsewhere were taking jobs away from whites at steel mills.

After struggling in their home series against the Mets, the Pirates used clutch hitting to their advantage in an abbreviated mid-May series against the Expos. For one of the first times in 1971, Roberto Clemente served up his own share of timely batting. Clemente smashed an eighth-inning home run to help bring the Pirates within one run of the Expos. Still trailing by one run in the ninth, the Pirates put two men on base, setting the stage for Clemente to face Montreal's relief ace, Mike Marshall. With two out and the game on the line, Clemente responded by smacking a triple off the center field wall, scoring Gene Alley and Dave Cash with the game-tying and go-ahead runs.

Earlier in the game, Clemente had experienced something he rarely heard at either Forbes Field or Three Rivers Stadium: a chorus of boos from Pirate fans. In fact, Pirate fans had not collectively booed their favorite right fielder over the first 14 years of his career, until a 1969 game against the Phillies when he committed an error and hit into two double plays.

Despite his late-game heroics against the Expos, the reaction of the fans clearly upset Clemente. After the game, a reporter from United Press International asked him about the boo-birds. "If I don't hustle, or something like that, I'd say that it would be good for me to get booed. The problem with me is hitting. You hit .280, it's a pretty good average. But I used to hit .350, so .280 is not good enough."

Clemente felt as if the fans had forgotten about those occasions when he had played despite being injured. "A lot of times in my career, I play when I shouldn't play," he told UPI. "One time I play with a shoulder [injury], it hurts so bad, I can't lift it. I hit into a double play. Then they hit a ball to the outfield and I can't bend down to pick it up, so they boo me."

The reporter then asked Clemente about the possibility of retirement. He explained that he had no intentions of retiring. And why should he? He had lifted his batting average to .295. Furthermore, his base running and fielding abilities remained top-notch, making him an overall asset to the Pirates.

The next night, the Pirates again beat Mike Marshall in the ninth inning before heading to Cincinnati for a rematch of the previous season's National League Championship Series. The first game at Riverfront Stadium offered another glimpse of classic Clemente. The Pirate right fielder, playing his best game of the season to date, collected four hits. The outburst included a triple and an inside-the-park home run, a rather stunning accomplishment for a 36-year-old. Clemente's lusty running and hitting spearheaded a 6-1 win, putting the Pirates in first place ahead of the Mets, who had lost to the Phillies.

The following day, May 20, the Pirates received a scare that made their pursuit of the National League East pennant seem trivial by comparison. Manager Danny Murtaugh, who seven years earlier had experienced heart problems, suffered pains in his chest and arm before the second game of the series against the Reds. Murtaugh was taken to Christ Hospital in Cincinnati, where he was kept for observation. After several tests, doctors determined that Murtaugh had not suffered a heart attack, but they were concerned enough to keep him in Cincinnati for a full week. Murtaugh then returned to Pittsburgh for more tests at Presbyterian-University Hospital.

In 1964, although Murtaugh had not experienced a heart attack, he had decided to stop managing after that season because of his health. He had subsequently moved into the Pirate front office to work as a scout under general manager Joe Brown. The latest round of medical concerns triggered speculation that Murtaugh might call it quits a second time. Murtaugh refused to offer any predictions, while Joe Brown showed proper perspective and restraint in an interview with *The Sporting News*: "I'm more interested in Murtaugh the man than Murtaugh the manager right now. The job of manager is Danny's as long as he wants it." Only one scenario seemed certain. If Murtaugh were to resign, hitting coach Bill Virdon would succeed him as the Pirates' full-time manager.

Prior to Murtaugh's hospitalization, Blass and other Pirate players had occasionally noticed their manager's somewhat haggard appearance. During the spring, Murtaugh had lost about 15 pounds, but had done so intentionally as part of a rigid diet. Did Steve Blass witness any symptoms that might have specifically foretold of a heart condition in 1971? "No, not to that degree," Blass says in retrospect. Yet, some of the Pirate players did notice wear and tear on their manager. "When we were on trips, back in that particular era," Blass says, "we didn't have the efficient airlines, we didn't fly all charters, we traveled some commercial [flights] and you could see fatigue with Danny, on occasion, after a long road trip or a trip to the coast. The season would kind of wear him down—physically." Two days before Murtaugh's admission to the hospital, the Pirates had beaten the Expos in the ninth inning. "These games are tough on my boiler," the frazzled manager admitted to UPI.

Like several other players, Blass felt very close to the popular Pirate manager. "Here's a man that, maybe, you care about more than you realize. When he goes into the hospital, [you realize] this stuff is more important than a baseball game." Richie Hebner says that Murtaugh's presence as a friendly father figure heightened the concern the players held for his physical well-being. "We all liked him," Hebner says. "He was the kind of guy when you were around him for a week or two, you'd say, gee, you know, this guy's like my dad. He was a nice, nice guy. And when he got ill, there was concern with everybody... We all missed him."

Although he personally did not understand why Murtaugh platooned him so often, Bob Robertson liked him and noted that the Bucs felt the absence of the manager who was often underappreciated by the masses. "Danny was the type of guy," says Robertson, "that you'd see him on the bench some times, and I've heard people say, 'Was Danny awake when this situation happened? Was he awake?' Yes, the Irishman was awake." Many observers had misinterpreted Murtaugh's calm demeanor as a sign of disinterest, or even more cruelly, as a symptom of advancing age.

"Danny was the type of guy that treated everybody equal, the way it should be," Robertson contends. "If you had a problem, you could always go in the door, the door was always open to Danny Murtaugh's office." Murtaugh also appreciated Pirate players who worked hard. "Danny Murtaugh always told me, 'You know, Robby, you can keep the players that make the great plays, the flamboyant stuff. Just give me a hard-nosed everyday-type ballplayer that will make the routine plays.' Danny Murtaugh could excuse the physical mistakes. But he could not stand to see a professional athlete come up with a mental mistake, like throwing to the wrong base or not hitting the cut-off man. He was a stickler on that."

Willie Stargell had known Murtaugh longer than most of the Pirates, except for Clemente, Mazeroski, and Veale. Stargell recalled for *Baseball Digest* the first time that Murtaugh had experienced heart problems: "When Danny first had to quit after the 1964 season because of his health, I felt I was losing somebody. He has a way of getting his point across. It's just like when you were in school. You liked certain teachers, and there were others who just couldn't get across to you. You liked the classes where you felt you were learning something."

Stargell lauded Murtaugh's ability to communicate with players, without having to speak too often. "If I were a manager," Stargell explained to the *Newark Star-Ledger* in July, "Danny Murtaugh is the kind of manager I'd want to be like. He doesn't demand respect; he commands it. He knows how to handle players, to get the most out of them. He doesn't say much, but when he does, you listen because you know it means something."

In spite of his general popularity, Murtaugh had repeatedly struggled in his relationship with the most prominent Pirate, Roberto Clemente. In previous years, Murtaugh had both directly and publicly questioned the severity of some of Clemente's many injuries, calling into doubt the toughness of "The Great One." On one occasion, Murtaugh had accused Clemente of "faking" an injury after he begged out of the lineup with one of his ailments. The lack of support from his manager tore at the proud Clemente.

By 1971, the two men had still not become friends, but they had learned to co-exist. Murtaugh realized how important Clemente's presence was to the franchise, how he helped unify the African-American, Latino, and white Pirates. Like few other players, Clemente served as a role model for all of his teammates, regardless of their ethnicity. With that in mind, Murtaugh often confided in his right fielder. Murtaugh knew that he could learn about his players, and communicate important messages to them, just by seeking out Clemente.

Without Murtaugh on hand, the Pirates had lost the second game to Cincinnati. They then dropped two out of three to the Expos in Montreal before facing the Reds in a quick rematch at Three Rivers Stadium. Interim manager Bill Virdon chose the inconsistent Bob Moose to start the first game against the Reds on May 25. Moose, who had alternated good starts with bad ones, gave up seven runs in an inning and two-thirds. Pirate fielding did not help matters, as Bob Robertson and Dave Cash committed errors in the first inning, and Moose added a miscue of his own in the second. The Pirates scored two runs in the third and two more in the sixth to close the gap, but a seven-run deficit proved too difficult to overcome.

Danny Murtaugh, who had tried to monitor the progress of the Bucs by listening to a radio broadcast, became so frustrated during the 7-4 loss to the Reds that he turned off the set in the second inning. The next night, out of concern for the aging skipper's medical condition, Joe Brown told Murtaugh not to listen to the game at all. As a result, Murtaugh missed out on an 11-strikeout performance by Steve Blass. Although the right-hander had pitched one of the best games of his career—a 2-0 shutout—he wondered if his manager would ever find out about it. Murtaugh had not only been blacked out from radio coverage; he had been prevented from reading about Blass' performance because of a continuing newspaper strike throughout Pittsburgh. "I pitch a shutout against the Reds and my manager won't even know it," deadpanned Blass in an interview with Charley Feeney. Workhorse Dock Ellis followed up Blass' performance by mastering the Reds on a complete-game seven-hitter, which the Bucs won, 5-2. Although overshadowed by the fast-starting Ellis, Blass had quietly entrenched himself as the Pirates' second-best starter.

With Blass and Ellis providing the impetus, the Pirates seemed to have turned a corner, only to stumble in the first of a four-game series against the disappointing Cubs. Luke Walker, the previous season's 15-game winner, fell to 1-6, giving up 11 hits and three runs, two of them earned, in four and two-thirds innings. In his previous seven starts, Walker had pitched creditably, but had suffered from poor run support; the Bucs' offense had scored a measly total of seven runs, or an average of one run per game. To make matters worse, Walker was hiding the fact that he was now suffering from a sore arm.

After Walker's loss, the Pirates rebounded to play three of their best games of the season. First came a 9-4 victory, followed by an impressive performance by the erratic Bob Moose, who throttled the Cubs on a complete-game three-hitter. In support of Moose, the Pirates' offense exploded for eight runs in the fourth inning of a 10-0 blowout at Three Rivers. The big inning included a three-run homer by Clemente, followed by a Stargell blast—the longest home run in the short history of Three Rivers Stadium. Six Pirates enjoyed multiple hit games, including Dave Cash, who banged out a four-hit barrage. The game also featured error-free defense by Pittsburgh, completing the baseball trifecta of pitching, hitting, and defense. The next day, the Pirates dealt the Cubs another early-season pennant blow when Steve Blass twirled a 6-0 shutout. Stargell's 17th home run and Richie Hebner's fifth longball provided the offense against a demoralized band of Cubs.

On May 29, the Pirates received some good news regarding Danny Murtaugh. Doctors at Presbyterian Hospital gave Murtaugh a clean bill of health, clearing him to leave the hospital within a few days. Team physician Dr. Joseph Finegold said that extensive tests showed no damage to Murtaugh's heart. The Pirates announced that Murtaugh would return to manage the club in a week, when he would guide the team in the final game of a series against the Houston Astros on June 6. "Because of the thoroughness of the tests," Joe Brown told UPI, "it was felt he should have an additional week to relax."

Thanks to the victories over the Cubs, the Pirates finished May with a record of 29-19 overall. With Stargell powering the offense, and Blass and Ellis anchoring the starting rotation, the Pirates had found an effective formula for taking leads in the early innings. In the bullpen, Mudcat Grant and Dave Giusti had helped the Pirates win almost every game in which they held the advantage after six innings. They were just two and a half games back of the suddenly surging Cardinals, who would be the Pirates' guests for the first series in June.

The fact that the Pirates could weather the absence of their manager for several weeks at a crucial point in the season was a credit to the players, collectively and individually. But they now faced their first big test—in terms of an intimidating opponent—of the season.

Chapter 6

JUNE

The St. Louis Cardinals had forged a seven-game winning streak and had taken command of the National League East. In the first game of a three-game series at Three Rivers Stadium, the Pirates quickly put into doubt any notion of Cardinal supremacy by scoring five first-inning runs off St. Louis starter Chris Zachary, who failed to last an inning. Dock Ellis, whose arm remained healthy, continued an amazing stretch for the Pirates' pitching staff by hurling a complete-game, three-hit, two-walk shutout, the team's third shutout in as many games.

Pittsburgh's streak of 35 innings without giving up a run ended on the next night, June 2, when Lou Brock scored on a sacrifice fly in the sixth inning off starter Luke Walker. Little did it matter, as the Pirates coasted to a 10-1 win. Walker and relievers Jim Nelson and Bob Veale combined on a seven-hitter, with Veale posting three impressive scoreless innings for his first save of the season. Offensively, the Pirates continued to manufacture runs, not so much with the long ball, but with sustained rallies. In the fourth inning, the Bucs managed five consecutive hits and a sacrifice fly. The rally included a Dave Cash double, singles by Vic Davalillo—subbing for the injured Bob Robertson at first base for the second straight game—Roberto Clemente, Willie Stargell and Richie Hebner, and an Al Oliver sacrifice fly, making it 4-0 in favor of the Bucs. The Pirates' bench continued to provide front-line production. Davalillo slashed out three hits against his former Cardinal mates, while Gene Clines, caddying for Clemente, chipped in with two hits and two RBIs.

The Pirates' offense—so dynamic in the first two games of the series—found itself stifled in the finale. Ace left-hander Steve Carlton, pitching on only three days' rest, became the National League's first 10-game winner by throwing a complete-game seven-hitter. Cardinals manager Red Schoendienst had originally sched-uled right-hander Mike Torrez to start, but Carlton, showing his competitive fire, volunteered to pitch after the Cardinals lost the first two games. The 7-1 Cardinal victory ended the Pirates' five-game win streak. Former Pirate Matty Alou haunted Joe Brown with an excellent all-around performance, which included three hits, three RBIs, and his first home run of the season. Meanwhile, Alou's successor in center field for the Pirates, Al Oliver, went 0-for-4 against Carlton's devastating fastball and slider.

Despite coming off this demoralizing loss, coupled with the absence of Roberto Clemente due to the flu, the Bucs managed to play a solid game when they faced the Astros at Three Rivers Stadium in their next series. Clemente's substitute in right field, Gene Clines, delivered run-scoring singles in the third inning and fifth innings to give the Pirates an early lead. Another Pirate back-up, Milt May, subbing for the resting Manny Sanguillen, accounted for a third run with a single that scored Richie Hebner. On the mound, Bob Moose made the lead hold up by allowing only two runs over eight and one-third innings with Dave Giusti relieving him to preserve a 3-2 win for the Pirates.

In contrast to relievers in the 1980s and beyond, Giusti rarely had the luxury of pitching only one inning in a closing role. While contemporary critics of relief pitchers have complained about save totals becoming deceptively inflated in recent years, they would be hard-pressed to draw similar conclusions of closers like Giusti. As with most star relief pitchers of the early seventies, Giusti usually pitched two to three innings per outing and often entered games with runners already on base. Unlike some of his bullpen successors, Giusti legitimately earned most of his 145 career saves, including a league-leading 30 rescues during the 1971 season.

After dropping a 4-1 decision to the Astros and 10-game winner Larry Dierker, the Pirates welcomed back the ailing Danny Murtaugh on Sunday, June 6. He had missed a total of 16 games, during which the Pirates went a middling 9-7. Looking leaner—he had dropped 10 pounds during his absence—Murtaugh stood anx-iously in the Pirates' dugout during the pre-game workout. Much to the chagrin of his doctors, he also chewed furiously on some of his trademark tobacco. One by one, Pirate players came over to Murtaugh, shook his hand, and welcomed him back to the National League East pennant race.

Murtaugh's first game back as manager did little to benefit his heart, or his nerves, as the Pirates eked out a 9-8 win over the Astros. The Pirates' offense lashed out 17 hits, including a combined 14 knocks from the first five hitters in the batting order: Dave Cash, Richie Hebner, Roberto Clemente, Willie Stargell (who belted his 18th home run), and Manny Sanguillen. In an unusual occurrence, the Pirates' two best relievers, Mudcat Grant and Dave Giusti, struggled in the late innings, but Bob Veale managed to collect the final out to stave off a ninth-inning rally. Without question, the return of the popular Murtaugh had provided the Pirate players with an emotional boost.

The Pirates flexed some more run-scoring prowess the next day, when Stargell and Robertson hit home runs in an 11-6 blowout victory of Milt Pappas and the Cubs at Wrigley Field. Although Nellie Briles lasted only two and one-third innings in a starting role, the Pirate relief tandem of Bob Veale and Dave Giusti combined for six and two-thirds of scoreless pitching. The effectiveness of Giusti had come as no surprise, but Veale was quietly emerging as a bullpen force after barely making the Pirates' staff during a shaky spring. "The reason we're in the race is because of our bullpen," Danny Murtaugh remarked to *The Sporting News*. "Dave Giusti and Bob Veale did the job today, and Mudcat Grant is capable of doing the same."

On June 8, Dave Cash's batting average stood at .356, tied for third with Joe Torre of the Cardinals, trailing only St. Louis' Lou Brock and the Dodgers' Willie Davis in the National League. Cash, who had scored four runs in Sunday's victory over the Astros, now totaled 37 runs on the season. Cash's impressive start prompted him to lay out some lofty goals. "I want to score over 100 runs," Cash boldly told the *Newark Star-Ledger*. "I want to bat between .340 and .360." Cash had certainly made a believer of Danny Murtaugh, the same man who had given Bill Mazeroski the Opening Day nod at second base after Cash's impressive spring performance. "Cash has to be considered for the All-Star team," proclaimed Murtaugh.

"You're supposed to pick them for their play now, aren't you?" Based on 1971 performance, and not on past reputation, Cash deserved to represent the National League All-Star team at second base.

On June 10, the Bucs opened up an important road series against the Cardinals, who had occupied first or second place in the National League East most of the early season. A run of minor injuries to Luke Walker, Bob Johnson, and Bob Veale, coupled with military reserve assignments for Jim Nelson and Bob Moose, had left Murtaugh with a recent shortage of pitching. At one point in June, Murtaugh was down to six healthy and available pitchers. In anticipation of the series

Signed by Pittsburgh as a free agent in 1958, Bob Veale made his big league debut in 1962. As a starting pitcher, he led the league in strikeouts in 1964. Moved to a fulltime relief role in 1971, Veale struggled with his weight and a 6.99 ERA, but did finish the season 6-0. (*National Baseball Hall of Fame Library, Cooperstown, NY*)

with the Cardinals, the Bucs recalled two pitchers from Triple-A Charleston, right-hander Frank Brosseau and left-hander Ramon Hernandez. Murtaugh promised that he wouldn't hesitate to use both unproven pitchers in the head-to-head matchups with St. Louis.

Murtaugh didn't need any extra pitchers in the first game of the series. Steve Blass went the distance, scattering seven hits in earning a 3-1 victory at Busch Memorial Stadium. The Cardinals had a chance to erase a three-run deficit in the sixth, when they loaded the bases with no one out. With the middle of their order coming to bat—Ted Simmons, Joe Torre, and Jose Cardenal—the Redbirds seemed primed to even the game. Simmons plated one run by lifting a sacrifice fly, but Torre and Cardenal both popped up weakly to end the inning. The Cardinals didn't score the rest of the way against Blass, whose clutch pitching was buttressed by Bob Robertson's 12th home run.

The second game with St. Louis provided some interesting strategy that would backfire on Cardinal manager Red Schoendienst. In the second inning, with two runners in scoring position, Schoendienst elected to intentionally walk the Bucs' No. 8 hitter, Gene Alley. The decision loaded the bases, but enabled the Cardinals to pitch to the weak-hitting Dock Ellis. The normally sound baseball strategy produced an unintended result. Ellis pounded out a bases-loaded two-run single, giving the Pirates the early lead. In the fourth inning, Schoendienst adopted the same approach, walking Alley once again to load the bases for Ellis. This time, Ellis responded with a less dramatic, but still productive base hit. An infield single by the Pirate pitcher brought home Pittsburgh's third run of the game, on the way to an 11-4 shellacking. The pitcher's spot in the batting order supplied a quartet of RBIs (Dave Giusti drove in a run later in the game).

The following night provided additional dramatics. The Bucs, who had raced out to a 3-0 lead, slowly allowed the margin to fritter away. The Cardinals scored single runs in the third, sixth, and eighth innings to tie the game at 3-3. With two outs and no one on in the top of the ninth, Al Oliver faced rookie left-hander Rudy Arroyo and supplied an example of his skill against southpaw pitching. A long home run against Arroyo gave the Pirates a 4-3 lead, and eventually the victory, after Mudcat Grant subdued the Cards in the ninth inning.

The Pirates primed themselves for a four-game sweep on Sunday afternoon, even though the odds of beating Steve Carlton seemed slim. Predictably, the Pirates trailed the Cards, 4-3, as the game moved to the ninth. Yet, Danny Murtaugh could take some solace in knowing that the top of his batting order would be coming to bat against a tiring Carlton. Meanwhile, the Cardinals' ineffective bullpen offered Red Schoendienst few options. Dave Cash led off the ninth with a single, Gene Clines followed with another single, and Clemente knocked in the tying run with a single of his own. A sacrifice fly by Willie Stargell scored Clines to give the Pirates a 5-4 lead, while also sending Carlton to the clubhouse. After a Manny Sanguillen single, Richie Hebner powered a game-salting three-run homer against reliever Chuck Taylor. Minor league refugee Ramon

Hernandez, working his second straight night of relief, pitched an unblemished ninth inning, as Murtaugh continued to use different pitchers to close out games. With the victory, the Pirates had swept the Cards and cemented their lead over both the Cardinals and the Mets in the National League East.

Although the flu had forced Roberto Clemente to the sidelines for a couple of days in early June, the Pirates' venerable superstar had enjoyed a period of resurgence at the plate. His rejuvenated hitting had altered the mood of many fans, writers, and broadcasters who had questioned the staying power of the 36-year-old Clemente in April and May. During that early-season slump, critics had taken shots at several facets of Clemente's game, in particular what appeared to be diminishing bat speed.

By the middle of June, Clemente had erased most concerns about the skills that he still featured as a hitter. On June 10th, his batting average stood at a healthy .313; his power numbers included six home runs and 31 RBIs. Despite some of the gloom-and-doom prophecies expressed by the media and fans early in the season, Clemente still possessed sufficient bat speed—among his many talents.

Even during his early season batting skid, no one had questioned Clemente's speed on the base paths, or in particular, his defense in right field. Even in his late thirties, Clemente's fielding remained of a Gold Glove caliber. Clemente provided further evidence of that on June 15, when he pulled off what may have been the most spectacular catch of his long career.

Playing at the Houston Astrodome, Clemente and the Pirates held a 1-0 lead as they headed toward the bottom of the eighth inning. With two outs and the fast-footed Joe Morgan leading off first base, Bob Watson stepped to the plate. A powerful right-handed batter, Watson stroked a hard liner that sliced severely as it headed toward the right field corner. In full gallop, Clemente raced toward the ball and neared the outfield fence.

Only a few feet from the wall, Clemente made a forceful leap. With his body fully extended off the ground and his back to home plate, Clemente snared the ball, just as it was about to clear the solid yellow line on the Astrodome wall. If the ball had hit above the line—as stipulated by the Astrodome's ground rules—Watson would have been credited with a home run.

Although the initial grab of the ball was impressive, it meant nothing if Clemente could not hold onto the ball upon colliding with the fence. He crashed hard into the wall, sending a shockwave through the crowd, and slumped to the ground, but the ball remained in his glove. Although Clemente had just deprived the Astros of a tie-breaking two-run homer, at the conclusion of the play, the 16,307 fans in attendance at the Astrodome produced an unusual reaction: they rewarded Clemente, an enemy player, with a standing ovation. He paid a price, however, with a badly bruised left ankle, a gashed left knee, and a swollen left elbow.

In an interview with *Sports Illustrated*, Astros manager Harry Walker, who had played in the majors for 11 years and had managed Clemente from 1965 to 1967, simply said this of the catch, "It was the best I'd ever seen."

Clemente's heroics preserved a 1-0 lead for the Pirates, who went on to win the game, 3-0, behind the pitching of Steve Blass. Afterward, the right-hander showed little interest in taking credit for his fourth shutout of the season, instead preferring to discuss the exploits of his teammate. "That shutout belongs to Clemente," Blass told John Wilson of the *Houston Chronicle*.

Although usually a confident player, Clemente himself had doubted whether he could make the catch. "I don't ever think I can get to it, but I have to try," Clemente said, while soaking his knee, ankle, and elbow in ice packs.

The remarkable play lacked only one element: it was not preserved on film or videotape, because this regular season game was not being televised. In order for the masses to fully appreciate his outfield skills, Clemente would have to repeat his defensive prowess much later in the season, this time with the cameras on hand to properly record the proceedings.

The following night, Roberto Clemente gave the Pirates another lift, this time with his bat. Clemente's two-run homer in the seventh inning provided the Pirates with the winning margin in a 6-4 decision at the Astrodome. Gene Clines, filling in for a resting

Willie Stargell, smacked four hits and stole two bases in support of Dock Ellis, who became the first Pirate pitcher to reach 10 victories. Although Ellis had pitched very well, he admitted to reporters after the game that he had experienced severe pain in his right elbow in stifling the Astros.

The Bucs returned to Three Rivers after a productive seven-win, three-loss road trip against the Cubs, Cardinals, and Astros, and now led the East by five and a half games. The Pirates began the new homestand against the young, building Montreal Expos, who started impressive youngster Steve Renko. The promising right-hander pitched effectively, holding a 6-2 lead over the Pirates at the start of the eighth inning. The Bucs plated two runs in the crucial frame, knocking out Renko in the process. Montreal responded with two runs in the top of the ninth, again increasing the lead to four runs. But the stubborn Pirates refused to yield to Montreal's relief ace, Mike Marshall. Manny Sanguillen doubled and scored on a pinch-hit by Bill Mazeroski. Dave Cash launched a two-run homer to draw the Pirates within a run, and Richie Hebner followed with his seventh home run of the season, tying the game. In the 11th inning, Gene Clines, pinch-hitting for Dave Giusti, poked a triple against Claude Raymond. With one out and the infield drawn in, Cash singled to drive in his third run of the night, giving the Bucs a dramatic extra-inning victory.

Cash, with two hits and three RBIs, had stretched his hitting streak to five games. Earlier in the month, Cash had endured an 0-for-18 slump. At the time, some Pirate fans had been pushing for Bill Mazeroski to play regularly, if for no other reason than to reach the 2,000-hit milestone that he had been approaching. Yet, Cash's rejuvenated hitting, which kept his average above the .300 mark, insured that he would continue to play every day at second base.

As the start of July loomed, the Pirates continued to hold their lead in the National League East; they also began pushing the Giants for the best record in the entire league. But Pirate attendance did not reflect the team's winning ways. Although the team's attendance was 147,000 fans ahead of the previous year's, nine National League teams owned better attendance figures than the Bucs. That fact partially explained why only one Pirate—Manny Sanguillen—

rated among the top two vote-getters for any position for the National League All-Star team. Willie Stargell, one of the leading contenders in the league's Most Valuable Player race, ranked only third in the outfield voting, behind Willie Mays and Hank Aaron. Even Roberto Clemente, the most popular of all the Pirates, ranked no better than sixth among National League outfielders.

Obviously not bothered by his showing in the All-Star voting, Stargell offered another glimpse of his awesome power on Sunday, June 20, against the Expos. The Pirates' left fielder, playing in the first game of a doubleheader, smashed a tape-measure home run into the highest deck of Three Rivers Stadium. The blast marked the third home run that Stargell had deposited in that section since the new stadium opened in the middle of the 1970 season. Estimates placed the latest home run at 430 feet, the longest ball that Stargell had struck in the young ballpark. Stargell's Ruthian shot overshadowed the longball heroics of Richie Hebner, who drove in four runs with a double and his eighth home run of the season.

After Blass won the first game, 7-1, Stargell once again contributed in the nightcap. Stargell hit a shorter, but more productive home run—a grand slam against the tormented Mike Marshall, who continued to be plagued by the Pirates' offense. Stargell's 24th home run of the season highlighted a seven-run seventh inning, which also included Milt May's second home run of the season. The 7-3 win gave the Bucs a sweep of the doubleheader.

Stargell's 25th longball came the next night in a 6-0 shutout of the Mets, now the second-place residents in the National League East. Stargell's two-run homer against left-hander Jerry Koosman helped make a winner of Dock Ellis. The Pirates' ace picked up his ninth consecutive win, and 11th in 14 decisions on the year. The hard-throwing right-hander logged the shutout despite continuing pain in his pitching elbow—and a lack of velocity in the early innings. Ellis not only pitched through recurring pain, but also recorded five putouts, matching the major league mark for most putouts in a game by a pitcher. In the meantime, Bob Robertson established a new major league record for most assists—eight—by a first baseman. Reserve outfielder Gene Clines, filling in for Al Oliver in center field, continued to make his value readily apparent with a

1-for-2 effort at the plate, two runs scored, and an RBI. Whether it was filling in for Oliver, Stargell, or Clemente in the outfield, or coming off the bench as a pinch-hitter, Clines was making Danny Murtaugh seem like a managerial mastermind.

In reality, Murtaugh did not possess the in-game smarts of an Earl Weaver or a Sparky Anderson, but he did possess the ability to motivate players to play hard—and well—for him. "Danny Murtaugh was not a strategical genius, by his own admission, although I still don't know how to define that particular term," says Steve Blass. "[But] he was a very good psychologist. He had a good sense of the people that worked for him as players, and his coaching staff." Unlike lesser managers, Murtaugh clearly understood the personalities of his players. "I think maybe the most unique thing about Danny that I can recall is the fact that whatever you approached him about never seemed to catch him off guard," Blass says. "He was always prepared for whatever you might come into his office with, in terms of a concern or a problem. He dealt well with people."

In 1971, Murtaugh dealt well with one of his most unpredictable players, Dock Ellis. General manager Joe Brown realized that Murtaugh had played a part in the emotional development of the talented right-hander. "I think Dock has matured," Brown told *The Sporting News*. "I think a lot has to do with his relationship with Danny. Dock respects Murtaugh." In part, because of Murtaugh's guiding hand, Ellis had finally harnessed his talents and become the best pitcher on the Pirate staff, and perhaps the best in the National League.

Just when it seemed the Pirates might start to pull away from the Mets in the divisional race, they succumbed in their next game, a disheartening 3-2 loss at Three Rivers. Trailing 3-0 in the bottom of the ninth, the Bucs rallied for two runs, only to fall short.

The loss turned out to be only a temporary setback, as the Bucs claimed the series finale. Stargell clubbed a three-run homer in the first, giving the Pirates a 3-1 lead. He later added a run-scoring double, giving him four runs batted in for the game and a league-leading total of 72, or 16 ahead of Atlanta's Hank Aaron. Not to be outdone, Roberto Clemente contributed four hits and Richie Hebner added three safeties to the attack, while Luke Walker and Mudcat Grant combined to pitch two-run baseball.

The Bucs opened a road trip in Philadelphia, where they took three out of four from the doormat Phillies. The weekend series included multiple-homer games by Richie Hebner and Jackie Hernandez (of all people), Stargell's 27th and 28th home runs of the season, and Clemente's 1200th career RBI, which came on a game-winning pinch-hit home run. Danny Murtaugh also continued to display a magic hand in filling out the lineup card. In the second game, Bill Mazeroski, making a rare start at second base, had banged out four hits, including his first home run of the season. Another ageless backup, Jose Pagan, had also contributed to the weekend onslaught, going 6-for-12 overall, including two homers and five RBIs in the nightcap of Sunday's doubleheader. As a team, the Pirates scored a total of 39 runs in the four-game set.

The Pirates continued to bulldoze through the National League schedule in June. The Bucs bombed the Cardinals, 11-5, burying them further in the Eastern Division standings. Mazeroski, subbing for Dave Cash—who had developed a leg infection—stroked two hits, the hot-hitting Jose Pagan collected three more, and Manny Sanguillen cleared the sacks with a bases-loaded triple. The Cardinals managed a split of the series by winning the next night, 8-3, but had already lost an opportunity to pick up some serious ground on the Pirates.

The loss to the Cardinals, coupled with the Mets' 3-0 win over the Phillies, drew New York within three games of first-place Pittsburgh. The latest results set the stage for an important two-game, midweek series at Shea Stadium. A crowd of 50,399 fans jammed into Flushing Meadow for the first game, anticipating a tantalizing pitching matchup between the veteran control specialist, Steve Blass, and the young fireballer, Nolan Ryan. The Mets dented Blass for a single run in the second inning, two more in the sixth, and a single run in the seventh, with a Ryan triple highlighting the Mets' scoring. Yet Ryan's pitching was even more impressive than his hitting. He overpowered the Bucs' lineup on nine strikeouts through seven scoreless innings, victimizing Willie Stargell three times. "You've got to outguess Stargell," explained Ryan in an interview with *Sports Illustrated.* "You can't give him the same pitch twice in a row." Even if you threw 95-100 mile per hour fastballs—like Ryan did.

Ryan eventually wilted in the 90-degree heat and humidity of the Queens night, giving way to Danny Frisella. New York's best right-handed reliever hurled the eighth and ninth innings to preserve an impressive 4-0 shutout for the Mets. With the home win, the Mets had clawed to within two games of the Pirates.

For the first time in several weeks, the Pirates felt some discomfort when looking at the National League East standings. A Thursday afternoon showdown with the Mets awaited them. If they lost, the Pirates' once-substantial lead would shrink to a single game. As fortune would have it, Dock Ellis' turn came up in the rotation. The right-hander, who had won nine straight deci-

Signed by the Pirates as an amateur free agent in 1964, Dock Ellis compiled a 96-80 record for Pittsburgh over nine seasons. The talented right-hander had his best year on the mound and at the plate in 1971. Known for his flamboyant self-expression and controversial candor, Ellis became a spirited personality in the Pirates' clubhouse. (*National Baseball Hall of Fame Library, Cooperstown, NY*)

sions, shackled the Mets for five innings. Unfortunately for the Pirates, the game was delayed three times by thunderstorms. After the second interruption, Danny Murtaugh decided to pull Ellis, who was holding a mere 1-0 lead. With his best starter now out of the game, Murtaugh called upon his least-known pitcher, the inexperienced Jim Nelson. Using his trademark palmball—the same pitch featured by relief ace Dave Giusti—Nelson struggled through two-thirds of an inning, giving up a walk and two hits to load the bases. Nellie Briles came on to register the third out and end the threat, then gave way to Giusti for the balance of the afternoon. The succession of relievers preserved a critical 3-0 victory that required four hours and 14 minutes to complete because of the intermittent showers. With the win, the Pirates had held their ground, maintaining a two-game lead in the East as they approached the Fourth of July weekend.

Chapter 7

JULY

As the 1971 season progressed, Danny Murtaugh continually found himself rotating players in making out his nine-man lineup. Major league teams like the Pirates had to concern themselves not only with the possibility of losing players to injury, but also to military reserve duty—something unheard of in today's sports. During the recent series with the Phillies, Jose Pagan had played third base in the absence of Richie Hebner, who spent his weekend in the Marine Reserves. In July, Dave Cash would miss several games while on reserve duty, which would allow Bill Mazeroski to return to the starting lineup at second base. The Pirates' bench— the deepest in either league—had consistently provided Murtaugh with capable backups. Pagan and Mazeroski, the two elder statesmen of the Pirates' bench, had played a doubleheader in Philadelphia in searing 90-degree heat. "This bench has no retirement plan," Murtaugh quipped to Charley Feeney of *The Sporting News*. Earlier, Murtaugh had been reluctant to call the 1971 bench brigade better than his 1960 group of reserves, but by June he was willing to step out on the limb. "This year's bench is the best I've ever had," Murtaugh said flatly. Its strength also provided plenty of motivation to the team's starters. "On this club, you have to be afraid to sit down for a day," Willie Stargell told the *New York Post*. "They held me out in Houston, and Gene Clines went 4-for-5 in my place."

Bob Moose became the next Pirate called up for two straight weeks of service in the military reserves. Equipped with a devastating slider, Moose had emerged as one of the Pirates' most effective mid-season starters. In his last outing, on Friday, July 2, in Chicago, he helped the Pirates best the Cubs 5-1. The gritty Moose never shied from taking the ball—either as a starter or a reliever. "Bob came from the old school," says Dave Giusti. "When he had a sore arm, you'd never know it, because he still wanted to go out there and pitch." Rather than pursue a trade for an established pitcher to replace Moose, the Bucs sought a boost from their own productive farm system when they recalled right-handed pitcher Bruce "Buster" Kison, who had forged a record of 10-1 at Triple-A Charleston during the first half of the season. Since beginning his professional career in 1968, Kison had achieved a record of 30-9 in the minor leagues, and had never experienced a losing campaign. Prior to the 1971 season, Kison had been considered two to three years away from major league competition, but his first-half minor league performance had accelerated his rise to Pittsburgh.

The baby-faced Kison arrived with a six-foot-four, 178-pound frame, and a waistline of only 33 inches. "I looked older than Kison the day I was born," Murtaugh told the Pittsburgh media. More important, Kison possessed a live fastball, a sharp curveball, and a deceptive motion.

The talented right-hander had developed his unusual pitching style by accident. As a Pony League pitcher at the age of 14, Kison had injured his elbow when he was hit by thrown balls on two successive days. When Kison returned, he began using a side-arm motion, which caused him less pain than throwing over the top. The side-winding style made him particularly effective against right-handed batters, and made him a top prospect in the minds of the Bucs' organization. Kison also arrived in the major leagues with a reputation for wildness. During a 1970 season split between Class-A Salem (Carolina League) and Double-A Waterbury (Eastern League), Kison had hit 21 batters with pitches, including seven batters in one game.

Looking out of place in the Pirates' skin-tight, double-knit pullover uniforms, the reed-like Kison made his major league debut against the Cubs on the Fourth of July. Kison pitched respectably in his debut, lasting six innings and giving up four runs. Although Kison left with the score tied at 4-4, the Pirates lost the game when the Cubs scored five runs in the bottom of the eighth inning.

After the tough loss, the Pirates won their next four games, including Kison's first big league victory on July 8. The following night, while playing against the Atlanta Braves, the Pirates executed the major leagues' first triple play of the 1971 season. Sonny Jackson and Hal King had opened the seventh inning with back-to-back singles against Nellie Briles. Eighth-place hitter Leo Foster, making his major league debut, stepped to the plate and promptly hit a ground smash down the third base line. Richie Hebner fielded the ball cleanly, quickly stepped on the third base bag for the first out, and fired to Dave Cash at second base for the second out. Cash immediately relayed to Bob Robertson at first base to complete the inning.

The triple play served as a mere sidelight to another impressive 11-2 Pirate victory. Briles pitched nine innings of two-run baseball, and a balanced Bucs offense managed 11 runs against a trio of over-matched Braves' pitchers. Hebner, Stargell, and Manny Sanguillen each rapped out three hits, with Stargell's 29th home run highlighting the blowout.

With nearly three months to play, Stargell appeared ready to make a run at Roger Maris' 10-year-old record of 61 home runs in a single season. In July, reporters repeatedly asked Stargell about the possibility of tying or breaking Maris' storied mark. At that, Stargell started to show slight signs of impatience with the comparisons to Maris. "No, I don't think about Babe Ruth or Roger Maris or anyone else," Stargell told a reporter from the *Newark Star-Ledger*. "I don't think about records or anything like that."

Before the Friday night win over the Braves, the Pirates had staged a special event at Three Rivers. The second annual Latino-American Baseball Players Day, which had been organized by baseball official Luis Mayoral, in cooperation with Commissioner Bowie Kuhn and National Association President John Johnson, honored several Latin Americans in attendance at the game. Six Pirate players of Latino descent, five members of the Braves (Orlando Cepeda, Gil Garrido, Felix Millan, Marty Perez, and Zoilo Versalles), and former major leaguer Vic Power received recognition during pre-game ceremonies.

The occasion provided an especially fitting tie-in for the Pirates, who featured more prominent Latin Americans on their roster than any other major league team. Roberto Clemente and Jose Pagan hailed from Puerto Rico, Manny Sanguillen and Rennie Stennett (recently recalled from the minor leagues) represented Panama, Vic Davalillo was of Venezuelan descent, and Jackie Hernandez came from Cuba. In other words, the Pirates' starting catcher, shortstop, and right fielder, and three of their top reserve players came from Latin American countries. These players comprised much more than a token presence on the Pirates; after all, Clemente and Sanguillen were regarded as All-Stars and team leaders, while Davalillo and Pagan were considered two of the most capable pinch-hitters in the game.

During the off-season, general manager Joe Brown and director of scouting Harding "Pete" Peterson had visited the Caribbean in an effort to scout younger prospects and sign those who were eligible to play in the States. Such scouting trips to Spanish-speaking countries were emblematic of the Pirates' organization. Longtime scout Howie Haak, who died in 1999 at the age of 87, served as Pittsburgh's point man in evaluating and obtaining Latino talent. "Howie used to go down and sign Dominican, Venezuelan, and Puerto Rican players," says Richie Hebner, who platooned with a Latin American, Jose Pagan, at third base. The prevalence of Latino players extended well beyond the major league level. "It was not just with our big league club," says Hebner. "You go down to Pirate City back in the early seventies. There was a lot of Latino kids and a lot of black kids. [There] was a lot of good talent down there, and I think Pittsburgh probably said, 'Hey, white, black, yellow, brown, whatever, we're gonna try to get the best players.'"

Playing the second game of the July series against the Braves, Willie Stargell continued his bombardment of National League pitching, having little difficulty with Phil Niekro's knuckleball, while connecting on his 30th home run of the season. In the bottom of the eighth inning, with the Pirates trailing 4-3, Vic Davalillo reached first on an infield single. After Niekro retired Al Oliver, Stargell deposited a dramatic two-run home run to provide the Bucs with the winning margin. With the landmark shot, Stargell established a single-season National League record—in the short era since the league had expanded to 12 teams—for the most home runs against any one club. Stargell had now hit 10 home runs against the pitching-poor Braves on the season, which still had nearly three months to go. Dave Giusti added his league-leading 19th save during the series with the Braves, and had clearly established himself as the National League's most consistent closer.

Yet, Giusti's impressive pitching during the first half of 1971 seemed to have little effect on Cincinnati Reds manager Sparky Anderson, who bypassed Giusti for the National League All-Star squad. Anderson instead picked his own closer, Clay "Hawk" Carroll, whose statistics did not measure up to Giusti's. Giusti did not handle the snub diplomatically. "This is the second straight year they've passed me up," Giusti complained to Charley Feeney of *The Sporting News*. "Last year they took Hoyt Wilhelm and now this year Carroll. I wish they'd figure out what the All-Star Game is supposed to represent. What's Carroll done? He's a good relief pitcher, but if he's so good, how come his team is in fifth place? Last year they passed me up because of sentiment for Wilhelm, who was on the verge of leaving baseball. This year they didn't pick me because Anderson favored his own man."

The Pirates' closer seemed to have a legitimate beef. Through games of July 8—only five days before the All-Star Game—Giusti had posted an earned run average of 2.25, better than Carroll's mark of 2.37. A much wider discrepancy could be found in the saves column. Giusti had saved 18 of the Pirates' victories, more than double Carroll's total of eight.

After a Three Rivers Stadium rainout against the Braves on Sunday, the Pirates welcomed the three-day rest provided by the All-Star break. All but four Pirates—All-Star selections Roberto Clemente, Dock Ellis, Manny Sanguillen, and Willie Stargell— would be free to do what they pleased over the next three days. Just a few weeks earlier, Ellis had made headlines by predicting that he would *not* be selected to start the All-Star Game. Ellis had reasoned that with American League manager Earl Weaver likely to select the sizzling Vida Blue as his starter, baseball's powers-that-be would want at least one white pitcher starting the midsummer classic in Detroit. "They wouldn't pitch two brothers against each other," Ellis told a reporter from the *New York Times*. Besides, according to Ellis, "Sparky Anderson [the National League manager] doesn't like me."

Much to the pitcher's surprise, Anderson announced that Ellis would start and would indeed face Blue in Detroit, marking the first time that black pitchers had started against each other since the All-Star Game's inception in 1933. Anderson denied that Ellis' comments had, in any way, swayed his decision. "His 14-3 record and the fact that he hasn't pitched since last Tuesday is what forced me to choose him," Anderson told the *New York Times*, while deflecting Ellis' comments: "I think everybody has a right to say what he wants."

In response to his outburst, Ellis received numerous angry letters from fans who criticized him for being so presumptuous about Anderson. "I don't mind those [negative] letters, but there was one letter I was particularly pleased with," Ellis told *The Sporting News*. "Jackie Robinson wrote me a letter of encouragement. I met him last April in New York, and then I received this letter from him."

On Tuesday, July 13, just hours before the start of the All-Star Game, Ellis offered no apologies for his recent remarks doubting the possibility of African-American pitchers starting the national pastime's showcase game. "When it comes to black players, baseball is backwards, everyone knows it," Ellis told a reporter from the *New York Times*. "I'm sort of surprised that I am starting, but I don't feel my statements had anything to do with it." Ellis also seized the opportunity to complain about the lack of endorsements for black athletes, compared to the commercial opportunities given to white players. A reporter asked Ellis if he had received any endorsement offers in light of his brilliant pitching in the first half of the season. "Aw, man, c'mon," Ellis said incredulously to Murray Chass of the *New York Times*. "Come to me for endorsements?"

Later in the season, Ellis would complain that black players received less attention from the media and less promotion from the front office than white athletes of similar ability. Ellis brought up several examples from the Pirates' own roster. "Bob Moose and I are the tightest," Ellis told Phil Musick of *Sport* magazine, "but when he came up, he was a phenom. Richie Hebner, he was Mr. Pie Traynor. Why don't they publicize black players like that?"

Throughout his life, Ellis had bristled at racist treatment. During his first spring training in 1964, Ellis said he had argued or fought with seven different teammates who had used ethnic slurs in conversing with him. Seven years later, instances of face-to-face racism still bothered Ellis, but he had learned to use restraint. During the 1971 season, Ellis and a friend visited a high school that had been affected by racial divisions. On the way to the school, a police officer called out to the two men, referring to them as "boys." "That's where I've changed," Ellis told *Sport* magazine. "Three years ago, I would've jumped on the cop's chest. But all I did was to correct him."

Ellis now found himself featured in the game's midseason showcase at Tiger Stadium, squared off against the game's other hot starting pitcher, Oakland's Vida Blue. In the bottom of the third, with the Nationals leading 3-0, Ellis faced Boston Red Sox shortstop Luis Aparicio, who had struggled through the first half of the season. Though barely batting above .200 in regular season play, the pesky Aparicio led off the inning by singling up the middle. Seizing the opportunity to use his bench in the All-Star Game, American League manager Earl Weaver called upon Oakland A's slugger Reggie Jackson to pinch-hit for his teammate Vida Blue. A last-minute All-Star Game replacement for the injured Tony Oliva, Jackson drove a mediocre Ellis fastball deep toward right-center field. The ball, still seemingly still on the rise, caromed off the light tower that peaked above the Tiger Stadium roof in right field. Some observers estimated that Jackson's home run had traveled 520 feet.

Ellis, despite his brilliant first-half pitching for the Pirates, would now be remembered more vividly for giving up a gargantuan home run on national television. Unfortunately for Ellis, his All-Star Game problems had just begun. After issuing a walk to Rod Carew, Ellis retired the next two batters on pop-ups, only to watch Frank Robinson club another one of his lazy fastballs into the right-field stands. F. Robby's blast gave the American League a 4-3 lead. Robinson, who had gone hitless in his last 14 All-Star Game at-bats, was on his way to winning the midsummer classic's Most Valuable Player Award. Ellis was on his way to a loss in his first All-Star Game appearance.

In the eighth, with the American League now leading, 6-3, Roberto Clemente strode to the plate to face Detroit Tigers left-hander Mickey Lolich. Although most of the 53,559 fans at Tiger Stadium were focusing on their hometown pitcher, their collective attention would soon shift to the batter's box.

Lolich, it seemed, wanted no part of facing Clemente. Even though Lolich was nursing a three-run lead, he threw two pitches far out of the strike zone. Visibly upset, Clemente stepped out from his stance in the batter's box and flipped his bat in the air. When Lolich fell behind in the count three-and-one, he delivered another errant pitch, one that appeared to be tailing high and away from Clemente, again clearly out of the strike zone. Yet Clemente swung at the rising fastball. Flicking his wrists with his customary quickness, Clemente lifted the ball toward right-center field. The ball seemed like it might be caught, but it carried surprisingly, landing in the Tiger Stadium bleachers beyond the right-field wall.

To the observant eye, it looked as if Clemente had challenged Lolich to throw him a strike, and when he refused, he simply expanded his strike zone, determined to hit the ball as hard—and as far—as he could. Clemente did not want to take a base on balls in an All-Star Game. Instead, Clemente wanted desperately to show the nationwide television audience that he could hit as well as anyone.

Clemente's home run was the sixth one hit that night in Detroit, as he joined Hank Aaron, Johnny Bench, Jackson, Robinson, and Harmon Killebrew in the long-ball parade. While Clemente's home run brought the National League no closer than two runs, it provided the television audience with a stunning example of the determination and athleticism of Roberto Clemente.

Still, the 1971 All-Star Game represented so much more—even beyond the exploits of Clemente and Jackson. Virtually every superstar of the late 1960s and early 1970s played in the game, indicating the era's depth of talent. The veritable who's who of baseball featured a flock of 18 future Hall of Famers who made appearances: Hank Aaron, Johnny Bench, Lou Brock, Ferguson Jenkins, Juan Marichal, Willie Mays, Willie McCovey, Clemente, and Stargell from the National League, and American Leaguers Luis Aparicio, Rod Carew, Reggie Jackson, Al Kaline, Harmon Killebrew, Jim Palmer,

Brooks Robinson, Frank Robinson, and Carl Yastrzemski. Black stars. White stars. Latin American stars, representing the best talent in baseball. Still, these were artificial teams playing an exhibition game. More meaningful integration would take place later in the season.

After the All-Star break, the Pirates welcomed the San Diego Padres to town. In one of the most compelling games of the season, the Padres forced the Pirates to play a 17-inning marathon, longer than any game to date in the National League that season. The Pirates trailed the Padres, 1-0, in the bottom of the ninth inning, but the lower third of the Pittsburgh order picked an opportune time to forge a comeback. A walk, followed by Jose Pagan's single, and Gene Alley's sacrifice fly tied the game at 1-1. In the top of the 13th, San Diego slugger Ivan Murrell gave the Padres their second lead, hitting his sixth home run of the season. In the bottom half of the frame, Willie Stargell prolonged matters by hitting his 31st home run. San Diego re-took the lead in the 16th inning, but Richie Hebner extended the game further, clubbing his 14th home run to tie the score in the bottom half. Then in the 17th inning, Roberto Clemente, struggling through an embarrassing 0-for-7 night, stepped to the plate against reliever Danny Coombs. With one out, Clemente finally brought an end to the proceedings, clearing the Three Rivers Stadium fences with his ninth home run. After a series of three comebacks in the bottom of the ninth, 13th, and 16th innings, the Pirates had found yet another way to win.

The victory gave the Pirates their seventh consecutive win and provided a springboard to the rest of the series against San Diego. Bob Johnson shut down the Padres on Friday night, July 16, and Dock Ellis continued his incredible run with his 15th straight win on Saturday. In so doing, Ellis became the first Pirate starter since Deacon Phillippe in 1910 to win 15 games in a row. Furthermore, Ellis continued to close in on the franchise record of 17 consecutive wins set by reliever ElRoy "Roy" Face in 1959.

Ellis, who would eventually be featured on the cover of the August 21 issue of *The Sporting News*, had emerged as one of the National League's most dominant pitchers—and one of its most intriguing personalities. While some black players shied away from public discourse of their own Afrocentric world views, Ellis reveled in such discussions. In an article in *Sports Illustrated*, Ellis explained the significance of his daughter's name, Shangaleza Talwanga, which meant "everything black is beautiful" in Swahili. In the Pirates' clubhouse, Ellis enjoyed listening to loud music that he labeled "funky." On the field, when preparing to take his at-bats during games he pitched, Ellis donned a fuzzy batting helmet, which he referred to as "velvetized."

Although Ellis often created controversy, he also strove to help others in the Pittsburgh community. Each week, Ellis visited the Western Penn Penitentiary and counseled inmates, often drawing on his own troubling experiences, which included a 1964 conviction of grand theft auto. Ellis also helped prison administrators in developing and improving recreation programs for the prisoners. Ellis believed that most of the inmates, whom he termed "residents," were worth the effort of rehabilitation. "What people tend to forget is that only about four per cent [of the prisoners] are in there for terrible crimes," Ellis told *The Sporting News*. "Most of the others will be out of there in a few years. These are the people we are especially trying to help."

Perhaps because of noble efforts such as these, Pirate players expressed fondness for Ellis, as both a person and a teammate. At times, the pitcher's own controversial, standoffish exterior hid a more approachable personality. "If Dock will let you inside that little atmosphere he's built around himself," Willie Stargell pointed out to Phil Musick of *Sport* magazine in 1971, "you'll find a sincere, warm person." Richie Hebner agreed. "Dock was good as a teammate. Every once in awhile, he wanted to say one and one was three, just to be different, I think. Dock would do things different. In the clubhouse, Dock was a good guy. I mean a lot of people outside of the clubhouse would probably say, 'I can't stand this guy...' But he was a good guy on the team."

"Personally, I think Dock Ellis is one fine human being," Bob Robertson says. "I'm gonna tell you about Dock. We used to be able to bring our family or our friends into the clubhouse at Three Rivers Stadium, and Dock and I got along great. He was a jokester in the clubhouse. Muhammad Ali—Cassius Clay—come in there one time, and he and Dock knew one another. Dock used to talk like him." During the 1971 season, Ali visited the Pirate clubhouse at Three Rivers Stadium. Ali proceeded to needle Ellis. "What's this I hear about you saying you're as pretty as me," Ali asked of the boastful Ellis. "Prettier," Ellis replied with a smile. "We used to laugh at Dock so much," Robertson says. "But Dock was the type of guy that if I brought one of my friends in there, and then all of a sudden I'd bring him back two months later, Dock Ellis would be the first person to go up and shake this man's hand and say, 'Nice to see you again.'"

The Pirates' mid-season mastery of the National League continued on July 18, when they swept the Dodgers in a doubleheader at Three Rivers. In the first game, rookie Bruce Kison and veteran Dave Giusti combined in holding the Dodgers to seven hits and two runs. In the nightcap, Luke Walker pitched the finest game of his career, narrowly missing out on the second Pirate no-hitter in two years. (Dock Ellis had thrown his masterpiece in 1970.) Walker held the Dodgers hitless until the ninth, when rookie catcher Joe Ferguson smacked the first home run of his major league career. Although Walker failed to hurl a no-hitter, he had helped the team forge a season-high 11-game winning streak, distancing the Pirates from National League East contenders Chicago, St. Louis, and New York.

Much to the surprise of most baseball writers who covered the National League, Pirate pitching had played a major role in the team's ability to open up space in the Eastern Division. Dave Giusti says that close observers of the team had begun to realize that the pitching was much better than originally thought. "We were known as the 'Lumber Company,' and as guys that could hit, but couldn't pitch, and that kind of thing," says Giusti. "As the year progressed we got a lot of respect in that we didn't give up a lot of runs. We were in the top of the league in pitching. I think that we found a way to win with our starting pitching and our short relief."

As the Pirates continued to pillage their rivals in the National League, their clubhouse continued to reflect the upbeat personalities on the team, which helped reinforce their winning ways. Prior to one game, Dock Ellis stood in the locker room listening to some of his favorite music, which he was playing at a high volume. Suddenly, one of the players turned down the level of the music, apparently in response to the entrance of The Great One, Roberto Clemente.

Ellis couldn't resist the opportunity to poke some fun. "Did you notice how the room went silent?" Ellis howled in front of a reporter from *Sports Illustrated*, before stepping into a physical imitation of Clemente. Ellis twiched his neck nervously and repeatedly, parroting the way that the aging superstar loosened his back muscles during at-bats. Ellis followed his demonstration by speaking in a Latino accent, "Oh, I not like I used to be. I a little bit of an old man." During Clemente's earlier major league days, a player might not have risked his wrath by mocking him in such fashion. A younger Clemente might have reacted to such a display with annoyance or anger. Yet, things were different now. By 1971, such humorous ribbing of the Pirate superstar was now considered acceptable behavior by Pittsburgh players—and by Clemente himself.

"It was a pretty close team," remembers Nellie Briles. "We all got along pretty well, even though you had some wild personalities, with a Dock Ellis and the Richie Hebners, and the Bob Robertsons, and the Sanguillens. It was a real diverse group. Even though the personalities were diverse, when that ballclub went on the field, I mean they were there to play baseball, and play hard. I think that's where we had a lot of respect for one another, because when it came time to play, we were ready to play."

The Pirates had played some of their best baseball of the season during the first half of July. The winning streak ended on Monday, July 19, when the Dodgers clubbed Briles and three relief pitchers to the tune of a 10-4 win. Although it was their first loss in 12 outings, the Pirates reacted as if they had lost the World Series, and sat in dead silence at their lockers.

The Pirates received another blow when starting second baseman Dave Cash left the team for his scheduled tour of military reserve duty. Murtaugh inserted veteran Bill Mazeroski into the lineup and brought up spring training sensation Rennie Stennett, recalled from Triple-A Charleston, to provide middle infield depth. By the time Cash returned, the Pirates had built up a lead of 10 and a half games.

On many talented teams, a strong corps of reserve players tended to create jealousies among players who clamored for additional
playing time. Looking back, Dave Cash says the Pirates featured
virtually no such dissension. "We had basically nine guys that started," Cash recalls. "We had about six or seven other guys that knew
their role, and they came in for defensive reasons, or they played
against left-handed pitching, such as Jose Pagan or Gene Clines.
Guys [like Davalillo] that gave Clemente a rest, gave Stargell a rest
now and then, picked up Hebner here and there... Each one of these
guys knew their roles, and I think that was one of the reasons why
there wasn't a lot of commotion. When a left-handed pitcher
pitched, the guys that didn't play against right-handers knew they
were going to be in the game against the left-hander." In fact, only
one Pirate player, a youthful Al Oliver, had sounded off publicly
about not receiving enough playing time.

When writers quoted Oliver's complaints about his status on the
ballclub, manager Danny Murtaugh refused to retaliate verbally. "I
wouldn't want a player on my team who didn't want to play everyday," Murtaugh told Charley Feeney. Although Oliver chafed at the
idea of not playing every day, he nonetheless enjoyed a good relationship with Murtaugh. "I never had any problems with managers,
as far as disliking them," Oliver says in recalling his major league
career. "It was just the way that I was brought up. My mother and
father didn't bring me up that way. With the spiritual type background that I had, I found it very hard to dislike people because they
didn't do the things that I would have liked for them to do." Still,
Oliver believes that he deserved to play more regularly in 1971.

Problems with platooning aside, the Pirates were threatening to
run away from the other teams in the Eastern Division. Perhaps the
West-leading San Francisco Giants, visiting Three Rivers Stadium
on July 20, 21, and 22, would provide a sterner test for the Bucs. In
the first game between the National League's division leaders, San
Francisco played more like lowly San Diego. After taking a 3-0 lead
in the top of the second inning and literally knocking Steve Blass out
of the game by hitting a line drive off his left calf, the Giants did
themselves in. Shortstop Chris Speier committed two errors that
handed the Bucs five unearned runs. The Giants came back with

five runs against Bob Veale, but watched their own middle relief combination of Don Carrithers and Rich Robertson give up a total of five runs of their own. With the Pirates now leading, Dave Giusti came on in the seventh and closed out an ugly 11-7 win by notching his 20th save.

On July 21, the Giants reversed their fortunes with a six-run, ninth-inning comeback, which started against Bob Johnson and climaxed against Giusti. The Pirates' closer walked Willie Mays with the bases loaded, forcing in the tying run. Giusti allowed matters to worsen quickly when he faced Willie McCovey. The feared left-handed slugger powered his 12th home run of the season—and the 13th grand slam of his major league career. McCovey's blast topped off an 8-4 win for the Giants.

In the rubber game of the series, the Giants sent a message that perhaps they—and not the Bucs—should be regarded as the best team in the National League. Pouncing on Dock Ellis for six runs in the first inning, the Giants seemed certain to end the All-Star pitcher's long winning streak at 15 games. Yet, Ellis settled down over the next six innings, holding the Giants scoreless. Now trailing by four runs as they headed to the ninth, the Pirates rallied to tie the score against a tiring Juan Marichal. In the 10th inning, Danny Murtaugh made an intriguing decision that would affect the game's outcome. He elected not to use his best reliever, Dave Giusti, who had pitched in the first two games of the series. Instead, Murtaugh opted for a well-rested Bob Moose, who promptly surrendered a leadoff triple to Ken Henderson (his second three-bagger of the game) and a single to light-hitting center fielder Jimmy Rosario. The two hits gave the Giants an 8-7 victory, making the Pirates' upcoming flight to the West Coast that much longer.

I n the opener of the Pirates' series in San Diego, rookie Bruce Kison quickly ended any possibilities of a sustained losing streak by hurling his first major league shutout. Home runs by Richie Hebner and Willie Stargell provided more than enough offense for Kison, who limited the Padres to a pair of harmless singles. With the complete-game victory, Kison improved his early record to 2-0.

After holding off a ninth-inning rally by the Padres in the next game, with Dave Giusti preserving Steve Blass' 11th win, Pittsburgh seemed primed for a doubleheader sweep on Sunday. In the first game, however, veteran left-hander Fred Norman, sporting an unsightly ledger of 0-6, held the Bucs to five hits. In the nightcap, struggling right-hander Steve Arlin, having lost 13 of his first 17 decisions, allowed only three hits in beating the Bucs, 2-0. The first doubleheader of the season could not have been more disappointing for the Pirates.

Still staggering, the Pirates then lost to the Dodgers in Los Angeles. After pitching a strong six innings, Dock Ellis suddenly weakened in the seventh, giving up RBI singles to Tom Haller and Maury Wills. Ellis gave way to Mudcat Grant, who promptly served up a grand slam to young right fielder Billy Buckner. The six-run outburst helped the Dodgers to an 8-5 victory. Ellis took the loss, ending his remarkable 15-game winning streak.

After the loss to the Dodgers, Pirate broadcaster Nellie King observed an unusual exchange in the Pittsburgh clubhouse between Roberto Clemente and Grant, who had given up the crucial home run in the Pirates' loss. "The club needed Mudcat Grant that year, and he was struggling," said King, who would tell the story to Pittsburgh area baseball writer Phil Musick many years later. "Anyway, I'm still in the clubhouse after almost everybody had left and Roberto got a stool and went over and sat beside Mudcat. He kept telling him, 'You can pitch! You can still get people out. Forget this game! It is gone!'" On most teams, no player would have dared to approach a veteran pitcher after such a loss, fearful of what might be an angry reaction. In this situation, Clemente had sensed that Grant was particularly down on himself and felt the circumstances mandated a pep talk—one professional to another.

The Pirates were clearly facing a major crossroads. A disastrous West Coast trip might provide a large enough window of opportunity for the Mets, Cubs, and Cards to sneak back into the race. Perhaps the Pirates had relied too much upon the power of Willie Stargell, who could not be expected to duplicate his home-run binge of the season's first half. Perhaps the Pirate pitching had over-achieved and would now return to the mediocre level of preseason expectation.

The powerful swing of underrated first baseman Bob Robertson would not allow the Pirates to fold. On July 28, he slugged his 20th home run, a solo shot against hard-throwing right-hander Bill Singer. Robertson tacked on a sacrifice fly in the eighth inning, accounting for half of the Pirate scoring in support of the brilliant pitching of Luke Walker. The streaky left-hander managed a four-hit shutout and continued his season-long domination of the Dodgers. The next night, Robertson collected his 21st longball during a six-run sixth inning, as the Bucs came from behind to post an 8-5 win at Dodger Stadium.

With his timely home runs against the Dodgers, Robertson had helped the Pirates stop the bleeding on the West Coast, but only temporarily. The Pirates headed to windy Candlestick Park for a four-game weekend series against the Giants, who continued to lead the West. The weekend soon turned into a disaster. The Giants, buttressed by a powerfully balanced lineup, torched Pirate pitching for 39 runs in the four games. None of the Pirate starters managed to survive past the fifth inning. Not even the power of Willie Stargell, who had supplied five more home runs during the series while also reaching the 100-RBI mark, prevented the Bucs from dropping all of the games in San Francisco.

The Pirates finished the West Coast trip with a disappointing 4-7 record. Just a week earlier it seemed the Bucs were on the verge of blowing out all of their divisional rivals. The Cardinals had now crept to within eight and a half games of the Pirates. It was the middle of the summer, and the heat of the pennant race was fast approaching.

Chapter 8

AUGUST

O n August 3, the Pirates began a three-game series north of the border in Montreal. Gene Alley, who only recently had discussed the possibility of retirement because of a weak bat, revived his hitting with a two-homer barrage in the opening game. Alley's second four-bagger highlighted a six-run eighth inning and contributed to a 10-6 come-from-behind win. Alley's batting average continued to hover around .200, but he had quickly raised his home run total to five, a fairly impressive number for a shortstop forced to share playing time with another infielder, Jackie Hernandez. Alley had also contributed to the Pirate cause with shrewd baserunning. Despite his lack of outstanding foot speed, Alley had successfully stolen nine bases in nine attempts.

After losing the next game in 11 innings, the Pirates managed to take the rubber game on Thursday. Unfortunately, they also lost one of their best bench players to a broken arm. After blasting a home run in his first at-bat, Jose Pagan fell victim to an inside fastball. The delivery from Montreal starter John Strohmayer nailed the Pirate third baseman, fracturing his left arm. The injury forced Pagan to the disabled list, and would keep him inactive for the next seven weeks. The unexpected loss of Pagan would keep Rennie Stennett on the major league roster for the foreseeable future.

With Dave Cash moving over to play third base for the injured Pagan, the Bucs suffered an unlikely defeat on Friday, August 6, when they entertained the dismal Phillies. The Phils, who had lost eight straight games at Three Rivers Stadium over the span of two seasons, managed 11 hits against Dock Ellis in posting a 3-2 win. The Pirates had led 2-1 in the top of the eighth inning, with Ellis seemingly in full control. But Ellis walked Deron Johnson, a right-handed batter, and then served up a two-run homer to the lefty-swinging Willie Montanez, one of the National League's best young hitters. The game also featured a bizarre but productive strategy by Phillies skipper Frank Lucchesi. With right-hander Billy Wilson on the mound and Stargell coming to bat in the bottom of the eighth, Lucchesi called for left-hander Joe Hoerner from the bullpen. Instead of taking Wilson out of the game, Lucchesi inserted him as the temporary third baseman and removed infielder John Vukovich from the game. Hoerner proceeded to strike out Stargell. Lucchesi then replaced Hoerner with Wilson, who returned to the mound to face a string of right-handed batters: Manny Sanguillen, Bob Robertson, and Gene Alley. Wilson held the Pirates scoreless for the balance of the game, giving the Phillies one of their rare—and most unusual—victories of the season.

The Pirates continued to struggle, falling behind the Phillies 5-0 in the next game and eventually losing, 5-3. On Sunday, the Pirates managed to split the doubleheader, as Bob Johnson pitched his first-ever National League shutout in the nightcap. The 4-0 win averted an embarrassing sweep at the hands of the league's worst team. Still, for the first time in 1971, the Pirates found themselves in the midst of a disastrous free fall.

In what amounted to their worst stretch of the season, the Pirates had lost 11 out of 16 games, including four straight losses to the Giants, the team they would likely have to face in the National League Championship Series—that is, if they even made it to the postseason. The Giants had dominated the Pirates in the regular season, winning nine out of 12 games overall, including five straight in San Francisco. If the two teams were to meet in the postseason, the Pirates would have to play the first two games at Candlestick Park and would face the undesirable prospect of meeting accomplished veterans like Gaylord Perry and Juan Marichal in succession. That possibility did not appeal to Danny Murtaugh, who tried to implant some humor into a depressed clubhouse. "If I were a drinking man," Murtaugh murmured to a reporter from *Sports Illustrated*, "I'd have one."

There were specific reasons for the drastic change in Pirate fortunes. At one point, the Pirates' bullpen sported a post-All-Star break ERA of 7.26, while surrendering 67 hits in 53 and a third innings. Bob Veale carried an ERA of over 7.00, belying his perfect won-loss record of 6-0. After pitching effectively in the first half, Mudcat Grant began to hang too many breaking pitches, a tendency that also plagued closer Dave Giusti. The unexpected struggles of Veale and Grant caused Murtaugh to call on Giusti more frequently. With his bullpen now faltering, Murtaugh tended to stay too long with his starters, who were becoming increasingly ineffective. No matter where Murtaugh turned for help, he found newly developing problems on his pitching staff.

Some general managers might have reacted to the kind of August slump the Pirates were now experiencing by holding off on possible deals, unwilling to overpay for a veteran pitcher in the trade market. That, however, was not Joe Brown's style. Nearly one year after acquiring Mudcat Grant, Brown now decided to dispatch the aging reliever, whose ERA had ballooned to 3.60 after an impressive early-season showing. On August 10, Brown pulled off a pair of related player moves. First, Brown sold Grant to the A's, the same team that had traded Grant to the Pirates the previous summer. Charlie Finley had tried to re-acquire Grant in March, but the Pirates had rejected the offer. Yet Brown had promised to consider Oakland's interest in Grant down the line. "I told Charlie we were counting on Grant," Brown told *The Sporting News*, "But if we ever decided to deal him, we'd try to give him first crack." The Pirate general manager proved to be a man of his word.

Having cleared a spot on his 25-man roster, Brown proceeded to ship off two minor league players to the non-contending Padres. In that deal, Brown acquired journeyman reliever Bob Miller and an undisclosed sum of cash for pitcher Eduardo Acosta and outfielder Johnny Jeter, both of whom had been toiling for Triple-A Charleston. Neither of the minor league players figured to help the Pirates down the stretch. Earlier in the season, no teams figured Miller could help them either. Even the pennant-contending Cubs, who desperately needed relief pitching, had released Miller on May 10. Several scouts claimed that Miller had ceased being a serviceable relief pitcher. A day after Miller accepted his release, Buzzie Bavasi, his former general manager with the Dodgers, did him a favor by signing him to a contract with the Padres. Miller justified

Bavasi's signing by posting a record of 7-3 with an impressive ERA of 1.41.

When Bavasi told him that he had been traded to the Pirates, Miller considered the possibility of quitting. "He spoke to me for a long time," Miller told *The Sporting News*, recalling his conversation with Bavasi. "I think when I entered his office I had the idea that I might not report to the Pirates. When Buzzie told me he was getting two good young players for me, I knew I couldn't do anything which would hurt him. He has been too good to me."

Some writers felt that Brown, by making two trades with his team still in first place, had pushed the panic button. Brown explained that he made the deal for Miller as a pre-emptive measure, in order to prevent a continuing swoon. "Why should we wait until we [really] need him?" Brown asked reporters rhetorically. The deal, while hardly a headline-maker or even popular with the media, would turn out to be another master stroke by the proactive Brown.

Yet, the trade did not have an immediate healing effect on the fading fortunes of the Bucs. The Pirates prepared for the arrival of the Cubs, who had re-entered the pennant race, thanks in part to Pittsburgh's recent problems. In the first encounter, the Cubs employed their surprisingly effective starter, converted relief pitcher Juan Pizarro, a onetime member of the Pirates. The veteran left-hander proceeded to shackle the Bucs on five hits. In pitching his third consecutive complete-game victory, Pizarro limited the Pirate scoring to Bob Robertson's 23rd home run and helped the Cubs move to within six games of their division-leading rivals.

The next night, the indomitable Dock Ellis shut down the Cubs with a complete-game win, while the Cards lost to the Braves. The Pirates now owned a seven-game lead on Chicago and an eight-game bulge on the Cardinals, who were coming to town for a three-game series. In the opening game, the Pirates faced red-hot left-hander Steve Carlton, who had already won 15 games. The Pirates supported their own left-hander, Luke Walker, with an early boost when they scored a first-inning run on a leadoff double by Dave Cash, a bunt single by Gene Clines, and a two-run double by Roberto Clemente. After walking Willie Stargell, Carlton struck out Manny

Sanguillen. Ted Simmons then threw Clemente out as he tried to steal third base. Carlton intentionally walked Bob Robertson before striking out Richie Hebner to end the inning.

With the Pirates leading just 2-0 heading to the top of the third, a defensive failing opened the floodgates. The suddenly error-prone Gene Alley bobbled Dal Maxvill's leadoff grounder, bringing Carlton to the plate. Cards skipper Red Schoendienst decided to forego the bunt and watched the fruits of his decision as Carlton delivered a line single. After forcing Carlton out on a fielder's choice, Walker surrendered a run-scoring double to Ted Sizemore and an RBI grounder to former Pirate Matty Alou. With two outs, the Cards' best hitter, Joe Torre, delivered a clutch single that scored Sizemore with the go-ahead run. Torre's RBI proved to be the game-winner, as St. Louis held Pittsburgh scoreless over the next seven innings. Carlton's 3-2 victory drew the Cards within seven lengths of the Pirates.

Cardinal pitching continued to dominate the Bucs. On Friday, August 13, Jerry Reuss held the Bucs to four hits and earned his 11th win. Another error by Alley in the second inning led to an unearned run against Steve Blass. The latest defensive shortcoming supplied the Cards with all the offense they would need in a 2-0 victory.

With the lead now down to six, in an apparent mismatch, future Cardinal Hall of Famer Bob Gibson faced the inconsistent Bob Johnson. Although the 35-year-old Gibson seemed well past his prime, with a middling record of 10-10, he was still regarded as a highly effective, and sometimes dominating, starting pitcher. The hard-throwing right-hander had achieved two one-hitters, two Cy Young awards, and a record-breaking strikeout performances in the World Series, but had never pitched a no-hitter or perfect game during an illustrious 13-year career.

On Saturday, August 14, against one of the best lineups in baseball, Gibson readied himself for one of the Cardinals' most important games of the season. Gibson struck out 10 Pirates, including Willie Stargell on three occasions. One of the strikeout victims, Milt May, reached base when catcher Ted Simmons failed to corral a wild pitch on a third strike. Three other Bucs made it to first base via walks. But none of the baserunners would get as far as second base.

And most notably, no Pirate would manage a hit against the nearly untouchable Gibson.

Not only did the 11-0 masterpiece mark the first no-hitter of Gibson's career; it also represented the first no-hitter thrown against a Pirates team since 1955, and the first major league no-no hurled in Pittsburgh since the 1907 season. "This was the greatest game I've ever pitched anywhere," Gibson exclaimed to a reporter from *Sports Illustrated.* "I never thought I'd throw a no hitter," said Gibson, "because I'm a high-ball pitcher. There are many more high-ball hitters than low-ball hitters."

"You can tell all those people who have been saying that Gibson was washed up," Stargell told Neal Russo of *The Sporting News,* "that they should have been at the plate with a bat in their hands." And for those who had been saying that the National League East pennant race was over, consider that the Cardinals had now crept to within five games of the Pirates.

In the series finale on Sunday afternoon, before a crowd of nearly 50,000, the Pirates endured another indignity. Pittsburgh held a 4-1 lead in the top of the eighth inning, with Bruce Kison seemingly in complete control. Kison retired Joe Torre to start the inning, but Ted Simmons and Joe Hague then banged out back-to-back singles, knocking the rookie right-hander from the game. Instead of summoning an overworked Dave Giusti from the bullpen, Murtaugh chose the well-rested Bob Miller, who was making just his second appearance with the Bucs. He allowed a single to the light-hitting Ted Kubiak, loading the bases. Miller then retired pinch-hitter Lou Brock for the second out of the inning. But Miller could not handle the next pinch-hitter, the little-known Jerry McNertney, who delivered a key two-run single. Miller now faced leadoff man Matty Alou, who had already picked up three hits against Pirate pitching. Alou, hardly known for his power, clubbed a three-run homer, providing the winning margin in a 6-4 decision. Alou finished the afternoon 4-for-5, with three RBIs and a run scored. Even two more home runs by Willie Stargell would not save the day.

Although their big lead had shrunk to four games, Blass says the Pirates refused to panic. Quite the contrary, Pirate players felt they had reached rock bottom and were ready to embark on a turnaround. "We felt when the lead got down to four or five games," Blass says, "that was as bad as it was going to get. It was not a comfortable lead, but it was still a lead. You had guys hurt, and guys away on military leave, but we never felt it was going to get any worse than that. We felt like we had enough strength, along with that bench. Even if we didn't pitch as well as wanted to, we could outscore people."

The loss to the Cardinals marked the low point of the Pirates' season. No one—except perhaps for the Pittsburgh players—would have been surprised if the Pirates were to go into a complete collapse and find themselves overtaken by both the Cardinals and the Cubs. An overworked bullpen, a fatigued starting rotation, and poor infield defense had led to the Bucs' undoing. Perhaps the 1971

Right-hander Steve Blass was signed by the Pirates in 1960. With his intellectual demeanor and wry wit, Blass emerged as one of the leaders on Pittsburgh's squad. His two complete-game victories in the 1971 World Series rank among the great performances in Fall Classic history. For unknown reasons, Blass suddenly lost his ability to throw strikes, forcing him to retire from the game in 1974 at the age of 32. (*National Baseball Hall of Fame Library, Cooperstown, NY*)

Pirates were not even as good as last year's divisional champions. Even a career season by Willie Stargell seemed like it might not be enough to preserve the Pirates' lead in the East. Along the latter lines, one of Pittsburgh's most important hitters issued a challenge to himself and the rest of the team's lineup. "Stargell's been carrying us all year," first baseman Bob Robertson remarked to *Sports Illustrated*, "and now that his shoulders have gotten tired, it's up to somebody to take over."

On Monday, August 16, the Pirates continued their homestand against the Astros, who featured Matty Alou's brother, Jesus, and other talented regulars like Cesar Cedeno, Joe Morgan, and Jimmy

Wynn. With their season on the brink, the Pirates responded with one of their most encouraging efforts. The superhuman Stargell rapped out four hits and four RBIs, bringing his season total to a career best 108. Vic Davalillo, playing right field for a resting Roberto Clemente, piled up two triples, a double and two RBIs. Bob Robertson plated two more runs with clutch sacrifice flies. Dock Ellis earned his 17th victory by working the first seven innings, before giving way to Dave Giusti, who provided two innings of scoreless relief. The Pirates also received good news from Cincinnati, where the Cardinals' winning streak came to an end. The Bucs' lead was now back up to five games in the East. Still, the Pirates' win over the Astros did little to erase the memories of their recent woes against St. Louis.

As if concerns on the field weren't enough, Dock Ellis stunned many baseball followers by revealing that he suffered from sickle cell trait, which team physician Dr. Joseph Finegold described to the Associated Press as a "non-fatal disease which has some of the symptoms of sickle cell anemia." Sickle cell anemia, a hereditary disease that primarily affects the African-American population and is sometimes fatal, had come to national attention partly through the public speaking efforts of Ellis' teammate Willie Stargell. "Dock may show a little bleeding now and then," Finegold told the AP, "and his blood count may go down, but all it takes is iron pills to get it back up again." Finegold said that Ellis would not require any special treatment as a carrier of sickle cell trait. Ellis told reporters that he suffered fainting spells and had passed blood at times, but believed that he did not have sickle cell anemia itself. "If I did," Ellis informed the Associated Press, "I'd probably be dead."

Continuing their series against Houston, the Pirates fell the following night by surrendering a seemingly comfortable 4-1 lead in the top of the seventh inning. Veteran relievers Bob Miller and Bob Veale failed to retire any batters, as the Astros rallied for five runs in the frame. The crucial seventh inning overshadowed a fine performance by Roberto Clemente, who returned with two hits and four RBIs. On the milestone front, Bill Mazeroski finally managed to collect the 2,000th hit of his career, a double to center field against starter Wade Blasingame. Unfortunately, the celebration of Maz' historic hit was marred by his own defensive miscue in the seventh. Mazeroski dropped a relay throw for an easy forceout at second base, a mistake that led to a crucial unearned run in the 6-5 loss.

The Pirates seemed ready to be overtaken by their divisional rivals. Yet, the cool hand of Danny Murtaugh would not permit it. Unlike other managers who ranted and raved in response to their teams' losing streaks, Murtaugh remained calm. As he once said, his performance as manager "hasn't changed much in 10 years." Murtaugh's response to slumps and injuries was usually the same: plug the holes in the lineup with the best available backup players, use long relievers and young prospects as spot starters, and hope the substitutes fill in capably for a few games until the front line players return to health or rebound from their subpar performances.

Murtaugh remained philosophical and chose not to hold any special team meetings, foregoing a strategy that many other managers had relied upon during extended slumps. "This is a time to keep the boys loose," Murtaugh maintained in an interview with Charley Feeney. "I see no reason to call a meeting to tell them what is at stake. They all know."

The Pirates rebounded to win the final game of the set against the Astros, thanks to the hitting of backup catcher Milt May, who supplied a home run and a bases-loaded single. The Pirates made it two straight wins by beating the Reds on Thursday night, thus expanding their lead back to six and a half games. The Bucs lost the next three games, however, shackled by the fine pitching of Reds starters Ross Grimsley, Jim Merritt, and Gary Nolan. Just when the Pirates had shown signs of revival, they had fallen back into an untimely offensive slump. But the Pirates were aided by the Cardinals, who earlier had lost three straight to the Reds and would proceed to lose two more in a row to Atlanta.

Injuries and illness were not helping matters. Richie Hebner, who had struck out eight straight times during the recent series against the Cardinals, was forced out of action with the Reds. Hebner had suffered severe chest pains during the night before the first game with the Reds, and ended up in the hospital, where doctors diagnosed him with a viral infection. The infection left Hebner feeling so weakened that he remained in the hospital for nine days and was sidelined for three weeks.

Hebner's weakened condition forced Danny Murtaugh to maneuver his infield. For the final game of the series in Cincinnati, Murtaugh inserted Bill Mazeroski at third base. After watching Maz go 0-for-4 against Gary Nolan, Murtaugh tried another infield alignment. With the talented but relatively untested Rennie Stennett playing second base, Murtaugh placed Dave Cash in the unfamiliar environs of third base, a position that required quicker reactions and a stronger throwing arm than second base.

Other manpower problems affected the Pirates' lineup. The chronically injured Gene Alley sprained his left knee, forcing him to return home for awhile. Alley's absence left Murtaugh with the inconsistent Jackie Hernandez at shortstop. Roberto Clemente, bothered by a sore shoulder, had been on the sidelines for a recent stretch of games, including the series in Cincinnati. Other key Pirate regulars, like Cash and Bob Robertson, had also missed games in August because of injuries.

On August 23, the Pirates continued their road trip with a twi-night doubleheader against the hard-hitting Braves. In the first game, the Pirates managed only one earned run against Braves ace Phil Niekro, but capitalized on shaky defense for three unearned scores in the sixth inning. The pitching of Steve Blass and Dave Giusti, who notched his 25th save, made the runs hold up in a one-run victory. In the nightcap, the Pirates enjoyed the relaxing glow of a blowout victory, exploding for 19 hits against three Atlanta pitchers. Al Oliver, who had been critical of Murtaugh over a lack of playing time, collected five hits—including two home runs and a triple—and five RBIs. Bob Robertson's breakout season continued with his 25th home run, while Roberto Clemente contributed his 13th roundtripper. With all of this offense, pitchers Bob Moose and Nellie Briles breathed easily during a 15-4 victory. Briles pitched four scoreless innings of one-hit relief to pick up the save. More important, he impressed Murtaugh sufficiently to be inserted again into the Pirates' starting rotation.

On Tuesday night, the Braves returned the favor to the Pirates, clobbering them, 15-5. On Wednesday, the Pirate offense piled up a season-high 21 hits, including eight singles in a six-run first inning. In the second inning, Willie Stargell and Bob Robertson cleared the fences with back-to-back home runs. Roberto Clemente went 5-for-6 and scored three runs. Despite Bruce Kison yielding five runs through two-plus innings, stellar relief pitching by Bob Moose and Bob Miller preserved a 13-6 win. Milt May, subbing for Manny Sanguillen and only hours after getting married in a pregame ceremony, played one of his finest games of the season, picking up three hits and three RBIs. With the win, the team had managed to take three out of four against the dangerous Braves. And for the first time in a month, the Pirates' offense had displayed its expected level of power and run production.

After his five-hit performance against the Braves, Clemente chose to talk about two of his favorite topics: injuries and fatigue. "I tire out a lot more quickly these days," Clemente insisted in a discussion with Charley Feeney. "My shoulder bothers me when I throw and I find I need a lot more rest." Clemente added that his heavy-hitting night against the Braves had actually worsened his condition. "A guy who doesn't hit so much doesn't have too run to much. Not only was I on base five times and scored three times, but how many times did I run on foul balls?" One could only wonder what Clemente might accomplish if he ever felt completely healthy and rested.

Clemente and the other Pirates had the next day off before concluding their road trip with a weekend series at the Houston Astrodome. In the opener, Dock Ellis earned his 18th victory and Dave Giusti recorded his 26th save while pitching against his original major league team. After losing the middle match of the series to the shutout pitching of flame-throwing Don Wilson, the Pirates snared the rubber game, 5-2. Bob Johnson provided an unusually good start and received relief support from the ever-improving Giusti.

Closing out what had been a dreadful month of August, the Pirates posted two of their most encouraging performances of the season. Opening up a homestand against the Phillies, Nellie Briles made his first start since July 19. The reliever-turned-starter held the Phillies scoreless before being betrayed by Gene Clines' drop of a sacrifice fly in the sixth inning. The miscue led to three unearned runs in the inning, giving the Phillies a 4-3 lead. But the Pirates, showing few signs of discouragement, rebounded quickly with a rally in the bottom of the sixth. In an unusual move, Danny Murtaugh allowed Luke Walker, his third pitcher of the night, to bat for himself. Walker rewarded the manager's confidence by drawing a walk. Even more unconventionally, Murtaugh then called upon Dock Ellis to pinch-run for Walker. A single by Rennie Stennett and a walk to Willie Stargell loaded the bases for Roberto Clemente. The right fielder stroked a two-run single to give the Pirates a 5-4 lead. With two outs, Manny Sanguillen sealed the game with another timely single, giving the Pirates' bullpen a two-run cushion. Dave Giusti, quietly regaining his early season form, pitched the final inning and two-thirds for his third save in four games.

On August 31, the Pirates displayed two characteristics common to most championship teams: bench strength, along with the resolve to come from behind to win games. In the bottom of the seventh, the Pirates trailed the Phillies 5-3. With the weak-hitting Jackie Hernandez scheduled to lead off, Pirate fans didn't expect much of a rally, but quickly changed their expectations after watching their shortstop work out a walk against a tiring Barry Lersch. Hernandez moved up to second base on a single by Bill Mazeroski, the first of three pinch-hitters that Danny Murtaugh would summon in the inning. Playing for the tie, Murtaugh elected to have Rennie Stennett bunt the runners into scoring position. With Vic Davalillo slated to face the deceptive slants of left-hander Joe Hoerner, Murtaugh properly went to his bench again. The Irishman called upon Gene Clines, who responded by pounding out a two-run double, knotting the score at 5-5. Clemente and Stargell followed with a pair of walks that loaded the bases, before Al Oliver struck out for the inning's second out.

Knowing the lack of depth in the Phillies' bullpen, Murtaugh decided to play his final trump card. He inserted Manny Sanguillen as a pinch-hitter for the lefty-swinging Milt May, and watched his Panamanian free swinger swat a two-run single. Murtaugh's strategy throughout the inning had paid off brilliantly. A perfectly executed sacrifice bunt, combined with three hits by three pinch-hitters, had enabled the Bucs to close out August in high style. For the month, the Pirates had won only 14 and lost 17, but they had managed to win seven of their last nine and maintain a five-game lead on the surging Cardinals. Little did anyone know that the Pirates would forge a new chapter in baseball history the following night.

Chapter Nine

SEPTEMBER

On the surface, the matchup of September 1 seemed like a relatively inconsequential game for the Pirates. While their poor play in August had posed a slight concern for their pennant hopes, a weeknight game against the doormat Phillies gave local fans little reason for excitement. The game also figured to receive less media coverage than normal, given the continuing strike by the Pittsburgh newspapers. Yet the evening of September 1 would mark one of the most historically and socially significant occurrences in major league annals.

Earlier that afternoon at Three Rivers Stadium, manager Danny Murtaugh made out his lineup card in preparation for a matchup against Philadelphia left-hander Woodie Fryman. Murtaugh's list read as follows:

Rennie Stennett, 2B
Gene Clines, CF
Roberto Clemente, RF
Willie Stargell, LF
Manny Sanguillen, C
Dave Cash, 3B
Al Oliver, 1B
Jackie Hernandez, SS
Dock Ellis, P

At first glance, the starters did not appear to represent anything out of the realm of the ordinary, other than the omission of the righty-swinging Bob Robertson against the lefty-throwing Fryman and the continuing absence of the ailing Richie Hebner. Upon further review, some writers and players noticed that Murtaugh had actually written out the first all-black lineup in the history of the major leagues. Not since the peak of the Negro Leagues had a team like this taken to the field.

What some critics have argued as sheer coincidence belies the importance of this lineup. A major league team beginning a game with nothing but black players (Latinos played in the Negro Leagues, and those with comparatively dark skin were commonly considered "black" at the time) would not have occurred without a team having a long-standing commitment to developing all players, regardless of background. It was fitting that the Pirates had become the first National or American League team to employ a lineup comprised exclusively of black and Latino players. No team had been more aggressive in signing Latin American and African-American stars from the mid-sixties through the early seventies. Such aggressiveness involved recruiting minority players for positions that had traditionally been reserved for white players. In fact, this event could have occurred even earlier. On June 17, 1967, the Pirates faced the Phillies at Connie Mack Stadium with *eight* black fielders and a white pitcher.

It has been suggested that the injured status of several Pirate players may have facilitated the all-black lineup. A *Sports Illustrated* article indicated that Robertson sat out the game with a minor injury, but the nature or severity of the ailment was not specified. According to Al Oliver, Murtaugh may have instead been looking to light a fire under a slumping Robertson, who had gone 2-for-14 in his previous four games. "Bob Robertson normally would have played that day, but Dave Cash had told me within the last [few] years, that Murtaugh was kind of disappointed in Bob for whatever reason. I don't know what the exact reason was, but he was disappointed in Bob, so he sat him down."

In the past, Murtaugh had never hesitated in doling out playing time to African-American and Latino players. Furthermore, he had gained a just reputation as a fair-minded man when it came to dealing with the concerns of minorities on the Pirates. After the game, a local reporter asked Murtaugh if he even realized that all nine starters were black. "Did I have nine blacks in there?" Murtaugh answered, feigning surprise. "I thought I had nine Pirates out there on the field. Once a man puts on a Pirate uniform, I don't notice the color of his skin." He explained, "When it comes to making out the lineup, I'm color blind, and my players know it."

Later that month, Gene Alley insisted that Murtaugh possessed no prior knowledge of the all-black lineup. "It was typical of him," Alley told Ed Rumill of the *Christian Science Monitor*. "That day he happened to start nine blacks in a game with the Phillies, he hadn't even thought about it or realized he had done it. They were, in his opinion, the nine best men available that day. And that's all that's ever important with him." Al Oliver supports Alley's contention. "In my estimation," Oliver says, "I think Danny was putting the best team on the field, and he probably didn't notice it until later. I didn't know it until about the third or fourth inning. Dave Cash mentioned it to me. He said, 'Hey Scoop, we got all brothers out there.'" Oliver pauses and laughs loudly for a moment. "You know I thought about it and I said, 'We sure do!'"

Steve Blass recalls that most of the Pirate players were fully aware of what was happening. "Oh yeah, we were aware. We saw the lineup on the wall. [And because] we had a loose group, we were all laughing and hollering about it, and teasing each other. I thought that was a great reaction."

At the time, Al Oliver thought the all-black lineup was interesting, but didn't appreciate the historical significance of the event until much later. "Of course, with us, I didn't even think anything about it," Oliver says. "Nothing about it at all. But now, of course it means something." Bob Robertson offers a similar perspective. "It was just another day in my baseball career as far as I was concerned," Robertson says. "That again was the type of ballclub that we had. It didn't make a difference if you were black, yellow, green, purple, whatever. We enjoyed each other's company. We got along fine. We had a lot of respect for one another. . . . I think it was good for our ballclub. I think it was good for the organization. I think it was good for the guys that got an opportunity that night to go out on a ball field."

Although Danny Murtaugh and Pirate players tried not to attach too much significance to the event at the time, the lineup of September 1, 1971, did represent a major milestone in the history of the game. Jackie Robinson had crashed through baseball's color barrier in 1947, but it had taken 24 years for a single major league team to field an entire lineup made up of African Americans and dark-skinned Latinos.

In the fifties and sixties, black and Latino players had gained reputations for being strong in specific areas of the game. "Latino players were always known for their defensive ability," Oliver says. "All of them could play great defense." As an example, Latin American middle infielders, particularly short-stops, had displayed outstanding defensive skills at the major league level since the early 1950s. Chico Carrasquel and Luis Aparicio of the Chicago White Sox and Willy Miranda of the Baltimore Orioles had emerged in the fifties, followed by slick-fielding standouts of the

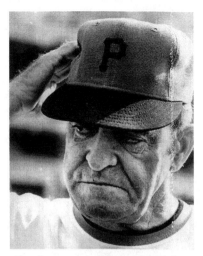

After having played for the Phillies, Boston Braves, and Pirates, Danny Murtaugh managed Pittsburgh on four different occasions from 1957 to 1976. Beloved by most of his players, the low-key Murtaugh guided the team to World Championships in 1960 and 1971. (*National Baseball Hall of Fame Library, Cooperstown, NY*)

sixties like Jose Pagan (San Francisco Giants), Leo Cardenas (Cincinnati Reds), and Bert Campaneris (Kansas City and Oakland A's). Although it was an exaggeration to label all Latinos as excellent defenders, the exploits of such players had cemented the Latin American reputation for fielding superiority.

Black players had been stamped with a different label by scouts and general managers. "And then the black Americans were known for their hitting ability," Oliver says. Offensive stars like Willie Mays, Hank Aaron, Frank Robinson, and Vada Pinson highlighted the statistical leaderboards, particularly in the National League. The Pirates, however, not only recognized blacks for their hitting, and Latinos for their defensive prowess, but also realized that African Americans and Latinos possessed all-around skills, and the intelligence to handle the cerebral game. "I tip my cap to the Pirates for doing that," Oliver says, thankfully. "You have to. . . not look at color; you have to look at talent. That's what the Pirates did."

The Pirates' lineup of September 1, 1971, was not merely a symbolic event. The starters were not a token collection of late-season call-ups, spring training invitees, or third-string utilitymen. The Pirates were in the midst of a still-undecided divisional pennant race with the Cardinals and Cubs, which left Murtaugh in no position to sacrifice crucial games for the sake of making history.

The contest began with an eruption. The Pirates offense accounted for nine runs in the first three innings, enabling the Bucs to take an early three-run lead. Stennett, Clines, Clemente, Stargell, Sanguillen, and Oliver each rapped out a pair of hits. Although Dock Ellis was knocked out of the game in the second inning, the Pirates were ably assisted by the relief pitching of Luke Walker, who capped off an impressive 10-7 victory. Yet the left-hander played down his presence as the lone white Pirate on the playing field. "All I saw on the field," the lanky Texan told *Sports Illustrated,* "were eight men and myself. I think all the guys on this team feel the same way."

After a day off, the Pirates began a home series with the Expos. Rennie Stennett, continuing to play in the absence of Richie Hebner, stroked four hits in the first game but made a critical ninth inning error that helped turn a 4-3 lead into a 6-4 defeat. The loss ended the Bucs' winning string at four, their longest streak since July. The Pirates played even shoddier defense the following afternoon, committing six errors. Somehow, the Bucs managed a win. On Sunday, September 5, the Pirates beat the Expos, 8-2, as Stennett clubbed the first home run of his major league career, and Willie Stargell added his 43rd of the season.

The Bucs now prepared for a series against the Cubs, who had fallen out of the Eastern Division pennant race. Once within six games of the Bucs, Chicago now trailed by double figures. In the first game of a twin bill, Nellie Briles continued to excel in his new role as a starter, shutting the Cubs down on three hits. Briles gave the Pirates their first complete game since August 19, ending a drought of 16 games. In the nightcap, a Willie Stargell grand slam—

his 44th home run of the season—gave the Bucs an easy 10-5 win. In four hours and 33 minutes of game time, the Pirates had buried the Cubs in the rubble of what was once a fairly tight race between the two teams. The Bucs then piled some more graveyard dirt on the Cubs, thanks to the complete-game pitching of Steve Blass and a five-RBI performance by Al Oliver. The three-game sweep left the Cubs 13 games out of first place with only three weeks remaining in the regular season. The Cardinals, at five and a half games back, were now the only team in the Eastern Division with a realistic chance of catching the Pirates

After the sweep of the Cubs, the Pirates traveled to Montreal and proceeded to lose two of three to the lowly Expos. They then moved on to Chicago and picked up where they had left off just a few days earlier, soundly defeating the free-falling North Siders, 5-1. Willie Stargell broke up a scoreless matchup between Steve Blass and Milt Pappas with a leadoff home run in the seventh, his 45th longball of the season. Throwing a complete-game six-hitter, Blass improved his season record against the Cubs to 4-0. The Pirate victory, coupled with the Cardinals' loss to the Phillies, lifted Pittsburgh to a six-and-a-half-game lead in the East.

The Pirates officially eliminated the Cubs the next day, September 14, by downing Chicago and 21-game winner Ferguson Jenkins, 4-3. Only a two-game series between the Pirates and Cardinals would offer the Redbirds a last gasp to move in on the Bucs.

In the first game against St. Louis, Danny Murtaugh handed the ball to staff ace Dock Ellis, who had not made a start since the first of September because of a sore elbow. Ellis' elbow, which had bothered him occasionally during the season, had become an increasing concern for Murtaugh. Meanwhile, the Cardinals countered with 18-game winner Steve Carlton, their best pitcher in 1971 and a summer-long nemesis of the Pirates.

The Pirates set the tone for the series in the first inning. After reaching base with a single against Carlton, Clines displayed the Pirates' game plan of speed and aggressiveness. Clines broke for second on a run-and-hit play; Clemente swung away and roped a single. Never breaking stride, Clines scored all the way from first.

The Pirates had seemingly borrowed the strategy from the offensive playbook of the Cardinals, whose offense featured the speed of Lou Brock, the hit-and-run execution of Ted Sizemore, and the line-drive hitting of Matty Alou and Joe Torre. The Pirates had proven that they could play the Redbirds' own aggressive style.

The Pirates added three more runs in the fourth inning against Carlton, who was surprisingly ineffective and quickly left the game for pinch-hitter Ted Kubiak. In contrast, Dock Ellis pitched more like the All-Star performer he had been during the first half of the season. He limited the Cardinals to six hits and one run through seven plus innings. Ramon Hernandez, recently recalled from the minors, finished off the game with two unblemished innings of relief. With the win, the Pirates increased their lead on the Cardinals to eight and a half games.

In the second and final game of the mini-series with the Cards, the Pirates pounded the Cardinals. In the bottom of the third inning, the Bucs proceeded to break up a scoreless game. Luke Walker and Rennie Stennett, two unlikely sources, drew walks. Clines followed with a single, Clemente delivered a sacrifice fly, and Manny Sanguillen drove in a run with a single, giving the Pirates an early 2-0 lead. The Pirates scored two more in the fourth, as Cardinals center fielder Jose Cruz misplayed a single by Jackie Hernandez. Cruz allowed the ball to roll past him into deep center field, enabling Hernandez to circle the bases and give the Pirates a 4-0 lead. The early runs would prove to be more than enough support for Luke Walker. With two and two-thirds innings of perfect relief, Ramon Hernandez posted his second consecutive save.

With the season now past the midway point of September and the Pirates up by nine and a half games in the standings, the divisional race was virtually over. A Pirate victory and a Cardinal loss would guarantee the Bucs of no worse than a tie for the National League East crown. Only one objective remained for the Bucs: an outright divisional win. The Pirates could then prepare for a Championship Series meeting with the winner of the Western Division: either the first-place San Francisco Giants, or the second-place Los Angeles Dodgers, who were just a game behind.

On Friday, September 17, the Pirates hosted the Mets, who had played so well for three months at the start of the season before collapsing in July. As late as June 10, the Mets had led the East. They proceeded to lose 20 of 29 games in July and 12 of 29 in August, despite the efforts of Tom Seaver. Seaver was on his way to one of the best seasons of his career, with an ERA of 1.76, 20 wins, 4 shutouts, and 21 complete games.

Out of the divisional race, the Mets would try to play the role of spoiler against the Pirates. New York's Gary Gentry bested Nellie Briles, 3-0, denying the Pirates at least a divisional tie with the Cardinals, who managed to pick up a game when Bob Gibson won a 7-2 decision over the Expos.

The following day, Danny Murtaugh elected to start September call-up Richie Zisk in left field, ahead of veteran Willie Stargell. Murtaugh reasoned that Zisk would fare well against the left-handed offerings of Mets starter Ray Sadecki. The rookie slugger responded with a walk, two runs scored, and two runs batted in. The hitting of Zisk supported the pitching of Steve Blass, who mastered the Mets on two hits and earned his 15th win in a 4-0 victory. With the Cardinals losing a 4-2 decision to the Expos, the Pirates now secured a divisional deadlock with the Cards, and were set to clinch a berth in the National League playoffs.

The Cardinals delayed the victory party, however, as Steve Carlton downed the Expos, 11-0, while the Pirates lost 5-2 at the hands of the Mets. With an off day on Monday, the Pirates and Cardinals would begin the final stretch of the regular season with a three-game set at Busch Stadium on Tuesday, September 21. St. Louis owned no realistic hopes of overtaking the Pirates, but wanted to prevent the Bucs from clinching on Cardinal turf. The Pirates raced out to a 4-0 lead, thanks in part to Dock Ellis' two-run single. But the Redbirds rallied for a quartet of tying runs in the bottom of the fourth, and jumped ahead in the seventh on a single by Ted Simmons and a two-run homer by Jose Cruz. The Cardinals' 6-4 come-from-behind win denied Ellis his 20th victory.

On Wednesday, September 22, Bob Gibson took the mound for the Cardinals against the inconsistent Luke Walker. Only five weeks earlier, Gibson had pitched a no-hitter against Pittsburgh, dominating the Pirates with his high-riding fastball. This time the Cardinals' defense undermined Gibson, as a Ted Simmons passed ball and a Matty Alou error in the first inning led to a run for the Pirates. Manny Sanguillen's fourth-inning RBI single gave the Bucs a 2-1 lead. In the top of the eighth inning, with the Pirates still up by just one run, the Cardinals' defense once again failed Gibson. A throwing error by backup shortstop Ted Kubiak accounted for three unearned runs, giving the Pirates a 5-1 lead. Dave Giusti, who had entered the game in the bottom of the seventh inning, needed just six more outs to clinch a playoff berth. With a four-run lead and a rested Giusti on the mound, the Pirates prepared for an inevitable division-winning victory party. Finishing the game off in his usual bulldog fashion, the Pirates' palmball specialist dusted off the Cardinals over the final two innings to record his 29th save of the season.

Bob Robertson, a major contributor with 26 home runs on the season, lumbered in from first base and Dave Cash dashed in from second base to greet Giusti at the mound. All-Star catcher Manny Sanguillen, with arms outspread and hands raised, raced from behind the plate to join Cash, Robertson, and Giusti. A few moments later in the Pirates' clubhouse, important role players like Vic Davalillo and Nellie Briles, who had been acquired in the much-debated Matty Alou trade, took turns dousing manager Danny Murtaugh with large bottles of champagne, which had been put into storage four days earlier.

The clinching was sweet vindication for Giusti, the National League's best reliever. It seemed fitting that Giusti had closed out the Cardinals, his previous team, after also pitching the division-clinching contest in 1970. Murtaugh was pleased that Giusti had once again saved a milestone game for the Pirates. "It's poetic justice that Giusti should wrap it up," Murtaugh shouted to Charley Feeney during the clubhouse festivity. "He has closed the door so often."

As he celebrated with his players, Murtaugh pondered the divisional race that his team had successfully concluded. He pointed specifically toward the team's 11-game winning streak in July. "That gave us the cushion we needed when things went badly," he told *The Sporting News*. After the long win streak, the Pirates had lost 23 of their next 35, but still didn't relinquish the lead to their closest pursuers, Chicago and St. Louis.

In 1970, the Pirates had not clinched until their 159th game of the season. Although the 1971 pennant chase had ended much sooner, Murtaugh felt it had taken a larger effort and been a harder struggle. "Last year we were dark horses," Murtaugh explained to Charley Feeney. "Not many people picked us to win. This year we were picked by almost everybody and when you're the favorites, the other clubs aim at you." As a result of their change in status, the Pirates had played stiffer competition in 1971. Yet, their own level of play had risen accordingly.

Although most historians accurately regard Roberto Clemente as the primary leader of the 1971 Pirates, Steve Blass observes that the leadership role was actually divided among three veterans. "You had a Latino player in Clemente, a black guy [in] Willie Stargell, and a white guy in Bill Mazeroski. We had the whole program covered," says Blass. "They were leaders—all three of them—and by that time in 1971, almost in terms of equal status. Neither one of them hollered a whole lot. Most of the hollering came from us young guys like Robertson, Hebner, Dock Ellis, Giusti, and myself. But those three guys—Clemente, Stargell, and Mazeroski—were very much the leaders of that team."

With the Pirate roster containing almost equivalent numbers of white, African-American, and Latin American players, it was helpful to have three leaders who essentially represented each one of those ethnic categories, according to Blass. "In looking back, it was great to have it. But I don't know that it was absolutely necessary. Even before you get to Latino, black, and white, the mix of personalities was good. Nothing was sacred in that clubhouse, including Clemente, who had that way he carried himself and was kind of an individualistic guy. We had the guys, who in a sense, would not allow that, and included him [in the clubhouse ribbing]. Giusti would holler at him. Dock would holler at him, and Hebner and Robertson. We had a continual mix that prevented divisive lines from ever emerging between Latinos, blacks, and whites."

According to Bob Robertson, Pirate leadership showed itself in the determined way in which players reacted to losses. "If we got our butt kicked," Robertson says, "say on a Sunday afternoon, well, I could guarantee you one thing. On Monday evening, when we went back out on that ballfield, that loss stuck with us. And I think it was just [that] everybody was a leader on that ballclub."

With the Pirates having clinched the Eastern Division, only two individual issues remained undecided: the race for National League Most Valuable Player, and Dock Ellis' quest for 20 wins. Baseball writers had mentioned Pittsburgh's Willie Stargell and St. Louis' Joe Torre as the two strongest candidates for the MVP Award. Stargell would finish the regular season with a league-leading home run total of 48, and the league's second highest total of RBIs with 125. Meanwhile, Torre would finish with a .363 batting average—which topped the National League batting race—and a league-leading 137 RBIs. Torre would also post his numbers while playing a more demanding position (third base) than Stargell, who played left field. In Stargell's favor, voters in the Most Valuable Player balloting did tend to gravitate toward players who had performed for pennant-winners, not for runners-up.

The suspense hanging over Ellis' assault on the 20-win plateau would end long before the announcement of the National League MVP Award in mid-November. Ellis would take his final regular season turn on September 28, against the last-place Phillies. Ellis pitched creditably, striking out 11 Phillies over eight innings, but he lacked his usually dominant curve. Shoddy defense by the Pirates also undermined Ellis' attack on his 20th win. An error by the slumping Gene Alley contributed to three unearned runs, representing the difference in a 6-3 loss. As a result, Ellis would have to settle for a record of 19-9, still the best of his career.

The Pirates had to wait more than a week to find out the identity of their Championship Series opponent. For most of the summer, it appeared that the Giants would be that team. On May 31, the Giants had owned a 10-and-a-half-game lead on the archrival Dodgers. During the final four months of the regular season, however, the Giants went only 53-58 and watched the Dodgers climb back into the race. In September, the Dodgers reeled off an eight-game winning streak, while the Giants lost 11 out of 12, including five games to Los Angeles. The contrasting streaks allowed the Dodgers to pull within one game of first place on September 14.

It remained a one-game lead as the Giants headed to the last series of the regular season in San Diego, while the Dodgers would host the Astros. On September 28, Gaylord Perry shackled the Padres, 7-1, while the Dodgers' Bill Singer bested Houston ace Don Wilson, 2-1. The next day, both the Giants and Dodgers lost their games, maintaining San Francisco's lead at one game. The two teams headed to the final day of the season, with Marichal on the mound for the Giants in San Diego, and Don Sutton taking the ball at Dodger Stadium. Sutton beat the Astros, 2-1, but the win didn't matter, as Marichal shut down the Padres, 5-1. Marichal's fourth consecutive winning start clinched the National League West for the Giants.

Offensively, the Giants were not led by either of their veteran mainstays, Willie Mays and Willie McCovey. Rather, their best offensive player was 25-year-old Bobby Bonds, who led the club with 33 homers, 102 RBIs, and a .288 batting average, and was regarded by some scouts as the fastest runner in the National League. McCovey, limited to 105 games because of a smattering of injuries, and Mays, held to 136 games, failed to produce their usual power numbers. The Giants still managed to rank third in the National League in runs scored (behind the Pirates and Cardinals), and featured the sixth-best pitching staff in the National League, just behind Pittsburgh. Juan Marichal led the staff with 18 wins, followed by Gaylord Perry's 16 victories. In addition, square-jawed right-hander Jerry Johnson emerged as an important pitcher in relief, with a record of 12-9 and an earned run average of 2.97.

As for the Pirates, Willie Stargell finished the regular season with monstrous numbers: 48 home runs, 125 RBIs, and a .295 batting average. Roberto Clemente, after his horrendous start, concluded the season at .341, with 86 RBIs in only 132 games. Bob Robertson finished second on the team, behind Stargell, with 26 home runs. Off the bench, Gene Clines batted .308, Vic Davalillo checked in at .285, and Rennie Stennett hit .353 in 153 at-bats. On the pitching staff, Dock Ellis forged a 19-9 record, while Steve Blass led Pirate starters with an earned run average of 2.85 and won 15 games. Bob Moose and Luke Walker also won in double digits, while Dave Giusti led the National League with 30 saves in 58 appearances.

As a team, the Pirates led the National League in hits, total bases, home runs, slugging percentage, and most importantly, runs scored (788). (They continued to show a lack of patience at the plate—ranking only ninth in walks drawn—but it didn't seem to matter much.) In terms of pitching, the unheralded Pirates finished a respectable fifth in team ERA (3.31), ranked third in both shutouts and walks allowed, and paced the league with 48 saves.

As soon as the Pirates clinched the National League East, writers and fans began drawing comparisons between the 1960 Pirates and the 1971 team. Bill Mazeroski, the starting second baseman for the '60 Pirates and a backup infielder on the '71 club, offered a succinct perspective on the comparison. "This [1971 Pirates team] is the strongest Pittsburgh team in my 16 years with the club," Maz told *The Sporting News* without hesitation. Yet, as impressively as they had played, the '71 Pirates could not validate Mazeroski's claim until they had completed two more steps: a victory in the National League Championship Series followed by a World Series triumph. Only then would Maz' words ring true.

The Pirates' team record of 97-65 (while not as good as the 1960 Pirates' mark of 95-59) was the best in the league, seven games better than the Giants' mark of 90-72. Given their record, the Pirates seemed to be the favorites. Yet the Bucs had their doubters. Although Pittsburgh had posted a better overall record, the Giants had won nine of the 12 head-to-head matchups, including the last six in a row. The Giants appeared to have more dominant and experienced top-end starters in Gaylord Perry and Juan Marichal. Finally, the Giants boasted loads of postseason savvy: Marichal, Mays, and McCovey (three future Hall of Famers) had all experienced the pressure of World Series play. Given these factors, the Pirates needed to play their best baseball in October to secure the championship.

Chapter Ten

THE NATIONAL LEAGUE CHAMPIONSHIP SERIES

With the playoff series against the Giants just days away, Danny Murtaugh and Joe Brown needed to settle on a 25-man postseason roster. They had decided to carry 11 pitchers—perhaps out of concern over the condition of Dock Ellis' elbow, which had been paining him during the final month of the regular season—so one of the backup infield positions would have to be sacrificed. That meant that Murtaugh and Brown would face a particularly tough decision. Would they keep the impressive rookie Rennie Stennett, who had compiled an 18-game hitting streak after his recall from the minors? Or would they choose the more experienced Jose Pagan, who had played in the postseason with the Pirates one season earlier and had also participated in a World Series with the Giants in 1962? Brown and Murtaugh elected to go with the veteran hand, activating Pagan for the National League Championship Series. When a *Pittsburgh Press* reporter asked Stennett about being left off the postseason roster, he responded quickly and to the point: "It was a shock."

After further, careful consideration, the Pirate brain trust decided on the following postseason roster of players:

> CATCHERS (3)—Milt May, Charlie Sands, Manny Sanguillen
> INFIELDERS (6)—Gene Alley, Dave Cash, Richie Hebner, Jackie Hernandez, Jose Pagan, Bob Robertson
> OUTFIELDERS (5)—Roberto Clemente, Gene Clines, Vic Davalillo, Al Oliver, Willie Stargell
> PITCHERS (11)—Steve Blass, Nellie Briles, Dock Ellis, Dave Giusti, Ramon Hernandez, Bob Johnson, Bruce Kison, Bob Miller, Bob Moose, Bob Veale, Luke Walker

With Pagan in and Stennett out, the Pirates opened the National League Championship Series on October 2 in San Francisco, where the Bucs had lost five straight games during the regular season. A crowd of 40,977 showed up at Candlestick Park to watch the battle of staff veterans, Gaylord Perry against Steve Blass. Danny Murtaugh had elected to start the series with Blass, who had never made a postseason appearance, instead of Dock Ellis.

The Bucs opened the scoring in the top of the third. Jackie Hernandez led off the inning by chopping a single down the line that eluded third baseman Alan "Dirty Al" Gallagher. Opting for the most fundamental of strategies, Murtaugh instructed Blass to bunt the runner over to second. Dave Cash then lifted what appeared to be a routine fly ball to right field. The winds of Candlestick Park, combined with the indecision of Dave Kingman in right field, turned the play into a strange misadventure. The iron-gloved Kingman badly misjudged the ball. He clumsily turned to his left, then shifted to his right, and ultimately watched the ball drop in for a ground rule double. Instead of having Hernandez anchored to second base with two out, the Pirates had scored the game's first run, and had moved another runner into scoring position, still with only one out. Richie Hebner then rolled a ground ball to Tito Fuentes at second base, but Willie McCovey dropped the throw at first base. The error allowed an attentive Cash to score all the way from second. Kingman's botched fly ball and McCovey's muff at first had given the Pirates the gift of two unearned runs.

San Francisco managed to narrow the gap in the bottom half of the inning. Chris Speier singled, moved up to second base on a Gaylord Perry sacrifice, and scored on a hard-hit double by Ken Henderson. Blass held the Giants scoreless in the fourth, but ran into more problems in the fifth. Speier reached on a leadoff single, before Blass retired both Perry and Henderson. With Willie Mays and Willie McCovey waiting on deck, the Pirate right-hander realized the necessity of challenging the singles-hitting Fuentes. Although the Giants' second baseman had batted a respectable .273 during the regular season, he had shown little discipline, walking 18 times, and almost no power, with only four home runs. Blass threw Fuentes a slider below the knees, a pitch that likely would have been called a ball had Fuentes not swung. Fuentes did swing, upper-cutting the errant slider. Surprisingly, the ball flew over the outstretched leap of Roberto Clemente—and over the fence in right field, for a two-run homer. Unnerved, Blass walked Mays on four pitches, and then served up another two-run homer, this time to McCovey. With two swings, the Giants had taken a 5-2 lead.

Now trailing by three runs, the Pirates would make a game of it in the seventh inning. Al Oliver contributed a two-run single, bringing the Pirates within a run. Unfortunately, Gaylord Perry would allow the Pirates no closer. Mixing his moving fastball with a good slider—and most likely his vintage spitball—Perry went the distance, scattering nine hits and walking just one. Perry featured such good control of his pitches that he went to a three-ball count only once during the Giants' 5-4 victory. In winning the first game of the Championship Series, the Giants had continued their season-long domination of Pittsburgh.

The loss in the first game placed more importance on the performance of Game Two starter Dock Ellis, who had touched off controversy with some critical remarks aimed at Pirate management. Ellis, referring to the Pirate front office as "The Establishment," chided the Bucs for failing to provide first-class air and hotel accommodations. The Pirates, on their way to San Francisco for the first game of the playoffs, had been forced to make a refueling stop in Omaha. The unexpected stopover delayed their arrival in the Bay Area until three o'clock in the morning. Once in San Francisco, the Pirates' players took up residence at the Jack Tar Hotel. Ellis found that the bed in his room was too small for his six-foot, three-inch frame, and was barely adequate for his wife, who was much smaller. Ellis then went to the front desk and asked for a suite. After being told by hotel management that none were available, he packed up and left. "I went to another hotel," Ellis said to the Associated Press, "got red carpet treatment, but paid $50 a day out of my own pocket. And to tell you how good that room was, me and my wife and baby slept in the bed."

The new hotel accommodations did little to appease Ellis' anger with the Pirates' brass. "'The Establishment' doesn't treat the players first class," Ellis railed in his interview with the Associated Press. "We don't travel first class, we don't get good rooms in a lot of hotels. They don't deserve to win the pennant," Ellis said of Pirate management. "They don't deserve to win the World Series. They don't deserve to win a thing."

General manager Joe Brown reacted to Ellis' sideswipe with restraint, refusing to address Ellis' complaints directly. "Dock is very outspoken," Brown told the Associated Press in response, "and like most of us, he's not always right." Ellis, for his part, insisted the Pirates would take the series—in spite of club management. "We're going to win because we have the best club. They [management] can't get out on the field. If we played the way they treated us, we wouldn't win a game."

Most of the Pirate players downplayed any controversy, having become accustomed to Ellis' tendency to sound off from time to time. Despite his vitriolic comments, the team knew they could count on him. "I think a lot of guys on our ballclub said, 'Dock is just being Dock right now,'" Richie Hebner recalls. "When you played with him, you knew the next day he's gonna come in laughing, smiling, be the same old Dock."

In the second game of the series, Ellis opposed left-hander John Cumberland, a onetime New York Yankees prospect who had pitched surprisingly well for the Giants as both a starter and reliever. Yet, Cumberland was not Charlie Fox's first choice to start Game Two. Fox would have preferred Juan Marichal; unfortunately the "Dominican Dandy" was not available to pitch any sooner than the third game because he had been needed in the regular season finale.

Against the unheralded Cumberland, Danny Murtaugh countered with his right-handed platoon. He inserted Gene Clines in center field and Jose Pagan at third base, while sitting down Al Oliver and Richie Hebner. Murtaugh's decision to bench Oliver against a little-known left-hander like Cumberland rankled the talented center fielder, who had hit well during the final month of the season. Oliver threatened to abandon the Bucs after the season if Murtaugh continued pairing him with Clines. "If I don't get the promise that I will play every day next season, I just might sit out the season," Oliver declared in an interview with *The Sporting News*. Pittsburgh beat writer Charley Feeney speculated that the Pirates might trade Oliver for a shortstop after the season and hand the center field job to Clines, who had already announced plans to try switch-hitting in winter league play.

One Pirate player who did not have to concern himself with being platooned, despite a late-season slump, was Bob Robertson. The slugging first baseman had missed 31 games during the regular season with a variety of knee problems. His aching knees had required cortisone shots in the middle of September. The injuries had at least partially accounted for Robby's long home run drought; he had not reached the seats since August 25.

In his first at-bat in Game Two, Robertson stepped in against Cumberland and delivered a double. Manny Sanguillen brought him home with an RBI single for a 1-0 lead. In his second at-bat, with the Bucs now trailing 2-1, Robertson sliced a Cumberland offering down the right-field line, chasing the uncertain Dave Kingman into the corner. Kingman raced to the foul line and lunged for the ball, at first appearing to make an impressive off-balance catch. As Kingman crashed into the foul pole, the impact knocked the ball out of his glove and over the fence—for a home run. Kingman's seemingly spectacular catch had suddenly turned into a Pirate run, which tied the game at 2-2. The Pirates then tacked on another run to take a 3-2 lead.

In the seventh inning, with the Pirates holding an uncomfortably close 4-2 lead, Robertson strode to the plate to face another left-hander, Ron Bryant. With two runners on base, Robertson powered a high drive over the left field fence. The three-run homer changed the tenor of what had been a tight game, giving the Pirates a 7-2 lead. Then in the ninth inning, with the Bucs leading 8-2, Robertson smacked a slider from a third left-hander, Steve Hamilton, over the wall in left-center field. With three home runs on the day, Robertson's unforeseen power barrage at Candlestick Park—five at-bats, four runs, four hits, and five RBIs—had suddenly given nationwide recognition to a player who had never before hit three longballs in a single game.

Robertson's performance had provided the Pirates with a comfortable cushion on a day when Dock Ellis struggled. In the first inning, the Giants scored a run and loaded the bases with one out against Ellis, who appeared on the verge of a knockout. But Ellis bowed his back, striking out the power-hitting Dick Dietz and forcing Dirty Al Gallagher to hit a weak infield tapper. Ellis gave up a second run in the second inning, before settling down over the next three frames. In the sixth, with the Pirates holding a two-run lead, Ellis hit Gallagher, the leadoff batter, with a pitch. Chris Speier followed with a single, putting the potential tying runs on first and second with no one out. Murtaugh, having seen enough from his ace right-hander, called upon Bob Miller to preserve the two-run lead. Miller retired Frank Duffy, who popped up a bunt on a sacrifice attempt. Miller then walked Ken Henderson to load the bases. With one out, Miller toughened. He struck out Tito Fuentes, the hero of Game One for the Giants, and retired Willie Mays on a fly ball to Roberto Clemente.

While most of the postgame focus centered on Robertson and Ellis, Murtaugh pointed to the sixth inning work of his long reliever as the turning point of Game Two. "The big play of the game was when Miller struck out Fuentes," Murtaugh said. "Miller did a helluva job for us. He has been off and on for us most of the time, but he was really outstanding today." Miller would give up two meaningless runs in the ninth inning, before giving way to bullpen ace Dave Giusti, who finished off the 9-4 victory. Another one of Joe Brown's quiet mid-season trade acquisitions had paid off for the Pirates.

Miller's clutch pitching had helped the Pirates accomplish their minimum goal of splitting the first two games in San Francisco. Robertson's power hitting had also helped make up for the lack of substantial contributions from the Pirates' most productive regular season hitter, Willie Stargell, who had gone hitless in nine at-bats.

After a day off for travel, the Pirates and Giants resumed the best-of-five series on October 5, at Three Rivers Stadium. San Francisco skipper Charlie Fox turned to longtime ace Juan Marichal, who had forged a record of 25-10 against the Pirates during his brilliant career. Yet the 33-year-old right-hander had been

Pirates first baseman Bob Robertson leans against his locker as he fields questions from reporters after his three-home run performance spurred the Bucs to victory in Game Two of the NLCS. Signed by Pittsburgh as an amateur free agent in 1964, "Robby" hit 26 home runs for the Pirates during the 1971 regular season. Affectionately nicknamed "Grumpy" by his teammates, Robertson was anything but after his record-setting performance against the Giants. "It made the flight from San Francisco back to Pittsburgh much more pleasant," said Robertson. (*National Baseball Hall of Fame Library, Cooperstown, NY*)

bothered slightly by a sore hip, ever since colliding with another player during a game with the Reds on September 26.

Danny Murtaugh decided to counter with Nellie Briles, who had pitched so impressively as a starter down the stretch. As Briles warmed up in the bullpen before the game, Briles aggravated his pulled hamstring muscle and told Murtaugh that he could not pitch. This was "probably the most difficult decision I had to make in my 14 years in the major leagues," Briles says. "I had pitched a couple of innings the last game of the [regular] season against Philadelphia, as kind of a tune-up, and that's where I pulled my groin. I didn't think it was very serious. . . . I went to the bullpen and warmed up for probably about 10 to 12 minutes. And it was just when I got ready to put the final touch [on the warm-up throws], I reached back to get that little extra fastball, and I could still feel it . . . my heart sank, because I knew that I wasn't going to be a hundred per cent. So I threw a couple of more pitches, it felt the same way, and I stopped, called the dugout, got ahold of Danny and said, 'Danny,

I'm only eighty per cent. You better get somebody else.'" Briles felt as if he had hit rock bottom emotionally. "That was probably one of the lowest points in my career," Briles recalls, "because I didn't know if I'd ever get to pitch in the playoffs, or if we got into the Series, if Danny would think about me getting in, or if I would just be in the bullpen."

With Briles unable to pitch, Murtaugh had to dip into his bullpen for an emergency starter: hard-throwing right-hander Bob Johnson. Given the unusual circumstances, Murtaugh asked the umpiring crew to delay the start of the game so that Johnson could have sufficient time to warm up, and the umpires agreed. Johnson had been one of the Pirates' few disappointments, failing to live up to the ballyhoo that had accompanied his arrival from the Kansas City Royals in a preseason trade. Johnson had finished the regular season with a mediocre record of 9-10 and an unspectacular earned run average of 3.45.

Pitching on extremely short notice, Johnson performed spectacularly. The young right-hander overcame several potential rough spots. In the second inning, with no outs, Johnson gave up back-to-back singles to Willie McCovey and Bobby Bonds. In what could have been a disastrous inning for the Pirates, Johnson responded by fanning Dick Dietz, retiring Dirty Al Gallagher on a groundout, and striking out Chris Speier.

The Pirates reached Juan Marichal early when Bob Robertson continued his postseason tear with a solo home run, his fourth of the Championship Series. The 1-0 lead stood up until the sixth inning, when Johnson and the Pirates' defense began to falter. Ken Henderson led off with a single and moved up to second when Tito Fuentes pushed a sacrifice bunt down the third base line. Charging in from third base, Richie Hebner tried to lead Dave Cash with his throw to first base, but ended up tossing the ball wildly down the right field line. Henderson raced all the way home on the overthrow, scoring the tying run, while Fuentes moved up to second base. With no one out, Johnson now prepared to face the heart of the Giants' formidable lineup: Willie Mays, Willie McCovey, and Bobby Bonds.

Expecting Mays to swing away, the Pirates played their infield back. Mays had a different plan in mind; he pulled his bat downward and squared to bunt. Mays punched the ball a few feet in front of home plate, where Pirate catcher Manny Sanguillen nabbed it quickly. Holding Fuentes at second base, Sanguillen threw to first base to retire Mays. With one out, Murtaugh now ordered Johnson to intentionally walk McCovey, the Giants' most feared hitter. Johnson then struck out the right-handed hitting Bonds for the inning's second out. After walking Dick Dietz, Johnson retired Dirty Al Gallagher on a routine ground ball to Jackie Hernandez. Johnson's clutch pitching maintained a 1-1 deadlock.

Murtaugh had displayed confidence in Johnson by staying with the right-hander throughout the frightful sixth. In the top of the eighth inning, Johnson encountered another critical situation. With two out and two runners on base, Johnson again faced Dietz, a dangerous right-handed power hitter. Johnson ran the count to two balls and no strikes, prompting a visit from pitching coach Don Osborn. "Listen, you big ape," Osborn told Johnson bluntly. "I don't have an SOB in the bullpen that's got the stuff you got out here today, so get this guy out." Johnson responded by retiring Dietz on a harmless ground ball, ending the threat.

With Johnson having maintained the tie, the Pirates came to bat in the bottom of the eighth inning. Marichal retired Vic Davalillo (who had pinch-hit for Johnson) and Dave Cash for the first two outs. With no one on base, Richie Hebner stepped up to bat. Carrying a reputation as a player who sometimes took his defensive problems to the plate with him, Hebner was only two innings removed from his sixth-inning throwing error.

Hebner didn't allow the memory of his defensive miscue distract him. He reached out for a Marichal pitch and lifted it high toward the right-field stands. Hoping that Hebner had gotten under the pitch, Bobby Bonds raced to the warning track and prepared to make a leaping grab. Bonds jumped, but the ball eluded his outstretched glove by a matter of inches and sailed into the bleachers. Hebner's home run gave the Pirates a 2-1 lead, with just one at-bat remaining for the Giants.

Now entrusted with a lead, Danny Murtaugh called upon Dave Giusti, who would take aim at his first save of the postseason. Giusti retired the Giants in order, giving the Pirates a 2-1 lead in the best-of-five series.

As had happened so often in baseball history, a pitcher called upon at the last moment had delivered an unexpectedly good performance to help his team win an important game. Afterward, Johnson attributed his success against the Giants to an improved fastball. "I think I threw harder today than I did all year," Johnson told the *New York Daily News*.

T hanks to Hebner, the Pirates had moved within one win of their first World Series appearance since the magical season of 1960. The fourth game of the National League Championship Series, set for October 6 in Pittsburgh, offered up a rematch of Game One starters: Gaylord Perry for the Giants and Steve Blass for the Bucs.

Blass, who had pitched poorly in the first game, again struggled in Game Four. In the first inning, Blass allowed a run on three singles and an error. Fortunately for Blass, the Pirates immediately bounced back with a pair of runs on a single by Dave Cash, a double by Hebner, and a two-run single by Roberto Clemente.

Unable to sustain the Pirate momentum, Blass allowed a home run to Chris Speier and a one-out single to Ken Henderson in the second inning. Tito Fuentes then lofted what seemed like a catchable fly ball to left-center field. Converging on the ball, Willie Stargell and Al Oliver failed to communicate with one another, allowing the ball to drop in for a gift single. The mental mistake put runners on first and second, placing Blass in a precarious situation. Barring a double-play ball, Blass would have to face his nemesis, Willie McCovey—and most likely with at least one runner in scoring position.

Blass did retire Willie Mays, but on a pop-up and not a twin killing. With two out, McCovey stepped into the batter's box. Moments later, "Stretch" rocked a fastball deep into the right-field stands. The three-run homer gave the Giants a 5-2 lead.

With Blass having failed, the Pirates' offense responded with championship resiliency in the bottom half of the second. After a single by Manny Sanguillen and a fielder's choice, Danny Murtaugh decided to pinch-hit for Blass with his 1960 World Series hero, Bill

Mazeroski. Taking an aggressive approach, Maz responded with a first-pitch single, putting runners on first and second. Taking his dramatic cue from Maz, Richie Hebner followed with his second home run of the postseason, matching McCovey with a three-run shot, which knotted the game at 5-5. Gaylord Perry, the Giants' winningest pitcher during the regular season, had failed to protect the sizeable early lead given to him by his offense.

With the game tied, Bruce Kison entered the game from the Pirate bullpen. The rookie right-hander, making his first postseason appearance, hurled four and two-thirds innings of spotless relief, keeping the game tied until the sixth inning. For the Giants, Perry recovered from his early-inning troubles to match Kison with three straight scoreless innings.

In the bottom of the sixth with one out, Dave Cash singled against Perry, and after an infield grounder, came home on Roberto Clemente's RBI—his third of the day. With two left-handed batters, Willie Stargell and Al Oliver, scheduled to bat next, Giants manager Charlie Fox lifted Perry in favor of his bullpen. Strangely, Fox chose not to bring in either of his southpaw relievers, Ron Bryant or John Cumberland. Instead, he summoned right-hander Jerry Johnson, who had begun warming up four innings earlier.

After a passed ball allowed Clemente to advance to second, Fox ordered Johnson to intentionally walk Stargell and pitch to Oliver. The unhappy center fielder, who had been benched in Game Two, hit a drive toward the right field stands, pushing Bobby Bonds to the fence. The Giants outfielder watched in frustration as the line drive traveled into the bleachers. The Pirates now enjoyed a 9-5 lead, with only three innings standing between them and the World Series.

Kison remained in the game to start the seventh. He recorded two outs, but also allowed two runners to reach base. With the game on the line, Murtaugh decided to place a call to his relief ace, Dave Giusti. Summoned in yet another crucial situation, Giusti stranded both runners to maintain the Pirates' lead.

In the eighth inning, Giusti allowed one runner to reach first, but held the Giants scoreless. Then, in the ninth inning, one more Giant reached base. It didn't matter, as Giusti once again stiffened, keeping San Francisco off the scoreboard. Two and one-third innings of scoreless relief by the Pirates' bullpen ace preserved a 9-5 Pirates victory. After losing the first game of the Series, the Pirates had won three consecutive games against a team that had dominated them so convincingly during the regular season.

In addition to the bullpen pitchers, several Pirate players had emerged as major factors in the National League playoffs, including Dave Cash, who led the Bucs in hits and runs scored during the four-game set. The list of heroes also included Bob Robertson. The powerful first baseman, previously unknown to many fans outside of the Pittsburgh area, had finished the series with seven hits in 16 at-bats, and a playoff record four home runs. Robertson's robust hitting had more than counterbalanced the lack of production from the Pirates' star power hitter, Willie Stargell. Over the span of four games, Stargell had gone hitless. Not only did Stargell go 0-for-14 against San Francisco pitching, but he also failed to drive in a single run. Then again, Stargell wasn't entirely to blame. The Giants had succeeded in pitching carefully to him throughout the series, as evidenced by two intentional walks and a hit-by-pitch.

In the meantime, Roberto Clemente had prospered with two singles and three RBIs in the clinching Game Four victory. Although Clemente was pleased that he had contributed to the pennant, he complained about both his physical condition and his performance. "I am happy, very happy, but I am not myself," Roberto told Harold Kaese of the *Boston Globe*. "I am not swinging [well], because my back is hurt. How many times do you see me strike out three times in a game?" Always demanding of himself, Clemente was clearly dissatisfied with his own individual achievement.

The four-game Championship Series win over the Giants appeared to represent the high point of the Pirates' 1971 season. After all, their World Series opposition would be provided by the Baltimore Orioles, the game's defending World Champions. The O's had fashioned the best record in the game during the regular season, sported an incredible rotation that featured four 20-game winners, and had just swept the Oakland A's in the American League Championship Series. Champagne flowed again in the Pirates' clubhouse, but the oddsmakers clearly thought that would be the last celebration for this team.

Chapter Eleven

WORLD SERIES GAMES ONE AND TWO: BALTIMORE

The Baltimore Orioles were a four-armed, slugging monster. They featured a full and balanced complement of four 20-game winners: right-handers Jim Palmer and Pat Dobson, and left-handers Mike Cuellar and Dave McNally. The Orioles' lineup boasted the power of Don Buford, Merv Rettenmund, Dave Johnson, Frank Robinson, Boog Powell, and Brooks Robinson. Powell and both of the Robinsons had each hit at least 20 home runs and driven in more than 90 runs during the regular season. Rettenmund, one of four Orioles to reach double figures in stolen bases, had led the team in hitting at .318. The Orioles' roster ran so deep that on any given day a solid player like Rettenmund, Buford, or fielding stalwart Paul Blair might find himself on the bench. Last, the Orioles' defense, anchored by the left-side infield combination of Brooks Robinson and Mark Belanger, and the masterful Blair in center field, made few mistakes in back of the team's stellar pitching staff. The game's defending World Champions ran away with the American League crown, cruising to a 101-57 record, including their last 11 games, the best record in the regular season, and swept the talented Oakland A's in the Championship Series. At seven to five, the oddsmakers made the Orioles considerable favorites to win the Series.

Nonetheless, the Pirates nervously anticipated the afternoon of October 9, when the World Series would open up at Baltimore's Memorial Stadium. With games one and two scheduled to be played in Baltimore, the World Series format had provided the Orioles with yet another advantage against the overmatched Bucs. Memorial Stadium possessed a particular quirk that figured to bother the Pirate hitters, most of whom had not played in the American League ballpark. A white stucco residence, stationed beyond the fence in center field, sometimes deceived hitters who lost the baseball as it dissolved against the similarly colored house. The background figured to be especially problematic for the Pirates when they faced Baltimore's tall right-hander, Jim Palmer. As Palmer released the ball from the top of an overhand motion, the ball tended to blend directly into the background.

Fortunately for the Pirates, Palmer's first start would have to wait until later in the Series; Orioles manager Earl Weaver surprisingly selected left-hander Dave McNally to pitch Game One. In the meantime, Danny Murtaugh hoped that he could call upon his most talented but often sore-armed pitcher, Dock Ellis.

Ellis' elbow had continued to bother him throughout the playoff series against the Giants. At 4:30 on October 7, two days before the start of the World Series, Ellis and Manny Sanguillen emerged from the Pirates' dugout at Memorial Stadium. After warming up, Ellis tested his elbow by making 25 long throws from second base to Sanguillen, who was waiting at home plate. Ellis then delivered 12 pitches from the mound—all fastballs—to Sanguillen. After Sanguillen shouted a few words of encouragement, Ellis proclaimed himself fit to pitch the opener of the Series. "My arm didn't hurt," Ellis told the *New York Post*. "It felt good. I'm ready."

Choosing the eve of the World Series as his forum, Ellis regaled the media with a stream of candid remarks. Reporters asked the pitcher about the importance baseball held in his life. "If it wasn't for baseball, I'd be in jail today," Ellis declared to reporters Red Foley and Phil Pepe, in recalling his own troubled youth in Los Angeles. "Thefts, that was my problem. Thefts and gang wars. Many a night I never went home. I slept in the park. . . . Who knows where I would be now if it wasn't for baseball."

One newsman asked Ellis to assess the keys to winning the Series. "Pitching is irrelevant," Ellis told reporters, going against the grain of conventional baseball belief. "Power will decide the Series." On another front, Ellis was clearly unimpressed by the Orioles' record, or the general caliber of play in the American League. "Baltimore is the only club in the American League that could play in our league," the shoot-from-the-hip right-hander pronounced to *The Sporting*

News. "That's why they call the American League the 'junior circuit.'" Danny Murtaugh could not have been thrilled to see those remarks in the newspaper.

With southpaw Dave McNally scheduled to face Ellis in Game One, Murtaugh decided to sit two of his most productive left-handed hitters, center fielder Al Oliver and third baseman Richie Hebner. Murtaugh replaced them with two of his right-handed platoon standouts, Gene Clines and Jose Pagan. These decisions represented a carryover from the way Murtaugh had made out his lineup during the regular season and the playoffs.

Still, some of the baseball writers covering the World Series questioned Murtaugh's decision to play both Clines and Pagan. After all, Oliver and Hebner had each hit three-run home runs in the clinching playoff win against the Giants. Oliver himself bristled at Murtaugh's benching him, especially at World Series time. Oliver told a reporter from United Press International, "I can see platooning if a guy can't hit one kind of pitching, but I always hit left-handers."

Murtaugh offered a curt response to the "first-guess" criticism. "I don't ask my players what they think," Murtaugh told UPI. "I make out the lineup and they read it." Earlier in the season, Murtaugh had indicated that he might eventually play Oliver on an everyday basis in center field, but the inspiring play of Clines had apparently changed his mind. "I go by the way I feel," Murtaugh said matter-of-factly. "Sometimes I play 'em, sometimes I don't. I make out the lineup to suit myself." Murtaugh saw no need to rationalize his starting choices. Furthermore, the Irishman was in no mood to let his players—or members of the media—dictate the way he filled out his lineup card.

Earl Weaver made an interesting lineup decision of his own when he opted to bench his best defensive outfielder, Paul Blair, in favor of Merv Rettenmund, a more productive hitter. "During the season, I went by the pitching charts. I'd play whoever I thought could hit the pitcher best. It was all very scientific," Weaver explained to a gathering of media. "Today, I didn't have any charts [since the Orioles hadn't faced Pirate pitching during the regular season], so I just looked up the batting averages and played the guys who had the best averages."

Baltimore's Dave McNally had won at least 20 games for the fourth consecutive season while posting the American League's highest winning percentage, despite spending 38 days on the disabled list with a strained elbow. Still, second-guessers deemed him a curious choice to pitch Game One, given that well-rested staff ace Jim Palmer had not pitched since the first game of the American League Championship Series.

Early in Game One, McNally struggled with his control. In the top of the second inning, Bob Robertson led off with a walk and advanced to second on a wild pitch. Manny Sanguillen followed by hitting a ground ball to Mark Belanger at shortstop. When the slow-footed Robertson unwisely tried to advance to third, Belanger fired the ball in the direction of Brooks Robinson. Fortunately for the Pirates, Belanger's throw struck Robertson in the helmet and bounced past Robinson into the Orioles' dugout. The errant carom enabled Robertson to score the first run of the Series, and allowed Sanguillen to move up to second base. After Jose Pagan's slow roller pushed Sanguillen to third base, Jackie Hernandez laid down a bunt. McNally fielded the ball quickly enough to have a chance to retire Sanguillen at the plate, but his throw eluded Hendricks, who claimed that he "never saw the ball" thrown by the pitcher. The official scorer charged Hendricks with the error, which not only permitted Sanguillen to score but also put Hernandez on second base. McNally then struck out Dock Ellis, but surrendered a line single to Dave Cash. Hernandez scored, giving the Pirates a surprising 3-0 lead.

Recovering quickly, the Orioles cut into the lead in the bottom of the second inning, when Frank Robinson led off with a home run into the left field stands. While the Orioles' offense showed signs of life, their largest worry remained McNally's mystifying inability to throw strikes. At the start of the third inning, McNally found no immediate relief from his control problems. He allowed a leadoff single to Roberto Clemente and compounded his woes by walking the lefty-swinging Stargell. That brought the dangerous right-handed bat of Bob Robertson to the plate. With the Orioles' bullpen already active, Earl Weaver seemed to be considering a pitching

Manny Sanguillen (No. 35) slides safely into home plate during the second inning of Game One of the World Series, beating an errant throw from Orioles pitcher Dave McNally that bounced away from catcher Elrod "Ellie" Hendricks. Sanguillen had reached first base on a fielder's choice and moved to second on a throwing error by Mark Belanger. The Pirates would score three runs in the frame on just one hit, thanks to the two Baltimore errors. (*National Baseball Hall of Fame Library, Cooperstown, NY*)

change. But Weaver, who tended to pitch his starters deep into games, decided to stay with McNally. In a postgame interview with *The Sporting News*, Weaver claimed that he never gave serious thought to lifting the left-hander "because Dave Cash's hit was the only ball the Pirates got out of the infield." McNally reinforced Weaver's faith by striking out Robertson, fanning Sanguillen, and retiring Jose Pagan on a fly ball to Don Buford in left. McNally had escaped the inning without any damage showing on the scoreboard.

McNally's reversal of fortune seemed to inspire the Orioles' offense. In the bottom half of the inning, Mark Belanger and Don Buford wrapped singles around a McNally strikeout, bringing the dangerous Merv Rettenmund to the plate. Dock Ellis tried to brush the outside corner with a breaking ball, but the pitch hung toward the middle of the plate. Seizing upon Ellis' mistake, Rettenmund powered the ball over the fence in left-center field. The three-run home run gave the Orioles a 4-3 lead. After Ellis walked Boog Powell, Danny Murtaugh came to the mound and signaled to the bullpen. As Ellis trudged to the dugout, he heard a rising medley of boos from the Baltimore fans, who remembered Ellis' pre-Series mouthings about the alleged inferiority of the American League. The Orioles later added an insurance tally in the bottom of the fifth inning, giving McNally a two-run advantage.

From the third inning on, McNally completely overmatched the Pirates' hitters. In one stretch, he retired 19 consecutive batters. In the top of the ninth, with the Bucs trailing 5-3, Bob Robertson led off the inning by flying harmlessly to Rettenmund in center field. Manny Sanguillen then bounded a chopper to the left side, which Belanger fielded cleanly but threw wildly past Boog Powell at first base. Belanger's second error of the game allowed Sanguillen to reach second base—ending McNally's streak of 19 straight outs— but more important, brought the potential tying run to the plate.

The scheduled batter was Jose Pagan. Although Pagan had managed only five home runs in 158 regular season at-bats, he had displayed significant extra-base power against left-handed pitching. The situation left Earl Weaver with an important decision to make. Should he stay with McNally or bring on his rested relief ace, Eddie

Watt, who used a deceptive three-quarters delivery and had led the Orioles in ERA during the regular season? If Weaver made the latter move, Watt would likely have to face the lefty-hitting Richie Hebner in a pinch-hitting role. In contrast to Pagan, Hebner had hit 17 home runs in 388 regular season at-bats.

After careful consideration, Weaver elected to stay with the matchup of McNally against Pagan. The veteran left-hander promptly missed with his first two pitches. With the count now in his favor, the free-swinging Pagan swung hard at the next pitch but popped a routine fly ball to Frank Robinson in right-center field. As Robinson cradled the ball in his glove, the Orioles moved within one out of victory in Game One.

With Pagan retired, Weaver's decision to stay with the left-handed McNally appeared even more favorable for the Orioles, what with the weak-hitting Jackie Hernandez the next scheduled batter for the Pirates. Danny Murtaugh, having already used World Series veteran Bill Mazeroski off the bench in the seventh, had run out of viable right-handed pinch-hitters. Gene Alley had batted a mere .227 with only six home runs during the season and Rennie Stennett was ineligible for the World Series. Murtaugh opted for his best available hitter: the lefty-swinging Al Oliver, who had been benched against numerous southpaws during the regular season. McNally ran the count to two balls and two strikes against Oliver, and then threw a knee-bending curveball over the outside corner. Oliver swung at the breaking ball but missed, becoming McNally's ninth strikeout victim. The heavily favored Orioles, after trailing by three runs, had taken the first game of the World Series, 5-3.

After Game One, McNally's turnaround became one of the popular topics of conversation. So did the performance of Dock Ellis. Oriole hitters expressed surprise at the lack of velocity on Ellis' fastballs. Several Orioles claimed to have seen Ellis throw much harder in the past. Danny Murtaugh agreed, although Ellis argued that he did not have to rely on fastballs to win games. "The scouting report on me happens to be that I'm a breaking ball pitcher," Ellis told Red Foley and Phil Pepe of the *New York Post* in the clubhouse. "Everything I threw was up, everything they hit was a hanging curve." Ellis had struggled with a flattening curveball during the final month of the regular season, perhaps because of the pain in his right elbow. In Game One, Ellis' curveball had once again rated as subpar.

Another post-game theme involved the lineup card made out by Danny Murtaugh. The Irishman heard some criticism for his decisions to bench Oliver and Hebner. Their replacements, Pagan and Clines, had combined to go 0-for-8 against a masterful McNally.

Game Two of the series was scheduled for Sunday, October 10, but was postponed because of a storm that resulted in two-and-a-half inches of rain. (The rain typified the summer of 1971 in Baltimore, where precipitation had become a dominant theme at Memorial Stadium.) The inclement weather in Baltimore produced the first rainout of a World Series game since 1962 (when the San Francisco Giants played the New York Yankees) and raised questions of when the second game might be played, either on Monday afternoon or Monday night. Baltimore owner Jerry Hoffberger proposed to play Game Two on Monday night, under the logic that Oriole fans who had been shutout by the Sunday rainout would have a better chance of attending the game in the evening, when they didn't have to work. The Pirates, however, had to give their approval to Hoffberger's idea before it could go into effect. General manger Joe Brown didn't like the proposal, which would have the two teams playing on Monday night, followed by an early turnaround for Game Three on Tuesday afternoon. Brown felt that a day game after a night game, with a trip to Pittsburgh sandwiched in between, didn't make sense. Thus, with the Pirates quickly rejecting the Hoffberger plan, the second game was rescheduled for Monday—in the afternoon.

On the rainy off day, several players met with the media, including a slumping Willie Stargell. The Pirates' left fielder, who had gone 0-for-3 in the first game against Dave McNally, had now gone hitless in his last 17 postseason at-bats. On the outside, Stargell remained calm and philosophical. "When I was going good, I didn't get excited," Stargell told reporters, "so when I'm going bad, I'm not going to hit the bottom of the barrel. . . . If I don't get a hit throughout the Series, I'll be able to say I did my best."

The next day, sunny and breezy conditions greeted Baltimore, with temperatures hovering near the comfortable 60-degree mark. Although the rain left the Memorial Stadium playing surface soggy in certain locales, particularly in the outfield, all of the larger puddles had dried up in time for the start of Game Two. The crowd of 53,239 fans included Patricia Nixon, the wife of President Richard Nixon, their daughter Julie, and son-in-law David Eisenhower. Mrs. Nixon threw out the first ball, and then stepped aside to watch 25-year-old right-hander Jim Palmer work his mix of fastballs and curves against the free-swinging Pirates' lineup.

Palmer faced off against Danny Murtaugh's surprising choice to start Game Two, Bob Johnson. Murtaugh had opted for the relatively inexperienced Johnson, even though Steve Blass was available on a full four days' rest. It seemed that Murtaugh had lost confidence in his veteran right-hander after two poor performances in the Championship Series.

Johnson, who had pitched so well as an emergency starter for Nellie Briles in the playoffs, retired the Orioles in order in the first inning. In the second, Johnson encountered his first jam. He allowed a single to Frank Robinson, a walk to Elrod Hendricks, and a single by Brooks Robinson, which produced the Orioles' first run. In the fourth inning, Johnson fell apart. He surrendered a line-drive single to Frank Robinson, hit Hendricks on the ankle with a stray pitch, allowed a walk to Brooks Robinson, and surrendered a two-run single to Dave Johnson.

With his Pirates down 3-0, Murtaugh decided to make a change, calling on rookie Bruce Kison. Given the circumstances, the Pirates could have excused the 21-year-old Kison for being nervous. After all, Kison was making his first World Series appearance, and was only six days away from an even more important occasion—his wedding. Not surprisingly, Kison proceeded to walk Mark Belanger and Jim Palmer, the eighth- and ninth-place hitters, to force in another run. The Pirates now trailed 4-0.

Danny Murtaugh later turned to Bob Moose and Bob Veale, but the veterans fared no better than Johnson and Kison. In the fifth inning, six singles, two more walks to Belanger and Palmer, and a Pirate fielding error contributed to six more Baltimore runs and an insurmountable deficit of 10-0. The disastrous inning confirmed Pirates fans' worst fears about their pitching staff's ability to suc-ceed against a powerful and deep lineup, one that didn't have to rely on one or two hitters to carry the load.

Throughout his major league career, Brooks Robinson had earned praise as the finest defensive third baseman in either league, with only Clete Boyer considered a fielding equal by some observers. His performance in the 1970 World Series against the Cincinnati Reds, which included an array of backhanded stabs and diving leaps, had only cemented the notion of fielding godliness. Yet, on this day against the Pirates, Robinson's offense would overshadow his usual defensive prowess. He banged out three hits and walked twice against Pittsburgh pitching. By reaching base five consecutive times in one World Series game, Robinson tied a record originally set by Babe Ruth in 1926, and matched by Lou Brock in 1967. As a team, the Orioles collected 14 singles against the Pirates, just one single short of the World Series record.

The top of the eighth inning provided a more typical spotlight for Robinson. Manny Sanguillen led off by driving a smash to the left side of the infield, between Robinson and Mark Belanger. Robinson moved quickly to his left, stabbed the ball on a hop, and fell to his knees, but still managed to make an off-balance toss toward first baseman Boog Powell. Incredibly, Robinson's throw beat the speedy Sanguillen. Although the outcome of the game had long been decid-ed, Robinson's play so impressed his teammates that they rewarded him with a standing ovation from the Orioles' dugout.

In the meantime, the Oriole offense overshadowed the pitching of Jim Palmer. In workhorse fashion, Palmer continuously overcame what he termed the "National League" strike zone being enforced by home plate umpire Ed Sudol. "I know that he did a fine job according to National League standards," Palmer explained to *The Sporting News*. "But in our league, we get the high strikes. In the National they don't give them." Sudol's unwillingness to call the "high" American League strike forced Palmer into deeper pitch counts, but the Oriole right-hander managed to keep the Pirates scoreless through seven innings. Palmer lasted eight innings, accu-mulating 168 pitches, thanks in large part to 10 strikeouts and eight walks.

Even though Baltimore had assumed a commanding lead in the Series, Oriole players offered no hints that they were ready to let down against the seemingly overmatched Pirates. When asked by *The Sporting News* if he considered Game Two a laugher, Frank Robinson offered a blunt response: "No, I didn't. We'll laugh only after we've won four games." In spite of his cautionary statement, most of the media considered Baltimore's prospects of winning four games merely a matter of time.

While Robinson's attitude reflected the businesslike approach of the Orioles, the comments of his right field counterpart, Roberto Clemente, seemed to display a different kind of attitude with the Pirates. After the defeats in Games One and Two, Clemente complained about the poor state of Baltimore's ballpark. A rainy late summer in Baltimore, coupled with a series of National Football League games at Memorial Stadium, had left the playing surface in less than ideal condition for the World Series. Criticizing not only the outfield surface but also the park's limited visibility, Clemente called Memorial Stadium the "worst field I've played on in the major leagues." In fact, Clemente considered it on a par with a minor league stadium. "This is not a big league ballpark. You cannot see the ball in the outfield. You can't see where it's going when they hit it in the air," Clemente told *The Sporting News*. "You don't do the things here that you usually do on good ground. You have to worry about the holes and the grass. You can't get to the ball."

In spite of his objections to Memorial Stadium, Clemente had played brilliantly during the first two games. At the plate, Clemente had rapped out four hits in nine at-bats. In Game Two, he had made a stunning defensive play from his post in right field. With no one out in the fifth inning and the fleet-footed Merv Rettenmund on second base, Frank Robinson had lofted a fly ball down the right field line. Even if caught, the fly ball seemed like it would easily advance Rettenmund to third. Clemente raced toward the foul line, all along battling the bright sun that glared in right field, and snared the ball at full speed, with his momentum falling heavily toward the right field line. Once Clemente gloved the ball, he stopped himself almost immediately, spun around completely, and fired the ball on one hop toward third base. Running hard from the moment of the catch, the speedy Rettenmund slid into third base, just as Richie Hebner applied a quick sweeping tag. The third base umpire ruled Rettenmund safe—the proper call—but Clemente had somehow made a routine second-to-third advance a close play. Orioles catcher Andy Etchebarren, who watched the play unfold from the Baltimore dugout, told sportswriter Dick Young that he considered it "the greatest throw I ever saw by an outfielder."

O ther than the performance of Clemente, Danny Murtaugh had witnessed few bright spots for the Pirates in the first two games. A reporter asked Murtaugh what he planned to do to inspire improvement in his team's play. "The leader of any team in professional sports has to play an important part in its success," Murtaugh told a reporter from *Sports Illustrated*. "Every manager must realize what his ballclub needs. We are all equal in this knowledge. We all make about the same moves. Eventually it is a question of strength."

One of the Pirates remembers Murtaugh providing his players with a stronger sense of motivation heading into Game Three. "One of the decisive things," says Dave Giusti, "was a headline that was in the Baltimore newspaper that said something like, 'It May Be Baltimore in 3.'" Murtaugh, insulted, hoped his players would feel the same. "Murtaugh took that out of the paper and put it in the clubhouse," Giusti says, "and I think that helped." Two other factors gave the Pirates a renewed sense of vigor. "We had Steve Blass going, who was probably the best pitcher that year, going for us in the first game at home," says Giusti. "We just knew how we played in the past at home."

It was now up to the Pirates themselves to turn this Series around.

Chapter 12

WORLD SERIES GAMES THREE, FOUR, AND FIVE: PITTSBURGH

While Danny Murtaugh had provided the Pirates with some motivation heading into Game Three, he had also ruffled some feathers with his batting-order selections and repeated lineup changes. A few hours before the third game, Richie Hebner took a look at the latest lineup card that was taped to the wall of the Pirates' dugout. "Well, I'll be a double-breasted blippety-blip," Hebner said out loud within earshot of the media, as he noticed his name was missing. With left-hander Mike Cuellar on the mound for the Orioles, Murtaugh had once again benched Hebner and countered with Jose Pagan at third base. Murtaugh explained that he liked the matchup of Pagan against Cuellar. "Jose has been around, and he has faced Cuellar a lot of times in the Caribbean during the winter. I think Pagan might do well against him." In other lineup developments, Murtaugh elected not to play Gene Clines against Cuellar, even though "Lil Angry" had hammered left-handers all season long. Thus, for the first time in the postseason, Al Oliver received a start against a southpaw. Murtaugh also benched Jackie Hernandez at shortstop, replacing him with the oft-injured Gene Alley, who had not played in the first two games of the Series. This move seemed surprising, given Hernandez' respectable 1-for-4 performance at the plate and flawless fielding.

The Pirates' hopes of forging a comeback in the Series rested on the shoulders of their blade-thin right-hander, Steve Blass, who had followed up an impressive regular season with two subpar performances in the Championship Series. To make matters worse, the versatility the Orioles had displayed in winning the first two World Series games had left Blass thoroughly confused. "I was charting pitches in the first two games [while watching from a ground-level monitor in the Pirate clubhouse]. In the first game, they hit a bunch of home runs, and in the next game they had all singles. As a pitcher, I'm trying to figure out if I'm going to be pitching against a power type of a team or am I going to be pitching against a singles team," Blass recalls. "Your approach is a little bit different. . . . So I had these two sets of notes, and probably best for me, I left both sets over top of my locker at Memorial Stadium." Without his notes, but with the full knowledge that the Pirates needed to secure a win, Blass felt enormous pressure. "I was so nervous the night before that I lay in bed for hours without being able to sleep," Blass revealed to *Sports Illustrated*.

At least Game Three offered Blass and the Pirates a home crowd of more than 50,000 fans ready to provide the Pirates with an emotional boost. On a more tangible note, the artificial surface of Three Rivers Stadium figured to aid the Pirates' slashing, line-drive hitting style.

As they had always done, Blass and Manny Sanguillen teamed up in determining which pitches would be thrown in certain situations during Game Three. "That was in the era when the pitch calls came from Sangy and I [and not the bench]," explains Blass. "We combined to call the pitches." The Pirates' battery decided on a pitching plan that would feature a mix of fastballs, sliders, and curveballs.

The teamwork between Blass and Sanguillen held the Orioles hitless until the fifth inning, when Brooks Robinson dunked a looping single in front of Willie Stargell in left-center field. Blass also kept the Orioles scoreless until the seventh, when he left a slider to Frank Robinson high in the strike zone. Taking advantage of the hanging pitch, Robinson homered into the second deck of the left-field stands.

By then, the Pirates had already done considerable offensive damage against Baltimore pitching. In the first inning, Dave Cash laced a double down the left field line off starter Mike Cuellar and moved to third on Al Oliver's ground ball to Boog Powell. On the play, Powell tried to toss the ball to Cuellar covering at first, but his throw sailed wide of the bag, allowing Oliver to reach safely. With the Orioles' infield playing back for a potential double play. Clemente seemed to give the Orioles what they wanted, hitting a ground ball to Dave Johnson at second base. Johnson forced Oliver at second, with Mark Belanger making the pivot and throwing to first. Hustling from the moment he hit the ball, Clemente beat the relay to first, as Cash crossed the plate for the first run of the game. In the sixth, the Pirates added another run on a leadoff double to right by Manny Sanguillen and a line single to left by Jose Pagan.

Leading off in the seventh, with the Pirates now ahead 2-1, Clemente tried to check his swing but the ball accidentally hit his bat, resulting in a weak tapper toward the mound. Cuellar fielded the ball cleanly, but was slightly off balance in front of the mound. Noticing that Clemente had started to run hard as soon as he hit the ball, Cuellar hurried his toss to Boog Powell. Cuellar's hastiness resulted in a poor throw; it pulled Powell off the bag and allowed Clemente to reach safely, turning a routine play into an error against Cuellar and a leadoff runner on base for the Pirates.

Perhaps rattled by his own mistake, Cuellar walked Willie Stargell, putting runners at first and second with no outs. Earl Weaver strode to the mound, apparently to bring in a right-hander to face the dangerous Bob Robertson. Weaver chatted with Cuellar, but left the veteran pitcher in the game.

Cuellar now prepared to face Robertson; he ran the count to one-and-one. Noticing that Brooks Robinson was playing deep at third, Murtaugh signaled to Frank Oceak, his third base coach. At first, Oceak found it hard to believe Murtaugh's sign, which called for Robertson, one of the team's most dangerous power hitters, to lay down a sacrifice bunt. Oceak was not the only member of the Pirates surprised by the decision. Clemente, who was leading off second, had his doubts, too. Waving his arms frantically in an attempt to call time, Clemente wanted to double-check that Oceak had signaled for a sacrifice bunt. Clemente's request came too late, as Cuellar offered his next pitch: one of his trademark screwballs. Based on Oceak's directions, Robertson should have squared around to attempt a bunt. Instead, he unleashed his best uppercut swing. Adeptly going with the screwball, which usually faded away from right-handed batters, Robertson drove the ball deep toward right field. The ball eventually landed above the 385-foot sign that marked the right-center field alley at Three Rivers Stadium.

A few moments later, fully anticipating congratulations from his teammates, Robertson greeted Stargell and Clemente at home plate. Stargell whispered to Robertson, "That's the way to bunt the ball," tipping him off as to the missed sign. Somewhat embarrassed, Robertson jogged back to the dugout and turned to Murtaugh, saying sheepishly, "I guess I fouled it up, huh?" Murtaugh responded in his typical deadpan. "Possibly," the ever-calm manager supposedly replied. "But under the circumstances, there will be no fine." Willie Stargell summed up the turn of events. "It was a helluva bunt," Stargell exclaimed to a reporter from the *Newark Star-Ledger*. "A perfect bunt. A beautiful bunt. You can be in this game all your life and never get a chance to bunt three runs in."

Regardless of the circumstances, Robertson's home run ensured a badly needed win for the Pirates. It also halted a 16-game winning streak for the Orioles, dating back to the final month of the regular season. And it demonstrated that the Pirates could beat an Orioles team that many observers felt was primed to sweep the Series.

As much as the Pirates enjoyed winning Game Three, they knew the outcome wouldn't mean much if they didn't post a win in Game Four as well. Apart from being a critical game, the fourth game also represented the first night contest in World Series play. The decision to make Game Four a nighttime affair was largely influenced by Commissioner Bowie Kuhn, who pitched the idea to NBC-TV. Kuhn felt that baseball could attract a larger television audience on a weeknight, as opposed to a typical mid-afternoon broadcast, when most fans either worked or attended school. (As testament to the historical significance of the game, the director of the National Baseball Hall of Fame and Museum, Ken Smith, paid a visit to the offices and clubhouses at Three Rivers Stadium that evening to collect artifacts for the museum's exhibits.)

A crowd of 51,378—a record for major league baseball in Pittsburgh—turned up at Three Rivers to witness baseball's history-making night. Although the forecast indicated a 30 percent chance of rain, gametime conditions were ideal: calm winds and a temperature of 72 degrees. The pleasant weather only enhanced the festive

With no one out, Roberto Clemente and Willie Stargell on base, and the Pirates ahead 2-1 in the bottom of the seventh inning of Game Three, Bob Robertson was given the bunt sign to advance the runners. Failing to pick up the sign, Robertson swings away and smashes Mike Cuellar's pitch into the right field stands for a crucial three-run homer. (*National Baseball Hall of Fame Library, Cooperstown, NY*)

atmosphere. Hall of Famer Stan Musial, a native of nearby Donora, Pennsylvania, threw out the ceremonial first pitch. Bing Crosby, a part owner of the Pirates, stood near the former St. Louis Cardinals' standout as baseball prepared to showcase its two best teams in the spotlight of prime-time television.

The attention given to *when* the game was being played removed some of the focus from Danny Murtaugh's unusual pitching choice.

Murtaugh gave the ball to left-hander Luke Walker instead of his regular season ace, Dock Ellis. Ellis seemed the logical selection, but Murtaugh was not convinced that he was healthy enough to pitch well, and he was concerned by Ellis' poor performance in Game One. "I don't feel we saw the real Dock Ellis in the first game, so I'm gonna stay away from him for these next two games," Murtaugh explained to the *New York Times*. "I don't think his elbow is good enough to throw the strong curve." Ellis reacted with surprising diplomacy to Murtaugh's decision. "I don't feel as though I've been passed over," said Ellis, who learned that he would not be starting Game Five either. "The dude [Murtaugh] sits down and picks his pitchers and he picked two other guys."

Walker, the little-used left-hander, had not pitched in three weeks. In fact, he had not worked at all during the postseason. Now his manager was asking him to pitch the Pirates' most important game of the season. Murtaugh's stunning decision to entrust Walker with the start left the manager open to a boatload of second-guessing.

Walker pitched poorly in Game Four. Failing to escape a first-inning jam, the young left-hander lasted only 22 pitches. The short stint included a leadoff single to Paul Blair, back-to-back infield hits by Mark Belanger and Merv Rettenmund, an intentional walk to Frank Robinson, and two deep sacrifice flies by Brooks Robinson and Boog Powell. Watching the Orioles take a 3-0 lead against Walker, Murtaugh sent his left-hander to the showers and brought in right-hander Bruce Kison to face Dave Johnson. The right-handed hitting Johnson pounded a routine grounder to Richie Hebner, finally ending the three-run uprising.

Down by three, the Pirates' offense now took its turn, facing right-hander Pat Dobson. Like Walker, Dobson had not pitched in the postseason, and last worked in a two-inning appearance on September 28. Praying that the 20-game winner had lost his precise control and sharp command, the Pirates began the inning with promise—a walk by leadoff man Dave Cash. Dobson then settled down, retiring Hebner and Roberto Clemente. Now just one out from completely discouraging the Pirates, Dobson buckled under. Willie Stargell drove a double into right-center field, scoring Cash from first base for the Pirates' first run. Al Oliver then blooped a fly ball into short center field. An excellent defensive center fielder who prided himself on playing shallow and catching short fly balls, Paul Blair raced in quickly to attempt a running catch. On this unusual occasion, Blair missed the ball, which bounced over his head for a double. Stargell scored easily from second, suddenly bringing the Pirates within a run.

In the top of the second inning, Kison kept the Pirates close. He retired catcher Andy Etchebarren on a ground ball to second base and then fanned his pitching counterpart, Dobson, on called strikes. With two outs, Blair looped a double into right-center field, beyond the reach of Clemente, but Kison was able to force Belanger to pop out to first to end the inning.

The Pirates continued their comeback in the bottom half of the third inning, but not before a controversial call in Baltimore's favor. With one out, Hebner grounded a single up the middle. Clemente next lined the first pitch from Dobson down the right field line. The ball caromed off the wall and back into the field of play. Assuming that the ball was either in play or had gone over the wall's yellow line for a home run, Pirate players climbed to the top step of the first base dugout and jumped in the air. Then, to their surprise, right field umpire John Rice ruled that the ball had gone foul. First base coach Don Leppert trotted toward Rice and argued that the ball had hit the wall in fair territory. "Fair ball," Leppert screamed over and over. "It hit the right-hand corner of the foul line." Danny Murtaugh jogged out to right field to support Leppert in the argument. Attempting to rationalize his decision, Rice indicated that the call was a close one. "If I called it fair, the other team would be argu-ing," Rice said. The closeness of the call did little to appease Murtaugh, who yelled back at Rice in disbelief. "What do I care about the other team?" cried Murtaugh.

But Clemente was unfazed by whether the call was correct or not. The tenacious Clemente simply lined another ball to right field in front of Frank Robinson—this one clearly fair. Clemente's hit advanced Hebner to second base. After Willie Stargell flied to Paul Blair in short center field, Al Oliver delivered the game-tying run with another line-drive single to right field.

Justifying Murtaugh's early call to the bullpen, Kison continued to retire Orioles batters with ease. In the meantime, Dobson continued to struggle. In the fourth inning, the Pirates threatened by reaching Dobson for a hit and a walk, but left the runners stranded. In the fifth, the Pirates loaded the bases with one out, but Bob Robertson popped out and Manny Sanguillen grounded harmlessly to shortstop.

In the sixth inning, the Pirates placed more pressure on Dobson. Jackie Hernandez led off by stroking a ground single to left field. With one out, Hernandez stole second and then moved up to third when Dave Cash lined a pitch back to the mound. The ball caromed off of Dobson's glove, putting Pirate runners at first and third. With the lefty-swinging Hebner batting next, Earl Weaver brought on southpaw Grant Jackson to replace the fading Dobson. Foregoing the pinch-hitting option of Jose Pagan, Murtaugh left Hebner in to face Jackson. Wisely going with the pitch, Hebner smacked a line drive to the left side of the infield. Unfortunately, Hebner picked on the wrong Orioles infielder. Brooks Robinson dove to his right and snared the ball on the fly for the inning's second out. Jackson then walked Clemente to load the bases, bringing another left-handed hitter, Willie Stargell, to the plate. Stargell managed only a ground ball to Dave Johnson, bringing the inning to a close. For the third straight inning, the Pirates placed at least two runners on base but failed to produce the go-ahead run.

In the top of the seventh, Kison yielded only his fourth baserunner of the game when he hit Andy Etchebarren with a one-out pitch. Kison recovered from his wildness to retire Tom Shopay, the pinch-hitter for Grant Jackson, on a forceout. Kison then escaped the inning when Paul Blair hit a deep fly ball to left field that landed safely in the glove of Willie Stargell.

With the game still tied, Earl Weaver elected to bring in his ace reliever, right-hander Eddie Watt, to pitch the seventh inning. Unlike in later years, managers in the sixties and seventies often summoned their ace relievers, or closers, to pitch in tie games. Watt struck out Al Oliver, a rare occurrence for "Scoop" against right-handed pitching. Watt then faced Bob Robertson, whose hit eluded the pitcher and skipped into center field. Manny Sanguillen lined another single to center field, putting runners on first and second with one out.

With Jackie Hernandez scheduled to bat, Danny Murtaugh considered the options on his bench. Murtaugh liked the matchup of his best pinch-hitter, the left-handed hitting Vic Davalillo, against the three-quarter and overhand deliveries of Watt. Even though Murtaugh knew that Weaver had left-hander Pete Richert available in the bullpen, he felt that the Oriole manager would be reluctant to remove Watt, his No. 1 reliever, in the seventh inning. To Murtaugh's delight, Weaver stayed with Watt, and the spray-hitting Davalillo lifted a fly ball into left-center field. The speedy Blair, who was shading Davalillo toward left field, raced over, and positioned himself to make the catch. Usually reliable, Blair dropped the ball, allowing Bob Robertson to advance to third base and Sanguillen to race toward second. After reaching second base, Sanguillen rounded the bag too aggressively. Mark Belanger, who had fielded Blair's toss from the outfield, realized that Sanguillen had strayed several feet from the base. Belanger fired to Dave Johnson, who applied a quick tag to an embarrassed Sanguillen.

If the Pirates were to lose the game, the media would likely blame the popular Sanguillen, normally a fine baserunner. Instead of enjoying a bases loaded, one-out situation, the Pirates now had runners on first and third, with two outs. Either way, Murtaugh felt he had to pinch-hit for Kison, even though he had hurled six and a third innings of unblemished relief. With his best and most experienced pinch-hitter having been burned, Murtaugh now called upon the untested bat of the youthful Milt May.

As a backup to the ironman Sanguillen, May had been productive in a limited role, accounting for six home runs and a respectable .278 batting average in 126 at-bats. Yet, the rookie receiver had never faced this kind of situation: a 3-3 tie in the bottom of the seventh inning of a critical World Series game.

Figuring that Watt would try to jump ahead of him with a fastball early in the count, May opted for an aggressive approach at the plate. As he held his bat high above his head—an unusual batting stance popularized by Boston Red Sox star Carl Yastrzemski—May awaited Watt's first delivery. As May expected, Watt threw a first-pitch fastball, over the outer half of the plate. Seizing the opportunity, May swung hard, but managed only a half-hearted line drive into right-center field. Paul Blair and Frank Robinson raced toward the ball, which was well placed by a fortunate May. Eluding both of the hard-charging outfielders, the looping fly ball dropped in for a run-scoring single. The 21-year-old May had become an instant hero of Autumn.

Although the Pirates now held a 4-3 lead, the seventh inning comeback had come at a price: the Bucs lost the services of Bruce Kison. Fortunately for Danny Murtaugh, he still had favorable options in his bullpen. Murtaugh turned the lead over to relief ace Dave Giusti, who had already pitched under substantial pressure in the Championship Series against the Giants. After working a perfect eighth inning, Giusti prepared himself to collect the final three outs. Those outs did not figure to come easily. Giusti would have to face Baltimore's fifth-, sixth-, and seventh-place hitters: Brooks Robinson, Boog Powell, and Dave Johnson. The key would be retiring Robinson, the leadoff batter in the inning. If the hot-hitting Robinson were to reach, the lefty-swinging Powell would come to the plate as the potential go-ahead run.

Giusti approached the inning with his typical bulldog style and retired Robinson on a leadoff grounder to shortstop. Giusti now had the luxury of pitching carefully to Powell, who was the Orioles' second-leading home run hitter during the regular season, but had been hampered by a sore right wrist throughout the World Series. Giusti ran up a three-ball count to Powell, throwing two palmballs that slipped out of his hand and a fastball that also went astray. When Giusti fired his next palmball over the plate, Powell decided to take a big swing. The mammoth slugger swung under the pitch, lofting a weak pop-up that Richie Hebner corralled near home plate. With the biggest threats of the inning now eliminated, Giusti faced Dave Johnson. Although not as feared as either Robinson or Powell, Johnson was regarded by some scouts as the most powerful second baseman in the major leagues. The owner of 18 home runs during the regular season, Johnson stroked a grounder to the left side of the infield. Moving in quickly, Gene Alley scooped up the ball cleanly and fired to Bob Robertson at first base—well ahead of Johnson's arrival. Despite having to work against a trio of Baltimore's best power hitters, Giusti had registered the final three outs with relative ease. Suddenly, a World Series that once appeared on the verge of a blowout had reversed momentum. The overmatched Pirates had drawn even with the mighty Orioles.

While the Pirates were pleased with the results of Game Four, so was baseball's hierarchy. The first night game in World Series history had produced a compelling matchup between two formidable teams. An estimated 61 million fans watched the game on NBC; television ratings for a World Series game during the daytime hours would not have come close to that. Even Orioles manager Earl Weaver realized the significance of the game, at a time when he might have been excused for dwelling on a Baltimore defeat. "They couldn't have written a better script," the Earl of Baltimore proclaimed to *The Sporting News*.

Whatever the final outcome of the series, Game Five would represent the final game of the season for the Bucs at Three Rivers Stadium. Pirate players realized they had to win their last home game in order to have a realistic chance of completing a dramatic Series comeback. A loss in Game Five would put the Pirates in the undesirable position of having to win two games on the road against a superior Baltimore pitching staff.

For the second straight game, Danny Murtaugh bypassed the ailing Dock Ellis and called upon an unlikely starter, 28-year-old right-hander Nellie Briles, who had started only 14 games during the regular season and missed his one scheduled playoff start because of a pulled leg muscle. Now, Murtaugh was asking him to pitch the most important game of his life.

Briles opened Game Five by retiring Don Buford, Paul Blair, and Boog Powell in order. In the second, Briles handled the first two batters, Frank Robinson and Elrod Hendricks, before allowing Brooks Robinson to reach on a line-drive single. The inning ended with a Johnson fly out to center field.

In contrast, the Pirates fared better against Orioles left-hander Dave McNally, who had pitched so brilliantly in Game One. Bob

Robertson started the top half of the second inning by launching McNally's first pitch over the center field fence, some 410 feet away. The leadoff home run gave the Pirates a 1-0 lead. Manny Sanguillen followed with a line-drive single and stole second base. Facing the lower third of the Pirates' lineup, McNally regrouped, striking out both Jose Pagan and Jackie Hernandez. With his counterpart, Nellie Briles, stepping to the plate, McNally appeared on the verge of ending the inning. He notched two quick strikes against Briles, but mysteriously missed with his next three pitches, filling the count. Showing Briles some respect, McNally and catcher Ellie Hendricks decided to throw Briles a breaking ball, and not a fastball. McNally unfurled a slider, which hung high in the strike zone. Briles swung, smacking the ball on a line into center field. The hard-hit single scored Sanguillen from second, giving the Pirates a 2-0 cushion.

In the third, the Pirates added to their lead. Gene Clines walked, moved to second base on a Roberto Clemente grounder, and advanced to third on a rare error by Brooks Robinson. Clines then came home on a wild pitch, giving the Bucs a three-run lead. In the fifth, the Pirates scored again, sending McNally to the clubhouse in favor of little-known reliever Dave Leonhard.

With four runs in his favor, Briles could pitch more comfortably. The veteran right-hander brilliantly spotted his pitches and exhibited remarkable control, especially given his recent lack of work. In the bottom of the eighth inning, Pirates fans showed their appreciation of Briles' World Series performance when he came to bat, giving him a thunderous standing ovation. As Briles listened to the crowd's response, he cried openly, remembering the difficult times that he had endured in St. Louis over the two previous seasons. "I've never done that before, but I couldn't help it," Briles told the *New York Times* in explaining his reaction. "I didn't know how to take it. All sorts of things flashed through my mind in a matter of seconds. All the people who were good to me, the people who gave me encouragement when I was down, my high school coach and the other coaches I had, my wife, my family, the things they've given me. I guess the main thing I thought in those seconds was that it had been two hard years with not much success and this was the culmination of all of it."

Nellie Briles demonstrates his unconventional follow-through as he falls to the ground while delivering a pitch in Game Five of the World Series. Briles would throw a complete-game, two-hit shutout against the high-powered Orioles. Originally signed by the Cardinals in 1963, Briles become a solid pitcher in St. Louis and pitched effectively in the 1967 World Series against the Red Sox. Taken by surprise when traded to the Pirates before the 1971 season, Briles became a key component of Pittsburgh's underrated staff, culminating in this performance against the Orioles—arguably the finest game of his career. (*National Baseball Hall of Fame Library, Cooperstown, NY*)

In the top of the ninth, Briles regained control of his emotions and retired the first two Orioles' batters, Mark Belanger and Merv Rettenmund. Briles then faltered, walking the patient Don Buford on four pitches. The sudden fit of wildness prompted a visit from pitching coach Don Osborn, along with some warm-up action in the bullpen, where Dave Giusti and Luke Walker began to stir. After the visit from Osborn, Briles regained his control, throwing two consecutive strikes to Paul Blair. Blair then hit a grounder to the left side of the infield. Jose Pagan fielded the ball cleanly and threw quickly to second base, where Dave Cash touched the base while barely avoiding the slide of the hard-charging Buford. In finishing off the masterful effort, Briles surrendered only two hits and two walks while extending the Orioles' run-scoring drought to 17 consecutive innings.

Four years earlier, Briles had won a World Series game with the St. Louis Cardinals, but his performance in Game Five against the Orioles exceeded even his initial Series victory. "I've gotta say that, for me, the fifth game of the World Series under that kind of pressure was the greatest game that I ever pitched." Statistics back up Briles' claim. The Pittsburgh right-hander faced only 29 batters; no one reached second base, a complete-game feat second only in World Series history to Don Larsen's perfect game in the 1956 Series.

While showcasing Briles at his best, Game Five also provided an intriguing example of the often strange and complicated relationship between a pitcher and a catcher. In this case, Briles teamed with Manny Sanguillen. "We're going into the seventh inning," recalls Briles, "and primarily we'd been blending our pitches very well, you know, spotting the fastball in and out, and mixing in our off-speed pitches, the slider and the palmball. Now I have a 4-0 lead going into the seventh inning, and we need just nine outs. And now is when I want to really take the game to the opposition. I wanna throw a lot of strikes, and I'm gonna go with a lot more hard stuff, get ahead in the count, take the game to them. Pitch good, high-percentage baseball and close out the game."

Sanguillen had another game plan in mind. The difference in opinion between pitcher and catcher led to a remarkable athletic display by Sanguillen. "So, Manny came out to the mound when we were starting the top of the seventh inning," Briles says, "and he told me in his English, 'Nellie, we going to throw the slide ball, we going to throw the palm ball, we going to get these guys out, OK?'

"I said, 'No.'

"He say, 'What do you mean, no? I call the game for six innings, you got the shutout, now you going to call the game. Are you nuts or something?'

"I said, 'No, let's take the game to them.'

"He says, 'You no like the way I call the game. I no call no pitch.'"

Sanguillen then returned to his station behind home plate. "He sat down," recalls Briles, "and he wouldn't put down a signal, and I said, 'Manny, come on, this is the World Series.' So then, he came back out, and I said, 'Manny, let's go, give me the sign.'

"Manny says, 'You no like the way I call the game, I no give you no sign. Besides, I no need no signs to catch your junk.' And so we went the [entire] seventh inning, and he didn't give any signs. Whatever you wanna throw, you throw. So I did. But Manny was so athletic he could do that. He would pick up the spin of the ball, react to the ball. And he knew that I was gonna be around the plate, because my control was exceptional that day."

Even the most hopeful Pirate optimist could not have foreseen the Pirates sweeping three games at Three Rivers, especially in the unexpected way they had done so—with strong pitching. Starters Steve Blass and Nellie Briles, along with Bruce Kison in relief, had all turned in stellar efforts. In the meantime, the mysterious defensive problems of the Orioles had opened doors for the Pirates' offense. Through five games, the O's had committed nine errors, accounting for five unearned runs. The sudden defensive deficiencies left Earl Weaver both confused and upset. "We don't [usually] give teams chances like we've given the Pirates," Weaver lamented to a reporter from *The Sporting News*. "This is not the way we play baseball."

In the meantime, Danny Murtaugh reveled in the Pirates' three-game win streak, and even took a slight swipe at the doom-saying writers. "I think most of you fellows had written us off after the first two games," he said in an interview with *The Sporting News*. "We've been written off before and we have always bounced back." In mid-August, the slumping Pirates' ability to maintain their lead had been questioned by legendary sportswriters like Jimmy Cannon. In the Championship Series, the loss in Game One to the Giants had prompted discussion of an early departure from the playoffs. In the World Series, defeats in the first two games had led to predictions of a four-game sweep by the Orioles. Yet, all of the doom-saying reports had proven false.

Chapter 13

WORLD SERIES GAME SIX: BALTIMORE

After watching his team endure a third consecutive loss, Orioles right fielder Frank Robinson delivered a response to Roberto Clemente's recent complaints about the uneven grass surface and dim visibility of Memorial Stadium. "I don't know why he's knocking ballparks," Robinson said in an interview with Jerome Holtzman of the *Chicago Sun-Times*. "Until they moved into this place [Three Rivers Stadium], he'd been playing in a coal hole [Forbes Field]. If you're a professional, you adjust to the different ballparks and don't complain." Robinson also reacted to Clemente's charge that the Memorial Stadium outfield forced him to play deeper than the close positioning he preferred. "Close?" Robinson asked sarcastically. "Every time I've seen him here in Pittsburgh, he's been near the warning track." Robinson then told Holtzman to pass along a message to Clemente. "Tell him he should watch me. He should watch where I play. We're going back to Baltimore, and maybe he won't want to play there. Maybe we should give him a ticket, and have him get a seat in the stands."

Rather than let Robinson's remarks pass without comment, Clemente decided to reply to the surprising diatribe. "Well, Frank Robinson is a better ballplayer than I am," Roberto said to Holtzman, with sarcasm readily apparent. "He's an American fellow. That makes him the best." Clemente wasn't done. "In Puerto Rico," Clemente recalled, "when I am a boy, I play without shoes. I am a professional. I can play anywhere."

With the Orioles facing their first must-win situation of the World Series, Earl Weaver chose Jim Palmer, the winner of Game Two, to pitch the sixth game back in Baltimore. Danny Murtaugh countered with yet another intriguing choice—his third consecutive surprise of the Series—right-handed swingman Bob Moose, who did most of his work out of the bullpen. Moose would become the sixth different Pirate starter in the six-game series, matching a record originally set by the Brooklyn Dodgers in 1955 in a victorious seven-game World Series against the New York Yankees.

In selecting Moose, Murtaugh once again bypassed Dock Ellis and also sidestepped another possible choice. Why didn't Murtaugh opt for Steve Blass, who had pitched so effectively in Game Three and would have been pitching the sixth game on three days' rest? "I like my pitcher to have four days in between starts," Murtaugh told the *New York Times*. "Moose was going to be my starter whether we were leading three to two in games, or trailing two to three, and I told him that before the fifth game. It's a sign of how much confidence I have in Moose."

The Pirates gave Moose an early cushion by scoring quickly against Jim Palmer. In the second inning, a double by Al Oliver and an RBI single by Bob Robertson produced the Pirates' first run. Roberto Clemente added an opposite-field home run in the third, making it 2-0.

In the meantime, Moose mowed down the Orioles through the first five innings, allowing only two hits and no runs. He no longer seemed like a risky choice to start the game, just as the selection of Nellie Briles for Game Five was no longer being questioned by the media.

In the bottom of the sixth, Moose faced Baltimore's leadoff batter, the switch-hitting and power-packed Don Buford. Moose threw a belt-high fastball to the stocky left fielder. Buford swung hard, lifting the ball deep toward right field. The line drive scaled the wall, giving Buford his second home run of the Series. More important, the home run brought the Orioles within a single run of the Pirates. Dave Johnson followed by hitting a high hopper to Richie Hebner, who dropped the ball for an error. A single by Boog Powell put Orioles runners on first and third with no outs, while also pushing Moose from the game. With only one run surrendered in five-plus innings, Moose had pitched creditably for the Pirates.

Murtaugh opted to bring the hard-throwing Bob Johnson into the game to face the trio of Frank Robinson, Merv Rettenmund, and

Brooks Robinson. Overpowering Frank Robinson with a high fast-ball, Johnson induced a weak pop-up to Jackie Hernandez at short-stop. One out. Johnson then struck out Rettenmund, who was caught looking. Two out. Johnson now faced Brooks Robinson, who bounded a routine grounder to Hebner at third. This time Hebner handled the ball without incident. He fired to Cash for the force at second. Three out. Yet another unlikely source had delivered clutch pitching for the Pirates.

In the bottom of the seventh, Mark Belanger dented Johnson with a one-out single to right field. Johnson then struck out Jim Palmer, but Belanger stole second base, putting himself in scoring position with two outs. When Johnson fell behind Don Buford 3-and-1, Danny Murtaugh walked to the mound and signaled for Dave Giusti. Murtaugh hoped that his No. 1 reliever could pull off anoth-er one of his multiple-inning saves—and end the Series.

Already behind in the count to Buford, Giusti threw ball four, putting runners on first and second. The right-handed hitting Dave Johnson stepped to the plate. With the count 2-and-2, Giusti opted for his best pitch, the palm ball. Using a one-handed swing, Johnson lofted the ball gently into short left field. The ball dropped in front of Willie Stargell, who was playing deep against Johnson, and scored Belanger with the tying run.

In the bottom of the ninth inning, the Orioles threatened to win the game. With two outs and Belanger on first base, Buford lined a double down the right field line. As Belanger rounded third, Clemente raised eyebrows throughout Memorial Stadium when he made a 309-foot throw from the depths of the right field corner to Manny Sanguillen at the plate—on one short hop. Wisely, Belanger returned to third base. Although no Oriole was retired on the play, the throw was still an incredible one, perhaps more impressive than Clemente's throw against Merv Rettenmund in Game Two.

Thanks to Clemente's arm, the game remained tied through nine innings. In the bottom of the ninth, Earl Weaver had lifted Palmer for pinch-hitter Tom Shopay, which forced him to go the bullpen. Rather than call on one of his regular relievers, Weaver elected to bring in Pat Dobson, usually a starter, to work the 10th. Leading off as the pinch-hitter for Dave Giusti, Vic Davalillo pulled a line drive—right at second baseman Dave Johnson. Dave Cash followed by serving a one-out single to right field. He then stole second base as Richie Hebner struck out. With the go-ahead run in scoring position, and Roberto Clemente at the plate, Weaver smartly decided not to tinker with "The Great One." Since Clemente had already powered a home run and a triple, Weaver had no interest in giving him a third chance to victimize the Orioles' pitching staff. After Dobson intentionally walked Clemente, Weaver made another pitching change. Deciding that his starting pitchers would provide more effective relief against the Pirates than his usually solid bullpen corps of Dick Hall, Pete Richert, and Eddie Watt, Weaver called on left-hander Dave McNally to face Willie Stargell.

Pitching from the stretch, McNally proceeded to walk Stargell, who was batting only .200 in the Series. The unintentional walk loaded the bases and brought another left-handed batter, Al Oliver, to the plate.

Danny Murtaugh had three quality right-handed pinch-hitters available to him: Gene Clines, Bill Mazeroski, and Jose Pagan. Murtaugh realized, however, that if he put one of those hitters into the game, Weaver could counter with an experienced right-hander like Watt or Hall. And since Vic Davalillo had already been used as a pinch-hitter to start the inning, Murtaugh possessed only one other lefty-swinging option in Milt May, the hero of Game Four. Would a rookie like May be able to strike lightning twice in the same World Series?

Murtaugh decided to stay with Oliver, despite the fact that he had struck out against McNally to end the first game of the Series. This time Oliver lofted a routine fly ball to Merv Rettenmund in center field, ending the Pirates' threat and keeping the score tied. To make matters worse, Murtaugh had also lost the services of his best relief pitcher, Dave Giusti, who had been replaced by the pinch-hitting Davalillo.

As the Orioles prepared to bat in the bottom half of the 10th inning, Murtaugh made an unconventional switch with his defense. He kept Davalillo in the game in center field—replacing Oliver, who had a stronger throwing arm. Murtaugh also called upon journeyman Bob Miller to take the mound. Miller, who had pitched inconsistently for the Pirates since joining them in a mid-season trade with the Padres, retired the first batter, Boog Powell, on a bouncer to second. Miller now faced the dangerous Frank Robinson. Pitching carefully, Miller walked the Orioles' most feared hitter on a three-and-two pitch. Some of the Pirates felt that home plate umpire John Kibler missed the call on ball four.

Merv Rettenmund followed the controversial walk by hitting a dribbler up the middle, past Miller. Although Rettenmund hit the ball rather slowly, neither Dave Cash nor Jackie Hernandez could knock it down. Robinson, one of the best and most aggressive runners in the American League, decided to make a hard run for third base, despite an injured Achilles tendon. He knew that Vic Davalillo, now playing center field, possessed the weakest throwing arm of all the Pirate outfielders. Although Davalillo charged the ball hard and made a surprisingly strong throw on the line to Richie Hebner, Robinson eluded the tag with a headfirst slide. In the process of making both a hard run and slide, Robinson pulled his thigh muscle. Yet, an injury for an extra base in a critical situation was a worthwhile tradeoff for Robinson. The Orioles simply had to win to extend the Series.

With runners on first and third and only one out, the Pirates moved their infielders and outfielders in against the power-hitting Brooks Robinson. Miller jumped ahead of Robinson, running the count to one ball and two strikes. Realizing the importance of putting the ball in play with a runner on third, Robinson understood that he now had to shorten his swing to protect against the strike-out. On the next pitch, Robinson lofted a fly ball to medium-depth center field. At first glance, the ball did not seem to have the distance to score a hobbling Frank Robinson from third base.

With the bottom of the order coming up, and the aging Davalillo having a weak arm in center field, Frank Robinson believed that the short fly ball represented the Orioles' best chance to score. Even with a weakened thigh muscle, Robinson decided to gamble. As Davalillo approached the ball, Robinson tagged up at third base. After making the catch in medium center field, Davalillo quickly fired in the direction of home plate and catcher Manny Sanguillen. The ball sailed to the left of home plate, a few feet off line. The ball

In one of the most memorable moments of the 1971 World Series, Frank Robinson, his helmet flying, slides under a leaping Manny Sanguillen to score the winning run in the bottom of the 10th inning of Game Six. With one out and another runner on first base, the injured Robinson decided to make a mad dash from third base on Brooks Robinson's short fly ball, rather than risk being stranded by the lower part of the Orioles' order. (*National Baseball Hall of Fame Library, Cooperstown, NY*)

bounced once, and then hopped unusually high on the second bounce. Sanguillen made a graceful leap and cleanly grabbed the ball. As the Pirate catcher hung in mid air, Robinson slid between and under his legs. As Sanguillen returned to the ground with a swipe tag, Robinson's feet scraped home plate. Umpire John Kibler

signaled Robinson "safe"—a close but correct call. The completion
of Robinson's mad dash around the bases had given the Orioles a
dramatic 3-2 win in extra innings.

As with most memorable World Series games, Game Six produced its share of controversy. Afterward, an infuriated Bob
Moose lashed out at the umpires. "I've never seen worse umpiring in
my life," Moose spewed to a reporter from *The Sporting News*.
Moose voiced extreme contempt for home plate umpire John Kibler,
who had apparently botched the three-two pitch to Robinson,
among other shortcomings. In fact, Moose was displeased with the
way Kibler had called balls and strikes throughout the game. "He
should go back to the instructional league," fumed an angry Moose.
Thankfully for the Pirates, the outspoken Moose would not be asked
to pitch again in the Series.

Danny Murtaugh was not pleased with Kibler's work, either. In a
little known post-game incident reported by Jerome Holtzman of the
Chicago Sun-Times, Murtaugh followed Kibler up the runway
toward the clubhouse. According to Holtzman's sources, Murtaugh
yelled at the veteran umpire because of his questionable balls-and-
strikes work behind the plate. "Murtaugh. . . apparently heaped
such abuse," Holtzman wrote, "that Commissioner Bowie Kuhn
asked Kibler to file a report." Another umpire told Holtzman that
Murtaugh would be fined for the unseemly outburst, which report-
edly lasted several minutes. After the World Series, Kuhn would
assess a $200 fine against Murtaugh for his verbal assault against
Kibler.

Murtaugh's diatribe toward Kibler was uncharacteristic of a
manager generally known for his placid demeanor. The painful ending to Game Six may have left Murtaugh in such a foul mood that
he had blamed the umpires for losing. Or perhaps Murtaugh simply
felt frustrated that he had just missed his best chance of winning a
World Series that many had considered unattainable from the
beginning.

Nonetheless, Game Six earned its merits as one of the true clas-
sics in World Series history. In the October 18 edition of the *New
York Daily News*, longtime baseball columnist Dick Young wrote the

following assessment of the sixth game between Pittsburgh and Baltimore: "Game Six ranks as one of the great ones. It was finger-chewing good. It had hearts pounding, harder, harder, incessantly, building to a crescendo. . . Baseball, a good baseball game, builds and builds its tension, its expectancies, its sustained frenzy." Game Six featured all of these qualities. As Young concluded about baseball, "When it is good, there is nothing like it."

Chapter 14

WORLD SERIES GAME SEVEN: BALTIMORE

While Bob Moose and Danny Murtaugh ranked as the angriest of the Pirates, perhaps no man was more disappointed by the outcome of Game Six than Steve Blass. "In that sixth game," Blass says, "Danny Murtaugh told me before the game, 'Moose is pitching today. If we don't win, you're gonna go tomorrow.' There was nobody that rooted any harder for Bob Moose to win Game Six than I did. I mean I had had my moment in the sun in Game Three, and I knew that I wanted us to finish it up right there, so I had no qualms about Bob Moose winning."

In the meantime, Roberto Clemente also tried to hide his own thoughts about his future in baseball. He confided to his wife Vera and his friend, longtime Pirate scout Howie Haak, that he would retire after the World Series—but only if the Pirates won Game Seven. Clemente told no one else about his plans.

Of immediate concern to Murtaugh was his lineup for Game Seven. With the Orioles throwing left-hander Mike Cuellar in the Series finale, Murtaugh made some changes. The biggest move involved a slumping Willie Stargell, who was dropped from the cleanup spot to the No. 6 position. Murtaugh also moved two other players up in the lineup, sliding Robertson and Manny Sanguillen to the fourth and fifth spots, respectively. From the Baltimore side, Earl Weaver announced that Frank Robinson would start the seventh game in right field and bat cleanup, despite his injured leg.

The pitching matchup of Mike Cuellar and Steve Blass seemed to give Game Seven a chance of approaching the suspenseful dramatics of the sixth game. Blass' heroic effort earlier in the Series had given the Pirates the most necessary win; Cuellar had earned a reputation as one of baseball's most respected veteran pitchers. The matchup also offered a contrast: Cuellar, the proven, playoff-tested left-hander who appeared calm and controlled despite his bizarre obsessions with superstition and ritual, against Blass, the outwardly nervous right-hander still trying to prove himself to the masses of fans who did not yet consider him a star.

Just minutes before the start of Game Seven, a smattering of large, darkened clouds appeared over Memorial Stadium. Weather reports indicated a 20 percent chance of rain showers that afternoon. While the umpires pondered the weather forecast, they ordered the field lights to be turned on at Memorial Stadium. Fortunately, the rain would hold off, allowing the game to start as scheduled.

The ominous weather—and the potential for an interruption at any moment—did not seem to bother Cuellar, who pitched efficiently through the first three innings. He retired every batter he faced, allowing only two balls to reach the outfield. Bob Robertson and Jackie Hernandez managed the hardest drives against Cuellar. One was a low-lying shot to Brooks Robinson at third, the other a line drive to Frank Robinson in right field.

In contrast, Blass labored considerably more than Cuellar did. In the first inning, Blass walked the leadoff man, Don Buford. Then, in a strategic maneuver that ran counter to the usual preferences of manager Earl Weaver, Dave Johnson tried to lay down a bunt. An unskilled bunter, Johnson popped the ball up to the mound, where Blass cradled the ball with a waist-level catch. Blass then faced Boog Powell, who pulled a lazy fastball into the farthest reaches of Memorial Stadium's upper deck—albeit dozens of feet foul. In the midst of Powell's at-bat, Weaver suddenly stormed onto the playing field. Weaver had several objections: Blass was illegally putting his hands to his mouth, he wasn't coming to a complete stop with Buford on first base, and he wasn't keeping his right foot in contact with the pitching rubber. The latter infraction grated Weaver the most. "Rule 8:01(b) says you have to be in front of the rubber or on it," an adamant Weaver explained later to *The Sporting News*.

Umpire Nestor Chylak agreed with Weaver's contention and informed Blass and Danny Murtaugh that the pitcher needed to comply with the rule. Blass threw one warm-up pitch, which skipped wildly off the outstretched glove of Manny Sanguillen, drawing some mock cheers from Baltimore's fans. After Blass threw a second warm-up pitch—this one for a strike—Weaver scurried out of the dugout again. "He was on the side," complained Weaver, who felt that Blass was continuing to pitch from a point off the rubber. "I told Nestor about it and he said, 'He's in front of it enough for me and it's got to be good enough for you.'"

Weaver's dual protests caused a delay of several minutes and rattled Blass. After Weaver's argument with Chylak, Blass threw two straight balls to run the count full, but recovered to strike out Powell on a nasty overhand curve. After enduring a long at-bat with Powell, he enjoyed a quicker at-bat with Frank Robinson. Swinging at the first pitch, Robinson hit a lengthy fly ball to right field, which Roberto Clemente handled deep in the corner. Although Weaver had hoped to disturb the excitable right-hander's rhythm, Blass had finished the inning unscathed.

In the second inning, Blass found himself in trouble again after yielding a one-out walk to Brooks Robinson and watching Elrod Hendricks reach first on an error by Bob Robertson. Mark Belanger followed by hitting a ground ball that looked like it might slip through the middle of the infield. Second baseman Dave Cash moved quickly to his right, backhanded the ball, and deftly stepped on the bag for the second out of the inning. Cash then pivoted, squared himself, and threw to Bob Robertson. The throw appeared to pull Robertson off the bag, but first base coach George Staller offered only mild protest to the completion of the unconventional 4-4-3 double play. Instead of working against a bases-loaded, one-out situation, the Pirates had escaped the inning entirely.

In the top of the fourth inning, Cuellar handled the first two Pirates' batters with ease. Dave Cash lined softly to Dave Johnson, who made a smooth catch on the run. Gene Clines then dropped down a bunt, which Cuellar fielded barehanded and fired to first, where Boog Powell neatly scooped up a low throw. Having set down 11 straight Pirates to start the game, Cuellar now faced Roberto Clemente. Hoping to keep Clemente off balance, the veteran left-hander threw him a curveball over the outside part of the plate.

Cuellar's attempted pitch location was consistent with the report provided by Orioles superscout Jim Russo. According to Russo, the best way to pitch Clemente was to throw him breaking pitches away while keeping the ball low.

Unfortunately for Cuellar, he failed to follow Russo's instructions to the letter. Although he kept the ball away from Clemente, he allowed the curveball to hang high, rather than keep it in its desired location below the belt. Clemente unleashed a long, powerful swing on the wayward pitch and cracked it into left-center field. Left fielder Don Buford and center fielder Merv Rettenmund raced toward the ball from opposite directions, each with thoughts of making the catch in front of the wall. Instead, the two outfielders watched the ball sail into the Memorial Stadium bleachers, just to the right of the 390-foot sign. Even the Pirate players were surprised that the ball had traveled as far as the left-field stands. "We saw the ball heading for the fence," Dave Cash remarked to *The Sporting News*. "All of us in the dugout had a sense of disbelief. We saw Rettenmund go back and we didn't think the ball would go out. You know, the ball doesn't carry too well in this park."

It was an intriguing coincidence that Clemente and Cuellar had met so dramatically in Game Seven. Just one year earlier, Clemente had managed Cuellar in the winter league. After a brief stint, the Cuban left-hander decided to bolt the team, unhappy with Clemente's disciplinary style. Clemente had been unhappy with the pitcher's unwillingness to listen to advice. Clemente cited an example: "Reggie Jackson, he is a good pull hitter who likes to jump on the pitch out over the plate. He hit a long home run off Cuellar and we tell him to try crowding Jackson, but Cuellar, he does not want to listen." Fittingly perhaps, Clemente had homered against the same kind of pitch—out over the plate—that had cost Cuellar in his confrontation against Jackson. In this case, the Clemente home run had done important damage.

Still, with only a 1-0 lead, the Pirates had to rely heavily on Steve Blass. Over the first five innings, Blass struggled with his pitching rhythm, but from the sixth inning on, as Blass began to mix in his moving slider more frequently, he became even more effective in turning back the Orioles' lineup.

The Pirates maintained their slim lead as the game moved to the top of the eighth inning. Leading off against Cuellar, Willie Stargell delivered a ground single to the left of Mark Belanger's failed backhand attempt. With the right-hand hitting Jose Pagan scheduled to bat, Weaver now had the option of making a pitching change. He could call on one of several capable right-handers in his bullpen.

Weaver decided to stay with Cuellar. The decision seemed reasonable, given Cuellar's effectiveness throughout the game. Other than the home run to Clemente, Cuellar had allowed only one other hit, a single by Manny Sanguillen. Pitching brilliantly, Cuellar did not appear tired. Weaver's strategy appeared above reproach.

Pagan walked to the plate to face Cuellar. Danny Murtaugh flashed the hit-and-run sign to third base coach Frank Oceak, who relayed the message to Pagan. Unlike Bob Robertson in Game Three, Pagan did not miss the sign from his third base coach. Shortly after the lumbering Stargell broke from first base, Pagan swung hard, banging a fly ball toward the left-center field fence. According to the basics of the hit-and-run, Pagan was supposed to hit the ball to right field, with the goal of pushing Stargell to third base. In this case, Pagan's long drive to left-center eluded both Merv Rettenmund and Don Buford, allowing Stargell to make it to third base easily.

As he neared third base, Stargell stopped for a moment to watch the ball, which had bounced off the wall, fielded by Rettenmund. With no one out, the slow-footed Stargell should have held his ground and remained at third. Instead, Rettenmund's momentary bobbling of the ball made Stargell more aggressive. He rounded third and headed for home. Rettenmund threw to Mark Belanger, who spun and fired toward home plate. First baseman Boog Powell made a questionable decision, cutting the relay off between the mound and the third base line. Although replays of the play are inconclusive, it appears that if Powell had let the ball go through, the Orioles had a chance of tagging out Stargell. With the ball instead cut off, Stargell crossed the plate without a play, giving the Pirates their second run of the game. Pagan had delivered one of the most important RBIs of the World Series—the most monumental hit of his long career, surpassing the home run he had belted for the San

Francisco Giants in Game Five of the 1962 World Series—after almost not making the Pirates' postseason roster in favor of Rennie Stennett.

With Pagan now at second base, no outs, and the Pirates threatening to put the game away, Cuellar faced a critical juncture. Fortunately for Cuellar, he was now working against the lower part of the Pirates' batting order. Cuellar retired Hernandez on a fly to deep right field, with Pagan making a questionable decision by holding his ground at second base. Cuellar now faced Steve Blass, who tapped the ball toward his counterpart for the inning's second out. Dave Cash followed by hitting a ground ball to Brooks Robinson, who tossed to Boog Powell to end the inning.

The Pirates had given Blass the margin of a two-run lead, but they had failed to score a third run after putting a runner on second base with no one out. A three-run lead, with Blass on the mound, and Dave Giusti waiting in reserve, would have seemed impenetrable.

Surely enough, Blass encountered his first emergency of the game in the bottom of the eighth. Elrod Hendricks led off by hitting a ground ball just a few feet to the left side of second base, where Jackie Hernandez would usually have been stationed against a left-handed hitter. But with the Pirates overshifting and Hernandez playing to the right of second base, Hendricks' routine grounder turned into a leadoff single. With Baltimore trailing by two and the sacrifice bunt no longer an option, the light-hitting Mark Belanger looped a limp single to center field. Suddenly, the Orioles had placed the potential tying runs on first and second, with no outs.

Earl Weaver now had options. He could have left Cuellar in the game to bunt both runners up. Instead, Weaver called on backup outfielder Tom Shopay, batting a respectable .267 as a pinch-hitter, to hit for Cuellar. Shopay took the first two pitches, one a ball, the other a strike. Then came a curious decision by Weaver, who asked the lefty-swinging Shopay to attempt a sacrifice bunt.

Weaver usually hated to give up outs through the sacrifice bunt, but he felt that the circumstances demanded it. Weaver's atypical strategy aside, Shopay successfully executed the sacrifice, moving Hendricks to third and Belanger to second. On the play, Sanguillen yelled to Blass to throw the ball to third to nail the lead runner. Blass thought better of it and threw to first. "Now I'm really nervous at that point," Blass recalls, "and my strong suit was not throwing to bases. . . . I'm coming to get that bunt, and I've got the whole play in back of me, and I'm thinking 'Sure thing, I'm gonna take the sure out.' Sangy hollered quite loud for me to go to third, and I just didn't do it. I still don't know how much of a play I had at third, because again, the play was behind me."

With runners now on second and third base, and the switch-hitting Don Buford scheduled to bat, Danny Murtaugh faced a difficult decision. Once Hendricks and Belanger had reached base, Murtaugh had instructed right-hander Dave Giusti and left-hander Luke Walker to begin warming up in the bullpen. Both pitchers were now ready to enter the game. If Murtaugh were to turn the game over to Giusti, few would have criticized him, giving Giusti's performance throughout the season. That would have been the safe choice.

Yet, Murtaugh didn't consider it the *right* choice. He elected to stay with Blass, who seemed to be tiring. With his emotional and physical energies almost spent, Blass prepared to face the top of the Orioles' order: first Buford and then Dave Johnson.

With the Pirates playing their infield back, Buford batted a hard ground ball down the first base line. Bob Robertson backed up a few steps and fielded the high-hopping grounder cleanly. He then ran to the first-base bag, recording the second out of the inning. As Robertson made the play, Hendricks scored the Orioles' first run of the game. In the meantime, Belanger, the potential tying run of Game Seven, moved up to third.

Although Robertson's play might have appeared rather run-of-the-mill to most observers, Blass remembers the reactions of his first baseman as far more than routine. "I threw Buford a slider," Blass says, "and he hit a real shot to Bob Robertson, who by the way, was a very underrated defensive first baseman. Bob Robertson might have been one of the best fielding first basemen that I had been around. He made a good play on the shot by Buford."

With two outs, a runner on third, and Dave Johnson coming to bat, Blass still faced a predicament. If he were to throw a breaking pitch, it might bounce in the dirt past Sanguillen and allow the fleet Belanger to score. If he were to throw fastballs, he would be playing to Johnson's strength. Still, Blass had to pitch aggressively to Johnson, what with Boog Powell waiting in the on-deck circle.

Manny Sanguillen walked to the mound to talk to Blass before he faced Johnson. Blass then paced slowly, eventually completing one of his many, nervous circular walks around the pitching hill. Blass returned to the rubber and proceeded to throw Johnson a series of sliders. After another visit by Sanguillen, Johnson hit another slider into the hole between short and third. As soon as Johnson laid bat on ball, Blass thought he had surrendered a run-scoring, game-tying single to left field.

Blessed with good range at shortstop, Jackie Hernandez moved quickly to his right and fielded the ball on a long hop. Setting himself quickly deep in the hole, on the back of the infield dirt, Hernandez unfurled a strong throw to first base. With the ball arriving chest-high, Bob Robertson caught the ball two steps ahead of Johnson's arrival. The fine play by Hernandez allowed Blass and the Pirates to move to the ninth inning with a 2-1 lead.

In the top of the ninth, the Pirates faced Pat Dobson, who had replaced Mike Cuellar on the mound. Dobson retired the first two Pirate batters, Gene Clines and Roberto Clemente, but then allowed a single to Bob Robertson and watched Manny Sanguillen beat out a topper—his 11th hit of the Series—to third base. With Willie Stargell scheduled to bat, Weaver walked to the mound and called on left-hander Dave McNally, the third 20-game winner to appear in the game for the Orioles. With a chance to drive home an insurance run, Stargell grounded to Dave Johnson at second base to end the inning. As a result, Steve Blass headed to the bottom of the ninth with a mere one-run lead.

Blass had spent the Pirates' half of the ninth inning in nervous anticipation. "When we're hitting in the top of the ninth," Blass recalls, "I go back in our clubhouse, because I can't sit still, and [Pirate broadcaster] Bob Prince is in there, and there's nobody else. Everybody else is out on the bench, and I walked in and said to Bob 'What the hell are you doing in here?' Bob says, 'What the hell are you doing here?' We kind of had a standoff. There's two of us in there so engrossed in what we're doing that we didn't know how to react to each other."

During the regular season, when the Pirates held a one-run lead, Danny Murtaugh might have replaced Blass with Dave Giusti to start the ninth inning. Would he make the change in the final game of the World Series? It was a tough call. Blass still possessed excellent stuff: a sneaky fastball, a devastating slider, and sharp control. He had also shown courage in working out of a dangerous, potentially game-tying situation in the bottom of the eighth.

"I went out to warm up for the ninth inning," Blass says, "and I got the ball back from third base. I looked into our dugout and it seemed to me like the only ones in the dugout were Murtaugh and the coaches. Then I looked out to the bullpen and it seemed like the whole Sioux nation was out there," Blass says with a laugh. "I never asked Murtaugh this, but I guess I had a feeling if anybody got on base, then obviously Dave Giusti would come in. He was our horse, and I had no problem with that."

As sunshine broke through the clouds for the first time that afternoon, Blass faced his first batter of the ninth, Boog Powell. The hulking first baseman, the Orioles' most intimidating presence, hit a bouncing grounder to Dave Cash at second base for the first out. Now Blass prepared to meet Frank Robinson, arguably the Orioles' best all-around hitter. Blass hung a slider, but according to the right-hander, Robinson "missed the pitch," popping up meekly to Jackie Hernandez in short left field. Next up came Merv Rettenmund, a quietly competent hitter who had enough power to reach the bleachers at Memorial Stadium.

It was now ten minutes after four o'clock. Blass delivered his eighth pitch of the inning. Rettenmund swung and grounded a ball up the middle. The ball was solidly hit. It bounced off the mound, veering slightly toward the right side of second base. "When Merv Rettenmund hits the ball," Blass recounts, "I always fall off quite dramatically to first base, and the ball was not that far from being right up the middle. I was sure when the ball left the bat that it was going to be a base hit."

Now shading Rettenmund toward second base after initially playing him as a pull hitter, Hernandez raced to his left—toward the other side of the bag. Situated a few feet beyond—and behind—the bag, Hernandez fielded the ball on the run. He was now near the lip

of the outfield grass, with a difficult angle to make a throw. Firing
the ball against his body, Hernandez steered the ball toward Bob
Robertson at first base. With Rettenmund still steps away from the
bag, the sure-handed Robertson squeezed the ball into his oversized
mitt. Game Seven was now over.

Blass ran toward Robertson and jumped in the air. Lifted by the
courageous pitching of the previously unheralded Blass, the clutch
hitting of the legendary Roberto Clemente, and the deft fielding of
the maligned Jackie Hernandez, the Pirates had won the World
Championship.

From his position at first base, Robertson enjoyed the perspective
of watching the final play unfold before him. "We're down to two
outs, and here comes Rettenmund up. Jackie Hernandez had moved
over because I had seen him move over—up the middle.
Rettenmund hit the ball, and where Jackie Hernandez fielded that
ball, he fielded that ball probably five feet back on the outfield
grass. And I seen the ball coming to me, and I knew it was gonna be
right there. I just caught it and I just threw my arms up in the air,
and I said, 'World Champs!'"

Just why was Hernandez shading Rettenmund so far up the middle? The positioning was dictated by Pirates farm director
Harding "Pete" Peterson and scouts Howie Haak and George
Detore, who had watched the Orioles extensively during the final
weeks of the regular season and in the playoffs against Oakland.
Prior to the Series, Danny Murtaugh had ordered his fielders to follow the scouting reports to the letter. Those reports had also been
responsible for Hernandez' positioning in the eighth inning, when he
had gone deep in the hole between short and third to throw out Dave
Johnson, ending an Orioles scoring threat. "I don't think many
American League clubs play Johnson to pull," Hernandez told *The
Sporting News*, while claiming that he had never played Johnson
deep in the hole during his days with the Kansas City Royals. If not
for the report put together by Peterson, Haak, and Detore,
Hernandez might not have been in position to make that critical
play against Johnson, or the final one against Rettenmund. "It was
one heckuva play that Jackie made," says Al Oliver, many years

later. Bill Guilfoile, the team's public relations director, offers the following: "Jackie Hernandez was one of my favorite players. He was just such a wonderful person, and a good shortstop. Our regular shortstop was injured and unable to play, and so, all of a sudden, here's the substitute shortstop who had only been in about half the games all season long. Now here he was playing in the seventh game of the World Series. I remembered Earl Weaver, the manager of the Orioles, was quoted as saying, 'The Pirates will never beat us with Jackie Hernandez at shortstop.'"

Back in March, prior to a spring training game against the Pirates, Weaver had made such an unsolicited attack while holding court with several beat writers for the two teams. Weaver suggested that the Pirates would be better off with Jose Pagan at shortstop, even though the aging infielder hadn't played the position regularly in years. In summation, Weaver had called Hernandez a "loser."

In the Pirates' clubhouse—just moments after Bob Robertson had secured Jackie Hernandez' throw for the final out of the World Series—Steve Blass, Roberto Clemente, Danny Murtaugh, and broadcaster Bob Prince stood on a podium as Commissioner Bowie Kuhn presented the Bucs with the World Championship trophy. The commissioner congratulated Clemente, who then took the time to acknowledge his parents in Puerto Rico in Spanish. After taking a turn on the podium, Danny Murtaugh received a telephone call from the President of the United States, Richard M. Nixon.

Immediately after the Game Seven victory, the residents of Pittsburgh began a massive celebration. Motorists throughout the city repeatedly beeped their car horns in unison. An estimated 100,000 people jammed into the downtown section of the city. Another 20,000 would drive to the Pittsburgh Airport to greet the Pirate players as they returned from Baltimore.

Blass would not fully appreciate his own pitching performance until after the Pirates took off from the Baltimore airport. "When everything had settled down on the airplane," Blass says, "Bill Mazeroski, whom I had roomed with for a period of time early in my career, came up to me. I always wanted to know how he graded pitchers, because I had, and still have, so much respect for him. Maz

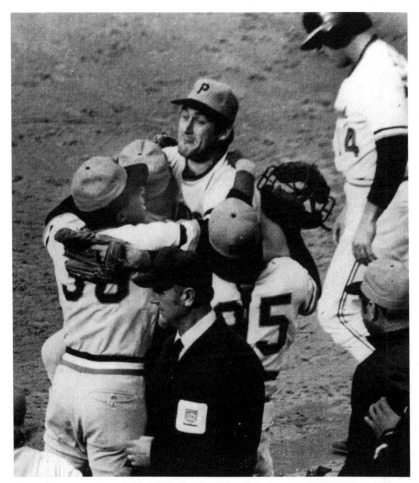

Steve Blass is embraced by teammates Manny Sanguillen (No. 35) and Dave Cash (No. 38) after recording the final out of the 1971 World Series. Despite tiring in the late innings, Blass limited the powerful Baltimore offense to one run and four hits in a gutsy complete-game performance. As Blass and his mates celebrate, Baltimore's Merv Rettenmund, the final batter of Game Seven, walks dejectedly back to the Orioles' dugout. (*National Baseball Hall of Fame Library, Cooperstown, NY*)

said 'My idea of a great pitcher is a pitcher who can win when he's pitching with a 2-1 lead. A lot of guys can pitch great games when they're down 2-1, but to me a pitcher who can pitch with a lead is the guy.' Maz came up to me on the airplane after the seventh game and he said to me, 'Now, you're that kind of pitcher,' and it made me feel like a million bucks."

No Pirate player was better equipped to frame the recently concluded World Series in historical perspective than Mazeroski. One of the longest tenured Pirates and an elder statesman of the team, Mazeroski stood at his locker and answered questions from the assembled press that had jammed into the clubhouse. Inevitably, a reporter asked Mazeroski to compare the 1960 World Championship to the one just concluded. Mazeroski had won the Series in 1960 with arguably the most famous home run in history—a Game Seven, ninth-inning, Series-ending blast—but had played only a bit part in the 1971 championship. In light of those facts, Maz' response to *Sports Illustrated* was mildly surprising. "Things are always supposed to be better when you look back on them from 11 years. But they might not be. They just might not be." Perhaps Maz realized that 1971 would likely represent his last World Series as a player. Or perhaps the camaraderie of the '71 Pirates, where black, white, and Latino players forged such an enjoyable union, had created a sensation that surpassed the champions of the previous decade.

During the pre-season, general manager Joe Brown had proclaimed the 1971 Pirates as superior in talent to the 1960 World Champs. At the time, critics might have accused Brown of owning a short memory. In retrospect, Brown was most likely correct. The '60 Pirates rated the edge at second base, shortstop, and third base, with Mazeroski, Groat, and Hoak all having enjoyed superior seasons to Dave Cash, Gene Alley, and Richie Hebner, respectively. The '71 Pirates, however, featured better players at catcher (Manny Sanguillen over Smoky Burgess and Hal Smith), first base (Bob Robertson slightly ahead of Dick Stuart), left field (Willie Stargell over Bob Skinner), center field (Gene Clines and Al Oliver ahead of Bill Virdon), and right field (where the '71 Roberto Clemente was a slightly better player than the '60 model, who had not yet fully developed into a clutch hitter and team leader). The Pirates' bench in '71 was deeper and more versatile than the 1960 group, and the pitching staff, while similar in quality to the '60 team, possessed a bit more depth in both the rotation and the bullpen. In addition, the '71 Pirates had pulled off an upset that was almost as impressive as the franchise's surprise dumping of the heavily favored New York Yankees some 11 years earlier. In winning that Series, the 1960 Pirates may have been greater overachievers, but the 1971 Pirates were most likely the better team—man-for-man.

As Mazeroski poured forth his emotions, another Pirates leader tried vainly to contain his. "Oh, my God, oh, my God," Willie Stargell whispered over and over in front of legendary baseball writer Dick Young. Stargell seemed to take special satisfaction in the Pirates' unexpected seven-game win over the favored Orioles. "Nobody thought we belonged," Stargell said as he choked back tears. "They said it would be another Little Big Horn, but we won! Oh, my God." Stargell sounded off on a theme that would become oft repeated by sports champions in future years: the "lack of respect" refrain. "I'm so happy about the way this turned out," Stargell exclaimed to Young. "When it began you would have thought the Pittsburgh Pirates were nothing more than the invited guests at the St. Valentine's Day Massacre."

Although Stargell had finished the Series with only five hits in 24 at-bats, his intimidating presence at the plate had nonetheless helped the Pirates. Stargell had drawn seven walks from Oriole pitchers, who had decided to pitch around the Bucs' cleanup man and take their chances against the likes of Bob Robertson and Manny Sanguillen. Robertson led the Pirates with five RBIs, while Sanguillen batted a robust .379 against Baltimore pitching. Much like the playoffs against the Giants, the Stargell "presence" had created more opportunities for the fifth-, sixth-, and seventh-place hitters in the Pittsburgh lineup.

Stargell also impressed many baseball writers with his dignified handling of a World Series slump. Stargell answered questions with patience and grace, refusing to snap at reporters who peppered him with inquiries about his struggles at the plate. "Stargell impressed me as a man," wrote Kansas City baseball writer Joe McGuff. "He never tried to hide from writers. He knew he was having a bad Series, but he always gave the impression that team winning was more important than any personal gains he could have in the Series."

Although they ranked as two of the most senior members of the Pirates, Stargell and Mazeroski received relatively little attention from the media horde in the clubhouse. For over an hour, the Pirates' other leader, Roberto Clemente, remained trapped on the NBC-TV platform, unable to move because of the mass of players, reporters, and officials that had packed into the Pirates' visiting clubhouse. At one point, Dave Giusti tried to sneak up on Clemente with a bottle of champagne. "Don't spray me," Clemente cried out, repeating his post-game refrain from the play-off series against the Giants. "I got a bad eye." In a more serious moment, Giusti praised his friend and teammate to members of the media. "When it means the big game, Clemente's gonna be the star of the game. I don't care what ballclub, what All-Star ballclub or what [ever], Clemente's gonna be the star."

An ebullient Roberto Clemente speaks with reporters following the Pirates' surprising World Series victory over the heavily favored Orioles. Named Series MVP after hitting .414 and slugging .759, Clemente had demonstrated to a nationwide audience his abilities as one of the game's best all-around players. (*National Baseball Hall of Fame Library, Cooperstown, NY*)

The Orioles didn't disagree. When Baltimore owner Jerry Hoffberger found Clemente in the crowded visitors' clubhouse, he congratulated the Pirates' superstar on his World Series performance. "You're the best of all," Hoffberger told Clemente, exhibiting true sportsmanship.

While on stage, Clemente conducted a host of interviews, expressing optimism that his World Series effort had changed people's opinions of him. The media had already begun to recognize Clemente's performance; *Sport* magazine named him the outstanding player in the Series. Roberto Clemente had hit a remarkable .414 in the Series, made several spectacular catches and throws, and had hit safely in all 14 World Series games he had played in his career. "This is what I want people to know, how I play, not that I am a hypochondriac, that I am a .300 hitter," Clemente told the Associated Press.

Prior to Game Seven, Clemente had informed Howie Haak that he would retire from baseball if the Pirates were to win. Now that the Pirates had won the Series, the timing seemed right for Clemente to announce his retirement officially. Yet, he said nothing about quitting. Apparently, Clemente had changed his mind. In an article by Pirates beat writer Charley Feeney, Clemente explained the reasons behind the change to Haak. "When I ran off the field after the last World Series game, I saw my wife, Vera, crying," Clemente told Haak. "She said to me: 'Roberto, don't quit baseball now. Please don't quit now. It's your life.'" The tears and words of his loving wife were enough to convince Roberto to keep playing the game he loved so much. The baseball world would have the opportunity to witness the splendor of Clemente for one more season.

Chapter 15

THE LEGACY

On the overcast, windy morning of December 31, 1972, a worn and overloaded DC-7 sat on the runway of Luis Munoz Marin Airport outside of San Juan, Puerto Rico. Over the din of the whirling engines, the 38-year-old Roberto Clemente crossed the tarmac and joined the pilot, copilot, and two other crewmembers aboard the craft. The plane was packed with much needed supplies for the victims of an earthquake that had ravaged Nicaragua a week earlier. The 6.5 magnitude disaster had sparked huge fires, destroyed whole communities, including most of the capital city of Managua, and had left nearly 10,000 persons dead and more than 300,000 homeless. All water and electricity were lost. Both telephone and telegraph links had been cut. As the news of the tragedy began to reach the United States and other countries, assistance was pledged from around the world.

Soon, discouraging reports began emerging that corrupt local officials were looting and redirecting badly needed supplies away from the victims. Those most passionately seeking aid were alarmed. One of those persons, Roberto Clemente, who had responded immediately to the disaster and had collected donations and given generously of his time and money, decided to personally make sure that food, water, blankets, and medicine reached the people who desperately needed it. This was bigger than baseball—this was bigger than all the honors and personal achievements accumulated across a brilliant career. Roberto Clemente would be there, there on the ground right where he would be most useful, where he could direct the aid and see to it that the neediest were not forgotten or ignored.

The plane rumbled noisily down the airstrip and slowly nosed up over the choppy Atlantic Ocean. Within minutes the plane began to shake and falter. Smoke poured from one of the engines and suddenly it exploded into flames. The doomed aircraft jerked and banked sharply before disintegrating into the dark surf. The Great One was gone.

Roberto Clemente had, despite his initial decision to retire, played baseball for another season after the World Championship, a season where he collected his 3,000th career hit. But now the game of baseball was deprived of one of its greatest stars and the world had lost a hero.

After the World Series, Clemente traveled to New York City to officially receive the *Sport Magazine* MVP Award, given to the outstanding World Series player. (He had also been named the winner of the Babe Ruth World Series MVP Award handed out by Major League Baseball.) Clemente used the opportunity to speak out on a variety of issues that mattered to him. First, he claimed that his World Series performance solidified his stature within the game. "I believe I'm the best player in baseball today," Clemente proudly told Ken Rappoport of the Associated Press. "I'm glad I was able to show it against Baltimore in the Series."

Clemente also expressed support for fellow outfielder Curt Flood, who was attempting to have baseball's reserve clause overturned. On October 9, 1969, the Cardinals had traded Flood to the Phillies, but the All-Star outfielder had refused to report to his new team. Flood subsequently took baseball to court over the reserve clause, which tied a player to his team year after year in perpetuity. "If I were ever traded, I would quit baseball," Clemente informed Maury Allen of the *New York Post*. "I have felt that way for 10 years."

Clemente clearly sympathized with Flood, who had enjoyed playing for a successful and racially harmonious team like the Cardinals. Flood expressed his contempt for baseball's reserve system, which he likened to slavery, and for the practice of trading players like properties without giving them any say in where they played. Flood's antitrust lawsuit had already been rejected by a U.S. Circuit Court, and subsequent appeals would be denied by a Federal appeals court and the U.S. Supreme Court. Yet by 1976, the players and owners would agree to a system of free agency, in large part due to Flood's willingness to fight the reserve clause.

Clemente also criticized the major league establishment for its failure to hire a black manager. "If a black player wants to become a manager," Clemente told Maury Allen, "the owners tell him he has to go to the minors to get experience. But a white player does not. And sometimes the white player has not even made it to the major leagues. I think that is a double standard." Clemente named several outstanding minority candidates to become managers, including both Ernie Banks and Frank Robinson, harboring no ill will against the latter for his critical verbal remarks during the World Series.

Clemente made further news when he announced his intentions to build a "sports city" for underprivileged children in his native land of Puerto Rico. Such a facility would provide children with an opportunity to receive practical instruction in baseball, swimming, and numerous other sports. The construction of three baseball fields, a swimming pool, basketball courts, and tennis courts would cost about $2.5 million in federal funding. "If I get the money to start this, if they tell me they'll give us the money this year," Clemente told Milt Richman of UPI, "I'll quit right now."

The drama of the '71 World Series had not only increased Clemente's credibility and recognition; it had helped elevate the overall popularity of baseball—at least for a short time. Longtime sportswriter Dick Young described this phenomenon in his *New York Daily News* column. "The 1971 World Series," Young wrote, "renewed for most people the assurance that baseball is indeed an exciting game, something, for some reason, they had been brainwashed into doubting." With likable players like Clemente, Steve Blass, and Manny Sanguillen prospering on the national stage, the game's image improved. Through their charisma and substantial on-field talents, the Pirate players had helped promote the appeal of baseball and its individual stars.

The legacy of the 1971 Pirates can be found on a number of levels: the greatness of Roberto Clemente, the impact of the World Series on baseball's popularity, and the importance of the team's pioneering level of integration.

Prior to 1971, major league baseball had never seen a World Championship, or pennant-winning team, as substantially integrated as the Pittsburgh Pirates. The Game Seven World Series lineup featured three black Americans (Dave Cash, Gene Clines, and Willie Stargell), four Latin Americans (Roberto Clemente, Manny Sanguillen, Jose Pagan, and Jackie Hernandez) and two whites (Steve Blass and Bob Robertson). The make up of the 1971 Pirates was a product of the organization's aggressive search for winning talent of any color, and the willingness to play that talent at any position—even if it meant that in any given game a lineup might be black, white, Asian, or Latino, or any combination of the four. This was the breakthrough that this Pirates team achieved—and their lasting contribution to the sport of baseball. "Obviously, we were looking for talent," said Joe Brown, the architect of the '71 Pirates, in an article that appeared in *Baseball Digest* in 1995. "We didn't care where they came from or what color they were. If they happened to be black, so be it." Unlike the Dodgers of the early fifties, the Pirates had not imposed a limit of four black players in their starting lineup. While other organizations, notably the Cardinal and Giants teams of the 1960s, had made progress in integrating parts of their major league rosters, the Pirates had taken a no-holds barred approach in populating their entire roster with talented players no matter who they were. The Pirates' philosophy not only helped the team win the World Championship in 1971, but also sent a message to other major league organizations: select the best players at each position regardless of color or background, and you will increase your chances of winning.

Prominent players from other teams took note of the composition of the Pirates' roster. Frank Robinson, often mentioned as a candidate to become the major leagues' first black manager, offered some admiring comments about the Pirates in a 1972 interview with *Sport* magazine. "Last year the Pirates may have had more black players than any team in baseball," Robinson said. "They became the first team to start an all-black lineup in a game. And they won a world title." Robinson described a direct connection between winning and the presence of minorities on a team's roster. "Color shouldn't matter anymore," said Robinson, "except it's clear if you have most of the top black players, you have a lot of top players, which gives you an edge in talent."

The success of the 1971 Pirates influenced other championship teams of the seventies and beyond. General managers in all sports copy what works: when they see a team succeed, they incorporate the reasons for that success in how they run their own teams. The Oakland A's, who won three straight World Championships from 1972 to 1974, featured a changing, increasingly integrated roster that reflected the Pittsburgh team. Although Cincinnati's championship teams of 1975 and 1976 were not as heavily populated with minorities as the aforementioned A's, the Pittsburgh strategy still applied: the most talented athletes available to a club would play. There was no pendulum to swing back and forth; this was a complete shift in how general managers and owners built winning teams. In 1977, the Yankees moved to the top of the baseball world, and did so with black players like Chris Chambliss, Willie Randolph, Roy White, Mickey Rivers, and Reggie Jackson in the starting lineup alongside white players Graig Nettles, Lou Piniella, and Thurman Munson, and Latino starting pitchers Ed Figueroa and Mike Torrez (who combined for 30 victories). Although White and Munson had come up with the Yankees, the other players had been acquired through trades and free agent signings since the 1971 season. In 1979, the Pirates won their second championship of the decade. Much like the 1971 team, the "We Are Family" Bucs did so with an intriguing mix of nationalities and colors—and it is not surprising that their team captain was Willie Stargell.

I still have the 1972 Topps baseball card depicting the 1971 Pirates as World Champions. It ranks as one of my most favored and cherished baseball cards. The card shows a half-smiling, half-grimacing Steve Blass in the middle of the frenzied scene, his expression reflecting both the joy of the moment and the emotional strain of pitching in the seventh game of the World Series. In larger photographs depicting the celebration seen on that card, there is Dock Ellis, wearing a Pirate windbreaker, smiling and stretching a gloved right hand onto the shoulder of Blass. Ironically, it was Blass who had emerged—ahead of Ellis—as the Pirates' No. 1 starter in the Series, yet there is no jealousy evident in the photo. Finally, one of my favorite players from the '71 Pirates, the heavily sideburned journeyman outfielder Vic Davalillo, appears (for some unknown reason) wearing Jose Pagan's No. 11 windbreaker, a fitting metaphor for the bond this remarkable group of players shared. Lifted by the spirit and determination of Roberto Clemente, the 1971 Pittsburgh Pirates proved conclusively, and really for the first time, that a pool of athletes, representing a variety of backgrounds and nationalities, could work together effectively and win a World Series championship. For that reason, they deserve to be called The Team That Changed Baseball.

(Author's Collection)

WHERE ARE THEY NOW

GENE ALLEY

Batted .254 with 55 HRs, 342 RBIs, and 442 runs scored in 11 seasons

The Pirates' soft-spoken shortstop played two more injury-scarred seasons in the major leagues before announcing his retirement in 1973 at the age of 33. Alley went to work for a Virginia printing company, just as he had indicated he would do while contemplating retirement during the 1971 season. Since his playing days came to an end, Alley has resided in Glen Allen, Virginia.

STEVE BLASS

103-76 with a 3.63 ERA and 896 strikeouts in 1,597 innings over 10 seasons

After enjoying a career season in 1972, Blass suddenly and mysteriously lost the ability to throw strikes, prompting a diagnosis that became known as "Steve Blass Syndrome." On March 27, 1975, the Pirates released Blass. Not wanting to pitch for another team, Blass decided to retire.

Although Blass never pinpointed the reason for his massive bout with wildness, he did not allow his sudden decline to hinder his post-playing success. Since his retirement, Blass has run a number of baseball schools for youngsters, hosted a sports talk show on a Pittsburgh radio station, and become a well-respected color commentator on Pirate broadcasts.

Blass has also contributed to a number of charities, including sickle-cell anemia, multiple sclerosis, and the Roberto Clemente Memorial Fund. All along, Blass has retained the sense of humor that made him one of the most popular Pirates in 1971, and one of Pittsburgh's most well-liked and respected sports celebrities.

Nelson "Nellie" Briles

129-112 with a 3.44 ERA and 1,163 strikeouts in 2,111 innings over 14 seasons

Briles pitched two more productive seasons with the Pirates before unexpectedly being traded to the Kansas City Royals. The well-traveled right-hander later spent time with the Texas Rangers before concluding a solid major league career with the Baltimore Orioles in 1978.

Having honed his skills as a drama student at Chico State College and Santa Clara University, Briles gained off-the-field attention as a well-rounded entertainer. During the offseason, Briles sang regularly in nightclub acts, signed several motion picture contracts, and worked as a television sportscaster. In perhaps his most notable public performance, Briles sang the National Anthem prior to Game Four of the 1973 World Series at Shea Stadium in New York.

After retiring as an active player, Briles joined the Pirates' television announcing crew as a color commentator for two seasons beginning in 1979. He later broadcast Seattle Mariners games before returning to the Pirates as the team's Director of Corporate Affairs in 1986. In 1999, the Pirates named him Vice President of Special Events. Briles also served as president of the Pirates Alumni Association.

On February 13, 2005, Briles was participating in a Pirates alumni golf tournament when he was struck by a fatal heart attack. Talented and amicable to the end, Briles was 61.

Dave Cash

Batted .283 with 21 HRs, 426 RBIs, and 732 runs scored in 12 seasons

Cash remained the Pirates' starting second baseman in 1972, but a logjam of second basemen eventually brought his career as a Pirate to a premature end. With players like Rennie Stennett and Willie Randolph in the Pirates' organization, the team traded Cash to the Philadelphia Phillies after the 1973 season. Cash went on to enjoy three productive seasons in Philadelphia, helping the Phillies to the National League Eastern Division title in 1976.

After the 1976 season, Cash took advantage of baseball's new free agent system and signed a five-year, $3 million contract with the Montreal Expos. A clash with Expos manager Dick Williams resulted in an eventual trade to the San Diego Padres, with whom he ended his playing career in 1980. Cash went on to work for an investment firm in San Diego and as a car salesman in Pittsburgh. In 1987, while working as an instructor at the Phillies' fantasy camp in Clearwater, Florida, Cash realized how much he missed the game. He accepted a position as an infield coach for the Phillies' Class-A minor league affiliate in the New York-Penn League. Since then, he has remained in baseball, becoming a minor league manager and then a major league coach with the Phillies before returning to the minor leagues as a manager, coach, and roving field instructor for the Baltimore Orioles' organization.

In 2005, Cash started the season as the bench coach for the Ottawa Lynx (the Triple-A affiliate of the Baltimore Orioles) before being promoted to the Orioles in August, when he became the major league team's first base coach.

Roberto Clemente

Batted .317 with 240 HRs, 1,305 RBIs, and 1,416 runs scored in 18 seasons

Fewer than three months after his tragic death on December 31, 1972, the Baseball Hall of Fame held a special election for Clemente, waiving the mandatory five-year waiting period. He was named on 93 percent of the ballots cast, well above the 75 percent needed for election. Later that summer, he was posthumously inducted into the baseball shrine. Clemente became the first of three 1971 Pirates—and the first Latin-born player—to be honored in Cooperstown.

As a lasting testament to his work as a humanitarian, the Clemente family operates the Roberto Clemente Sports City in his hometown of Carolina, Puerto Rico. The 304-acre athletic complex provides underprivileged children in Puerto Rico with an opportunity to participate in sports while learning the ideals of competition and sportsmanship. The Roberto Clemente Foundation is an official Pittsburgh Pirates charity.

Gene Clines

Batted .277 with 5 HRs, 187 RBIs, and 314 runs scored in 10 seasons

After batting .334 in 1972 and following up with a strong start to the 1973 season, Clines became the Pirates' everyday right fielder, replacing a struggling Manny Sanguillen. Soon after, Clines tore ligaments in his right ankle, forcing him to the sidelines. When he returned, he had difficulties at the plate and became a victim of the numbers game in the Pirates' outfield. After the 1974 season, the Pirates traded Clines to the New York Mets. He later played for the Texas Rangers and Chicago Cubs before being placed on waivers in mid-1979, ending his playing days.

Clines remained with the Cubs' organization as a coach. He later served as a coach with the Houston Astros, Seattle Mariners, Milwaukee Brewers, and San Francisco Giants. When Giants manager Dusty Baker left the organization to become manager of the Chicago Cubs, Clines joined him in the Windy City, becoming the team's first base coach. Prior to the 2005 season, the Cubs promoted Clines by naming him their hitting coach.

Vic Davalillo

Batted .279 with 36 HRs, 329 RBIs, 509 runs, and 125 stolen bases in 16 seasons

Arguably the Pirates' best regular-season bench player in 1971, Davalillo enjoyed an even more productive season in 1972. After starting the season on the bench, Davalillo became the Pirates' regular left fielder against right-handed pitching, batted .318 in 368 at-bats, and swiped 14 bases.

A slow start in 1973 ended his tenure in Pittsburgh, as the Pirates sold Davalillo's contract to the pennant-winning Oakland A's. In the decisive fifth game of the American League Championship Series, Davalillo delivered a key RBI triple, helping the A's clinch with a 3-0 victory. Davalillo also took part in Oakland's World Series victory over the Mets.

The A's released Davalillo early in 1974, but he continued his career in the Mexican League. In the middle of the 1977 season, he returned to the major leagues with the Los Angeles Dodgers, becoming a key pinch-hitter for the eventual National League champions.

Davalillo concluded a vagabond but productive career in 1980, finishing with one All-Star Game berth, a single-season pinch-hitting record, 95 career pinch-hits, World Series appearances with three teams, and two World Championship rings. Now retired, Davalillo lives in his native Venezuela.

DOCK ELLIS

138-119 with a 3.46 ERA and 1,136 strikeouts in 2,127 innings over 12 seasons

The most colorful of the 1971 Pirates, Ellis remained a productive pitcher for the Bucs through the 1975 season. Despite elbow and knee trouble, he helped the Pirates to Eastern Division championships in 1972 and 1975, and did not allow an earned run in either playoff series.

A run-in with manager Danny Murtaugh in 1975 led to an off-season trade to the New York Yankees. Ellis went 17-8 in his first season with New York, helping the Yankees to their first postseason berth in over a decade. The following year, Ellis' critical remarks directed at Yankee owner George Steinbrenner resulted in another trade, this time to the Oakland A's. A subsequent trade to the Texas Rangers capped off Ellis' most traveled major league season, as he played for seven managers over the course of the year.

In 1979, Ellis pitched for the Rangers and New York Mets before rejoining the Pirates at the tail-end of the season. Appearing in three late-season games, Ellis pitched effectively in relief for Pittsburgh. Although the Pirates qualified for the playoffs, on their way to their second World Championship of the decade, Ellis' late arrival left him ineligible for postseason play.

Ellis' major league career ended after the 1979 season, the same year that he checked himself into a drug and alcohol rehabilitation center. As a result of his own experience, Ellis became a counselor to drug abusers and alcoholics. "What we need to educate our young about is the abuses of alcohol and drugs," Ellis emphasized. "When I say young, I mean starting with kindergarten. That's the time when little bitty kids with little bitty eyes start watching and following adults."

Sadly, Ellis's efforts in discouraging drug abuse were cut short. In November 2007, he was diagnosed with advanced cirrhosis of the liver and informed that he would need a transplant. During the spring of 2008, Ellis publicly revealed the severity of his condition and his desperate need for a new liver.

The transplant never came, and on December 19, 2008, Ellis died in a Los Angeles hospital. He was 63 years old.

Dave Giusti

100-93 with 145 saves, a 3.60 ERA, and 1,103 strikeouts in 1,716 innings over 15 seasons

In 1972, Giusti once again excelled in his role as closer, posting 22 saves with a career-best earned run average of 1.93. Giusti prolonged his run as the National League's most consistent closer the next season, recording 20 saves and an ERA of 2.37. Then, in 1974, Giusti began to unravel. He blew several save opportunities, which led to episodes of depression.

After the season, Giusti underwent an elbow operation, from which he recovered to pitch well in 1975. The following season, Giusti suffered a muscle tear and a pinched sciatic nerve in his right leg and lost the closer's role to Kent Tekulve. After the season, the Pirates added Rich Gossage, Terry Forster, and Grant Jackson to their crowded bullpen, which made Giusti expendable. On March 15, 1977, the Bucs sent Giusti to the Oakland A's as part of a massive nine-player deal.

Giusti pitched well in middle relief for the A's, posting an ERA of 2.98 in 40 appearances. On August 5, the noncontending A's decided to unload Giusti's contract, selling him to the Chicago Cubs. Surprisingly, Giusti pitched poorly for Chicago, posting a 6.04 earned run average in 20 appearances. The Cubs released Giusti, ending his playing days.

In 1979, Giusti began a three-year stint in sales with Millcraft Products before assuming a managerial position with American Express. In his post-baseball life, Giusti has remained close to Steve Blass, his best friend on the 1971 Pirates. Giusti has maintained his ties to the Pirate community by living in the Pittsburgh area and serving as vice-president of the Pirates' Alumni Association.

Jim "Mudcat" Grant

145-119 with 53 saves, a 3.63 ERA, and 1,267 strikeouts in 2,441 innings over 14 seasons

After his mid-season trade to the Oakland A's, Grant finished out the

1971 season in the Bay Area. Grant pitched effectively in middle relief for manager Dick Williams, posting an earned run average of 1.98 in 15 appearances. Although Mudcat appeared to have life left in his 36-year-old arm, the A's released him after the season ended. When no other major league team would give him an opportunity, Grant pitched briefly in the Cleveland Indians' farm system before retiring.

After a short stint as a broadcaster and community outreach representative with the Cleveland Indians, Grant became a special marketing director for the Anheuser-Busch Company and a contributor to the speakers' bureau of the NBA's Cleveland Cavaliers. Grant returned to the national pastime in 1984, when he was chosen as an assistant venue director for baseball at the Summer Olympic Games in Los Angeles.

About a month after the Olympics ended, Grant ran into Hall of Famer Hank Aaron, who was serving as the Atlanta Braves' director of player personnel, and accepted an offer to become a pitching coach in Atlanta's minor league system. Six years later, Grant began operating a nationwide program called "Slug-Out Illiteracy, Slug-Out Drugs" where he encouraged former players to put forth an anti-drug message during baseball instructional clinics. In the early 2000s, Grant helped promote a book about African-American pitchers with 20-win seasons in the major leagues called *The Twelve Black Aces*. Grant and his cohorts welcomed a 13th ace to their fraternity when Dontrelle Willis posted a record of 22-10 for the Florida Marlins in 2005.

All the while, the personable Grant has continued to pursue one of his life-long loves: singing. Mudcat, who began his professional music career at the age of 30 with a group called Mudcat and the Kittens, still performs at nightclubs throughout the country. When not performing or traveling for a variety of causes, Grant resides in Los Angeles.

RICHIE HEBNER

Batted .276 with 203 HRs, 890 RBIs, and 865 runs scored in 18 seasons

After the 1971 season, Hebner continued to improve his power production, hitting 19 home runs in 1972 and a career-high 25 the following summer. All the while, Hebner established a reputation as Pittsburgh's most eligible bachelor. Meanwhile, some Pirate officials criticized him for a lack of concentration, which may have caused some of his defensive problems at third base.

Hebner remained in Pittsburgh for three more seasons, before signing a free agent contract with the Philadelphia Phillies. Later, when the Phillies signed Pete Rose as a free agent, Hebner became expendable. On March 27, 1979, the Phillies traded him to the New York Mets, who hoped that Hebner would fill their long troublesome third base position. Unfortunately, his stay in the Big Apple turned into a disaster, as New York fans booed him lustily during his turns at bat. On October 31, just a few days before his wedding day, the Mets traded Hebner to the Detroit Tigers.

While in Detroit, Hebner failed to take advantage of Tiger Stadium's right field porch and never did justify manager Sparky Anderson's initial confidence in him as Detroit's cleanup hitter. On August 16, 1982, the Tigers sold Hebner's contract to Pittsburgh. He played two seasons for the Pirates as a pinch-hitter and utilityman and then signed as a free agent with the Chicago Cubs, where he contributed as a backup infielder to the team's 1984 National League East championship. Hebner remained with the Cubs until April 1, 1986, when he drew his release.

Since his playing days, Hebner has remained active in baseball, working as a major league coach with the Phillies and the Boston Red Sox. In 1995, Hebner became the manager of the Toronto Blue Jays' Triple-A affiliate, the Syracuse Chiefs. He lost the job two years later, only to return to his first professional organization, the Pirates, as a minor league hitting instructor. In 2002, Hebner became the hitting instructor of the Durham Bulls, now the Triple-A affiliate of the Tampa Bay Devil Rays. When not coaching for the Bulls, Hebner resides in Walpole, Massachusetts.

JACKIE HERNANDEZ

Batted .208 with 12 HRs, 121 RBIs, and 153 runs scored in 9 seasons

In 1972, Hernandez batted just .188 in 72 games as a backup to

Gene Alley. He also struggled defensively, committing 22 errors. In 1973, Hernandez improved to .247 at the plate, but played even fewer games in a reserve role and drew his unconditional release from the Pirates after the season. The release ended his playing career at the age of 33.

After retiring from the game as a player, Hernandez has lived and worked in the Miami area. He has coached baseball at the Little League level and has worked as a coach in the independent Northern League. Hernandez has also played regularly in old-timers' games across the country, forever remembered as the man who made the final play of the 1971 World Series.

RAMON HERNANDEZ

23-15 with 46 saves, a 3.03 ERA, and 255 strikeouts in 430 innings over 9 seasons

After helping the Bucs down the stretch in 1971, especially in head-to-head matchups against the St. Louis Cardinals, Ramon Hernandez enjoyed his best season in 1972. By the end of that summer, Hernandez had emerged as the Bucs' left-handed relief ace, with a 5-0 record, 14 saves, and an earned run average of 1.67. From 1973 to 1975, Hernandez continued to pitch well, establishing himself as one of the National League's best left-handed relievers of the mid-1970s.

On September 8, 1976, the Pirates traded Hernandez to the Chicago Cubs, a move that drew criticism from several Pirate players. The stylish southpaw lasted less than two months into the 1977 season before the Cubs traded him to the Boston Red Sox for outfielder Bobby Darwin on May 28. Hernandez struggled in most of his 12 appearances with the Sox, thus ending his nine-year major league career.

Retired from baseball, Hernandez lives in his native town of Carolina, Puerto Rico.

BOB JOHNSON

28-34 with a 3.48 ERA and 507 strikeouts in 692 innings over 7 seasons

After his disappointing 1971 season, Johnson posted one of his best major league campaigns in 1972, forging an earned run average of

2.96 as a long reliever and spot starter. But Johnson returned to mediocrity in 1973. On December 7, the Bucs traded him to the Cleveland Indians.

Later in his career—and well after his tenure with the Pirates had ended—Johnson announced publicly that he had struggled with a severe drinking problem. Johnson said he had begun drinking while with the Kansas City Royals in 1970, and only increased his drinking habit during his three-year stay with the Pirates. "It was affecting my behavior. I was saying things I shouldn't have been saying," Johnson revealed in a 1977 interview with *New York Daily News* baseball writer Phil Pepe.

In October 1975, Johnson vowed never to take another drink. Two years later, he made it back to the major leagues for a brief but unsuccessful stint with the Atlanta Braves.

In his post-playing days, Johnson has owned and operated a construction company, while staying active in the game as an American Legion coach and local umpire in southern Oregon. "I am staying in baseball at a lower level, but I am still in baseball," Johnson told *Sports Collectors Digest* in 1997. "I really love the game."

BRUCE KISON

115-88 with a 3.66 ERA and 1,073 strikeouts in 1,809 innings over 15 seasons

After several years of alternating between starting and relieving, Kison finally became a regular member of the Bucs' starting rotation in 1975. Aided by a change-up that he had learned from Steve Blass, Kison won a career-high 14 games in 1976. Three years later, Pirates manager Chuck Tanner selected Kison to pitch Game One of the World Series against the Baltimore Orioles. Unfortunately, he lasted only one-third of an inning and took the loss. The cold weather in Pittsburgh that night aggravated a circulatory problem in his right arm, which went numb. Kison did not pitch again in the Series.

One of a handful of Pirates to play on both the '71 and '79 World Champions (along with Dock Ellis, Manny Sanguillen, Willie Stargell, and Rennie Stennett), Kison left the organization in 1980. He joined the California Angels as a free agent, but developed arm problems. In July, Kison underwent surgery on damaged nerves in his elbow and wrist.

After an up-and-down tenure with the Angels, Kison once again became a free agent, signing a one-year contract with the Boston Red Sox, with whom he finished his pitching career in 1985. In his post-playing days, Kison was a pitching coach for the Kansas City Royals and Baltimore Orioles before becoming an advance scout with the Orioles in 2000. In 2005, the Orioles gave Kison their Jim Russo Scout of the Year Award.

MILT MAY

Batted .263 with 77 HRs, 443 RBIs, and 313 runs scored in 15 seasons

Following the death of Roberto Clemente, manager Bill Virdon moved Manny Sanguillen to right field, making room for May as the No. 1 catcher. Although the switch of Sanguillen to the outfield did not last long, May still managed to play in 101 games.

After the 1973 season, the Pirates decided they could no longer afford the luxury of carrying two catchers the quality of Sanguillen and May. In need of a starting pitcher, the Bucs sent May to the Houston Astros on October 31 for left-hander Jerry Reuss. In 1975, May gained national attention when he drove in teammate Bob Watson, scoring the one millionth run in major league history.

After his overall mediocre stint in Houston, the Astros sent May to the Detroit Tigers as part of a seven-player deal. Ten games into the 1976 season, May broke his ankle, sidelining him for the balance of the year. In 1977 and 1978, May reclaimed his starting job with Detroit, but the emergence of top prospect Lance Parrish eventually made him expendable. May was traded to the Chicago White Sox on May 27, 1979, before signing a free agent contract with the San Francisco Giants at the end of the season. In 1983, he returned to the Pirates, finishing out his career.

In 1985, May went to work as the vice-president of a bank in Bradenton, Florida. May missed the game, however, and applied for a job in the Pirates' organization that winter. Joe Brown—who returned to the Bucs as interim general manager—hired May as a minor league catching and hitting instructor. Since then, May has worked as a coach for Jim Leyland with the Pirates, the Florida Marlins, and the Colorado Rockies, earning a World Championship ring with the Marlins in 1997. He later returned to the Pirates' organization as a minor league hitting instructor, before being named the batting coach of the Tampa Bay Devil Rays in the winter of 2001. A resident of Bradenton, May is now retired from baseball.

BILL MAZEROSKI

Batted .260 with 138 HRs, 853 RBIs, and 769 runs scored in 17 seasons

Maz returned to the Pirates for the 1972 season, in what would be his final major league go-round. He served as a backup to Dave Cash and Rennie Stennett at second base and Richie Hebner at third base. In June, Mazeroski announced that he would retire at the end of the season. On October 1, the Pirates honored their longtime second baseman with a special day at Three Rivers Stadium. After the season, the Pirates named Mazeroski as their third base coach, replacing Frank Oceak, who was released from Bill Virdon's staff.

Mazeroski served as a Pirates' coach for only one season. In 1979, he returned to the game briefly as a coach with the Seattle Mariners, and later, as a minor league instructor with the Montreal Expos before deciding to leave organized baseball. In his post-baseball career, Mazeroski has owned and operated a nine-hole golf course in Rayland, Ohio.

On August 7, 1987, the Pirates officially retired Mazeroski's uniform No. 9, which spurred more discussion of Maz' nationwide legacy. Fourteen years later, Mazeroski was elected to the Hall of Fame. Now a spring training instructor for the Bucs, Mazeroski became the third member of the 1971 Pirates to make the grade in Cooperstown, joining Pittsburgh legends Roberto Clemente and Willie Stargell.

BOB MILLER

69-81 with an ERA of 3.37 and 895 strikeouts in 1,151 innings over 17 seasons

In 1972, Miller put together one of his finest seasons. Pitching mostly in middle relief, Miller forged an earned run average of 2.65 in 36 games and became the Bucs' second best right-handed reliever behind Dave Giusti.

Budgetary concerns forced the Pirates to release Miller on March 27, 1973. He joined the San Diego Padres on April 1 before being passed along on waivers to the Detroit Tigers on June 22. When he joined the Tigers, Miller equaled Dick Littlefield's record for most teams played with during a major league career—10. (The record has since been matched by Tommy Davis and broken by the ultimate journeyman, vagabond pitcher Mike Morgan.) In 1974, Miller concluded his 17-year major league career with an effective tenure in relief for the New York Mets. He returned to Pittsburgh that season as a batting practice pitcher prior to the All-Star Game. Miller then went on to coach for the Toronto Blue Jays, followed by a stint with the Padres. In 1982, Miller moved up the coast to San Francisco to begin a long association with the Giants.

On August 6, 1993, Miller was killed in a car crash when the driver of the other vehicle apparently suffered a seizure and ran a red light. The well-liked Miller, who was working as a Giants scout at the time, was 54.

Bob Moose

76-71 with a 3.50 ERA and 827 strikeouts in 1,304 innings over 10 seasons

After spending most of 1971 as a swingman, Moose became a full-time starter under Bill Virdon in 1972. Moose went 13-10 with an ERA of 2.91 during one of the best seasons of his career. Moose's fortunes, however, turned sour in the postseason. In the ninth inning of the final game of the Championship Series against the Cincinnati Reds, Moose uncorked a low fastball that eluded catcher Manny Sanguillen, allowing Hal McRae to score the series-winning run.

Moose's teammates applauded him for the way he handled himself after the wild pitch that ended the Pirates' season in 1972. "Moose didn't go into hiding after that pitch," Al Oliver told *The Sporting News*. "He walked off the field with his head high. Later in the clubhouse, he didn't hide from reporters. He answered every question and he didn't alibi. He was a pro."

The following year, Moose underwent a knee operation to remove some cartilage. The next summer, a blood clot near Moose's collarbone necessitated two operations and sidelined him for most of the season. Although Moose struggled to regain his pitching form after the surgeries, he seemed destined to become the Pirates' No. 1 relief pitcher.

Unfortunately, on October 9, 1976, his 29th birthday, Moose was driving to a party in his honor when he lost control of his car on a rain-slickened, narrow, twisting road. Police said that Moose, who was driving too fast given the wet conditions, crashed head-on into an oncoming vehicle. Two women in Moose's car and the other driver escaped with injuries, but Moose was pronounced dead at the scene.

JIM NELSON

6-4 with a 3.06 ERA and 53 strikeouts in 103 innings over 2 seasons

One of the most obscure players on the 1971 Pirates, Nelson pitched fairly well in long relief during the early months of the season, but his lack of control led to a mid-season demotion to Triple-A Charleston. Although he forged an ERA of 2.34 in 17 games with the Pirates, he would never again pitch in the major leagues. A variety of arm injuries, including rotator cuff problems, set Nelson back, forcing him to spend time on the disabled list in 1972 and 1973. The following season, the Pirates released him.

After his professional career came to an end, Nelson went to work for the United Parcel Service. He left UPS after 13 years to spend more time with his father, who had fallen gravely ill. Nelson maintained a residence in California in his post-playing days. On August 22, 2004, Nelson passed away at the age of 57.

AL OLIVER

Batted .303 with 219 HRs, 1,326 RBIs, and 1,189 runs scored in 18 seasons

Despite switching between the outfield and first base, Oliver remained a productive player for the Pirates through the 1977 season. Overloaded with quality outfielders and in search of pitching, Pittsburgh traded him to the Texas Rangers on December 8, 1977, as part of a four-team trade that also brought Bert Blyleven to the Steel City.

In four years with the Rangers, Oliver batted .324, .323, .319, and .309. In the spring of 1982, Oliver asked for a trade after the Rangers refused to renegotiate or extend his contract. At the end of spring training on March 31, the Rangers traded him to the Montreal Expos for Larry Parrish and Dave Hostetler. Oliver responded to the trade by leading the National League in batting average, hits, RBIs, and doubles. His power fell off in 1983, prompting the Expos to trade the seven-time All-Star to the San Francisco

Giants. After a short stint in the Bay Area, Oliver was dealt to the Philadelphia Phillies. He later played for the Los Angeles Dodgers before finishing his career with the Toronto Blue Jays in 1985. In the '85 Championship Series, Oliver went 3-for-8 and produced two game-winning hits.

After his retirement, Oliver became a board member for an organization in Arlington, Texas, called Suicide Is Not Painless, that helps youth to avoid suicide. In 1991, Oliver returned to baseball when he became the first head coach in the history of Shawnee State, located in his hometown of Portsmouth, Ohio. Oliver has remained active as a motivational speaker, often touring the country to address young people and students.

Oliver also became a deacon in his post-playing days. In an emotionally charged address, he delivered the invocation at the 2001 Hall of Fame Induction Ceremony—the same event that saw his onetime teammate, Bill Mazeroski, officially enter the Hall of Fame. Still active as both a deacon and a public speaker, Oliver lives in Portsmouth.

JOSE PAGAN

Batted .250 with 52 HRs, 372 RBIs, and 387 runs scored in 15 seasons

After the World Series, Pagan played for the San Juan Senators in the Puerto Rican Winter League. He endured a near-replay of a regular season injury —when he suffered a fracture in his right arm when he was hit by a pitch (earlier it was his left arm). Pagan returned to health in time for the start of the 1972 season, but once again played the role of utilityman. Pagan came to bat only 127 times, his lowest full-season total in a Pirate uniform. After the season, Pagan expressed his displeasure over the lack of playing time and indicated that he would prefer a trade to the American League. On October 24, the Pirates officially released him and Bill Mazeroski, but offered Pagan a managerial position in their farm system. Pagan instead decided to sign a player contract with the Philadelphia Phillies.

The Phillies planned to use Pagan as an occasional fill-in and tutor for a promising young third baseman named Mike Schmidt. The Phillies also decided to room Pagan with another youngster, first baseman Willie Montanez, who had suffered through a "sophomore slump" in 1972 and had struggled to fit in on a team that featured no other Spanish-speaking players. Pagan played very little for the Phillies in 1973, compiling an average of just .205 in only 78 at-bats. On August 16, the Phillies waived Pagan and announced plans to make him a fulltime coach. Although he hadn't hit much in limited duty, several Phillies players credited Pagan with helping to improve the play of both Montanez and late-blooming outfielder Bill Robinson.

Pagan returned to the Pirates' organization the following spring, when the team named him third base coach to replace Bill Mazeroski. Pagan served as a third base, first base, and infield coach until October 1978, when Joe Brown's successor, Harding "Pete" Peterson, decided to fire him. Pagan then managed the Oakland A's affiliate at Ogden, Utah, in 1979 and 1980. Now retired from baseball, Pagan lives in Sebring, Florida.

Pagan eventually realized that he would never become a major league manager and decided to give up managing entirely. He watched as other black and Latino candidates, like Frank Robinson, Cito Gaston, and Felipe Alou, earned opportunities at the major league level. Would Pagan have been successful as a big league manager? It's hard to say with certainty, but Pagan possessed all of the necessary qualifications: strategic intelligence, the ability to communicate in both English and Spanish, and the experience of playing for a World Championship team.

Bob Robertson

Batted .242 with 115 HRs, 368 RBIs, and 283 runs scored in 11 seasons

After his performance in '71, Robertson seemed on the verge of stardom. Robertson hit well at the outset of 1972, raising his average to the .300 level. Then, during a game at Wrigley Field, Robertson chased a pop-up off the bat of Ron Santo into foul territory. Near the dugout, Robertson ran into a small puddle of mud and slipped momentarily. Initially, Robertson felt little pain, but after the game his right knee swelled up. Robertson eventually underwent surgery to repair ligament damage.

During the course of his career, Robertson underwent two more operations on the knee, and three surgeries on his back. In 1974, he endured surgeries to both of his knees. The injuries and the operations curtailed Robertson's production, preventing him from becoming the "next Ralph Kiner" as the Pirates had once hoped. After hitting a combined 53 home runs in 1970 and '71, Robertson reached the seats only 48 times from 1972 to 1975.

On March 31, 1977, the Pirates released their one-time budding star. Robertson missed all of 1977 while rehabilitating himself after back surgery. In 1978, he made a comeback with the Seattle Mariners, and then spent a short time with the Toronto Blue Jays before retiring.

Robertson decided to start his own advertising agency, and also conducted motivational seminars. In 1990, he returned to baseball as the hitting instructor for the Columbus Mudcats of the Southern League, the Double-A affiliate of the Houston Astros. After retiring from baseball completely, Robertson has maintained connections with the game by attending many of the Pirates' alumni events and keeping close ties with the organization from his home in Maryland.

CHARLIE SANDS

Batted .214 with 6 HRs, 23 RBIs, and 15 runs scored in 6 seasons

Perhaps the least-known member of the Pirates' base 25-man roster in 1971, Sands struck out in his only World Series plate appearance and then went on to enjoy a productive season in the Dominican Winter League. When Bill Virdon decided to carry only two catchers in 1972, Sands failed to make the team's Opening Day roster. Outside of one pinch-hitting appearance in Pittsburgh, he spent most of the year at Triple-A Charleston. On April 2, 1973, the Pirates dealt Sands to the Detroit Tigers' organization for Chris Zachary; within three weeks, the Tigers sent him packing to the California Angels. Sands spent parts of two seasons in California before being released. He signed on with the Oakland A's, his last major league stop, in 1975. Sands finished out his playing career in the Pacific Coast League and the Mexican Pacific League.

After retiring from the game, Sands started up a chain of restaurants called *Charley's* throughout North Carolina and Virginia. He later sold the restaurant franchise and now lives in Fort Myers, Florida.

Although Sands played sparingly over a career that stretched from 1967 to the mid-1970s, diehard fans of Pittsburgh have not forgotten his timely pinch-hits during the championship season of 1971.

MANNY SANGUILLEN

Batted .296 with 65 HRs, 585 RBIs, and 566 runs scored in 13 seasons

After the Pirates' World Series victory, 1971 continued to be a prosperous year for Sanguillen. In December, his wife, Kathy, gave birth to the couple's first child, Manuel, Jr. The arrival of an eight-pound, 10-ounce baby boy capped off the best year of Manny's baseball life. With his personal life and baseball career at a high level, Sanguillen remained a durable and productive catcher for the Pirates from 1972 through 1975, save for an unsuccessful stint as the Bucs' right fielder in the aftermath of the death of Roberto Clemente. "I feel bad being here," he told *The Sporting News* in discussing his placement in Clemente's old stomping grounds. "I know I don't belong." It soon became obvious that Sanguillen did not fit in the outfield, as he committed six errors in the team's first 34 games in 1973. Bill Virdon wisely decided to move Sanguillen back to his regular position behind the plate.

Quickly re-acclimating himself to his favorite position, Sanguillen enjoyed his best offensive season in 1975, when he displayed increased patience at the plate and batted a career-high .328. After he had an injury-riddled 1976 season, the Pirates made an unpopular move by sending Sanguillen and $100,000 in cash to the Oakland A's for manager Chuck Tanner. Sangy played one productive season with the A's, as a catcher, first baseman, outfielder, and designated hitter. Unfortunately, Sanguillen did not fit in with the A's movement toward youth. On April 4, 1978, the rebuilding A's traded Sanguillen—this time back to the Pirates.

As a part-time player in 1979, Sangy contributed to the Pirates' "We Are Family" championship season. In Game Two of the World Series against the Baltimore Orioles, Manny lined a ninth-inning pinch-hit single against Don Stanhouse to score the game-winning run.

Sanguillen played one more season with the Pirates before being included in a trade that sent Bert Blyleven to the Cleveland Indians for four players on December 9, 1980. Sanguillen never played for the Indians, who brought his career to a halt when they released him on February 18, 1981. Later that year, Sanguillen declared that his sporting goods store in downtown Pittsburgh had gone bankrupt. One year later, he filed for personal bankruptcy. Although Sanguillen has had his share of financial problems, he has retained his ever-present smile and remains a popular figure around the country, often appearing in old-timers' games. Now retired, he lives in Del Ray Beach, Florida.

WILLIE STARGELL

Batted .282 with 475 HRs, 1,540 RBIs, and 1,195 runs scored in 21 seasons

Just two months after the 1971 World Series, Stargell underwent surgery for a cartilage tear in his left knee. Doctors who performed the repair expressed amazement at Stargell's willingness to play through the injury, which had bothered him most of the 1971 season. Stargell himself had complained very little about the pain in his knee; he had decided to finish out the season, realizing that the Pirates needed him to reach the playoffs.

After moving to first base in 1972, Stargell returned to the outfield in 1973 and led both the National and American leagues with 44 home runs, 119 RBIs, 43 doubles, a .646 slugging percentage, and 28 game-winning hits. Yet he again finished as the runner-up in the MVP balloting, this time to Pete Rose.

In the spring of 1974, Danny Murtaugh rewarded Stargell for his increasing leadership role—coming in the aftermath of the Roberto Clemente's death—by naming him team captain. Stargell became the Pirates' first captain since Bill Mazeroski, who had served in the role from 1962 until his retirement. In 1979, Stargell's leadership abilities became a national story. Now fully entrenched at first base, Stargell put up numbers that were far less impressive than the ones he had compiled in 1971 and '73, but he shared the MVP Award with Keith Hernandez of the St. Louis Cardinals. Stargell's vocal leadership abilities played as large a part in winning the MVP as his statistics. Becoming a father figure to the team's younger players,

Stargell popularized the practice of handing out gold stars (known as "Stargell Stars") to certain players and coaches after each game, for anything from advancing a runner to delivering the game-winning hit.

Unlike his post-season struggles in 1971, Stargell emerged as the star of the 1979 World Series. He batted .400 and powered three home runs with seven RBIs. During the Series, Stargell discussed the Pirates' remarkable unity, reminiscent of the great '71 team. "We have shown what men can do together," Stargell told a reporter from the *Washington Star*. "We have blacks, whites, Latinos, but we were family." Images of Stargell became synonymous with the "We Are Family" theme of the 1979 Pirates.

Stargell finished out his career with three seasons of part-time play before retiring at the end of the 1982 campaign. In 1988, in his first year of eligibility, Stargell gained election to the Hall of Fame. Stargell became the second 1971 Pirate to gain enshrinement in Cooperstown, joining the late Roberto Clemente.

After Stargell retired as an active player, he remained with the Pirates as a coach for one season, before moving on to the Atlanta Braves' organization in 1986. Stargell served as a coach and roving minor league instructor for Atlanta, while remaining active in community-oriented projects. As both a player and coach, Stargell successfully mobilized public awareness of a disease that had received very little publicity in the 1960s: sickle cell anemia, an illness that attacks blood cells, mostly in African Americans. Stargell made numerous public appearances in efforts to raise money to combat the disease.

In 1997, Stargell returned to the Pirates' organization as a special assistant to general manager Cam Bonifay. In the years after his return to the Pirates, Stargell became increasingly ill, stricken with both kidney disease and the onset of diabetes. With his weakening condition becoming noticeable, a frail Stargell appeared at the final game in Three Rivers Stadium on October 1, 2000.

Stargell's condition worsened during the winter, so much so that he was unable to attend the dedication of a bronze statue in his honor, which was revealed to the public on the last Saturday before the start of the 2001 season. Two days later, on April 9, 2001—the same day that the Pirates played their first-ever game at the new PNC Park—Stargell passed away at the age of 61.

RENALDO "RENNIE" STENNETT

Batted .274 with 41 HRs, 432 RBIs, 500 runs, and 75 stolen bases in 11 seasons

After batting .353 in 153 at-bats for the Pirates in 1971, the hard-hitting Panamanian batted .286 as a semi-regular in 1972, while splitting time between second base, the outfield, and shortstop. After the 1973 season, the Bucs alleviated their logjam at second base by trading Dave Cash and opening up an everyday position for Stennett. In 1974, Stennett responded to the challenge by hitting a solid .291 in a whopping 673 at-bats.

On September 16, 1975, Stennett enjoyed the finest moment of his major league career. He established a modern-day record when he went 7-for-7 against the Chicago Cubs at Wrigley Field. Two years later, with his batting average at .336 and his career ascending, Stennett fractured a bone in his right leg and suffered a dislocation of his right ankle. The mid-August injury ended his season— and the Pirates' pennant hopes.

Stennett returned to the Pirates in 1978, but he was clearly not the same player. Relegated to bench duty, Stennett remained with the Pirates through the championship season of 1979 before signing a free agent contract with the San Francisco Giants. In two seasons with the Giants, Stennett played poorly in the field and at bat, prompting his release. An unsuccessful comeback in the Montreal Expos' organization led to his premature retirement.

Eight years later, Stennett attempted a stunning comeback when he signed a minor league contract with the Pirates. Stennett went 2-for-3 as a pinch-hitter during the exhibition season, but had obviously lost much of his speed and defensive skills. When the Pirates released him on April 3, 1989, the team's director of minor league operations, Chuck Lamar, commented on Stennett's comeback attempt in an interview with the *New York Times*. "Rennie is one of those people who will think he can hit forever," said Lamar.

Now fully retired from the game, Stennett lives in Boca Raton, Florida.

Bob Veale

120-95 with a 3.07 ERA and 1,703 strikeouts in 1,926 innings over 13 seasons

In his first five appearances in 1972, a slimmed-down Veale struggled, giving up seven walks and 10 hits in nine innings. The Pirates responded by placing Veale on waivers. When no other major league team claimed him, Veale agreed to report to the Bucs' Triple-A affiliate at Charleston. On September 2, the Pirates sold Veale's contract to the Boston Red Sox, who were contending for the American League East title. Veale pitched extremely well in six games for Boston, hurling eight scoreless innings of relief, while picking up two wins and two saves. Veale pitched well enough for the Red Sox in 1973 that he became their second-best reliever, but his performance fell off in 1974, bringing an end to his 13-year major league career.

At the time, very few black men held managing or coaching positions at the major or minor league level, but Veale expressed a desire to continue in baseball. In 1976, Veale signed on as a minor league pitching instructor in the Atlanta Braves' organization. After a one-year stint as the pitching coach for the New York Yankees' affiliate at Greensboro, North Carolina, Veale landed in Utica, New York—Dave Cash's hometown—in 1984. There he served as pitching coach for the independent Utica Blue Sox, the champions of the New York-Penn League. Veale is now retired and living in Birmingham, Alabama.

Luke Walker

45-47 with a 3.65 ERA and 558 strikeouts in 824 innings over 9 seasons

Despite possessing a live arm and a fine curveball, Walker would win only 16 more games over the next three seasons—the last three of his major league career. Control problems, a bad back, and an occasionally sore elbow also plagued Walker, whose Pirate days came to an end in 1973, when the team sent him to the Detroit Tigers for slightly more than the waiver price of $20,000. He remained with the Tigers until April 6, 1975, when he was released at the age of 31, ending his career.

Unlike many of the 1971 Pirates who have remained in baseball after their playing careers ended, Walker decided to leave the game completely. Since his playing days, Walker has lived in Wake Village, Texas, where he has served as a sheriff.

MANAGER DANNY MURTAUGH

W–L record of 1,115-950 (.540) over 2,068 games and 15 seasons

After the World Series, Murtaugh told reporters that he would make a decision about returning within the next several weeks. "We'll have a family meeting, and discuss it—my daughter, my two sons, and my dear wife," Murtaugh told Joe Durso of the *New York Times*. "We'll sit down and vote. Of course, my vote will be the deciding one."

On November 23, Murtaugh announced that he would not return, marking the third time he had left the Pirates' managerial post. The Bucs tabbed coach Bill Virdon as his successor, and named Murtaugh a superscout, a job that would involve far less travel and stress.

Two days after his retirement announcement, Dick Young of the *New York Daily News* wrote a poignant tribute to Murtaugh. "This beautiful man," Young wrote, "related to all people, young, old, white, black, purple, star or 'scrubini.' He ran a loose clubhouse by most standards, I guess, but it was his, and the players didn't question it. Nobody on the Pirates hides in the trainer's room. There is always some kind of hilarity, wisecracking, practical joking going on in the clubhouse before a game. You walk in and you can't tell if the team is first or fourth. Same way with Danny Murtaugh. It had to be a reflection of him."

In 1973, with the Pirates struggling under the burden of losing Roberto Clemente, Bill Virdon's job fell into jeopardy. On September 6, with the Bucs having fallen three games back of the first-place St. Louis Cardinals, general manager Joe Brown once again called upon Murtaugh. The Pirates won eight of their first 11 under Murtaugh, prompting players like Dock Ellis to sing his praises. "He's a master of psychology," proclaimed Ellis in an interview with Murray Chass of the *New York Times*. "He doesn't tell you how bad you are; he tells you how good you are." Although the Pirates played well under

Murtaugh, they failed to make up the three-game deficit on the St. Louis Cardinals and finished second in the National League East. In 1974, the Pirates continued to play well for Murtaugh, who helped the club to the divisional title before falling in the playoffs.

Murtaugh guided the Bucs to a second straight Eastern Division title in 1975, only to lose to the World Champion Cincinnati Reds in the playoffs. In 1976, the Pirates fell back to second place. At the end of the season, Joe Brown announced his decision to retire as general manager. Only 48 hours later, Murtaugh followed with his own announcement. Having experienced a series of dizzy spells, he had grown tired of the day-to-day regime of managing. On October 1, just a few days before his 59th birthday, Murtaugh retired from the Pirates for a fourth time.

Unfortunately, Murtaugh's retirement did not last long. On November 31, 1976, Murtaugh suffered a serious stroke at his home in Woodlyn, Pennsylvania, and was taken to a nearby hospital in his hometown of Chester. Two days later, he died. Although Murtaugh looked much older—the effects of repeated heart trouble—he was only 59 years old.

Four days after his death, Murtaugh's funeral drew approximately 700 people. Several members of the 1971 Pirates paid their respects, including Manny Sanguillen, Bob Robertson, Jose Pagan, Willie Stargell, Al Oliver, Steve Blass, Bruce Kison, and Dave Giusti.

Throughout his career, the humble Murtaugh downplayed his own managerial skills. While he was blessed with a large supply of talent during his various terms of office in the 1970s, Murtaugh was smart enough not to undermine the success rates of those Pirates' teams. And given the unpredictability of baseball in general, and the penchant for player performance to fluctuate wildly from year to year, the Pirates' record under Murtaugh stood as a testament to his ability to extract the most from his players. He never overmanaged, and his teams rarely underachieved.

Pittsburgh Pirates Final 1971 Individual Statistics

Player	G	AB	R	H	BB	SO	HR	RBI	BA	OBP.	SLG.
Gene Alley	114	348	38	79	35	43	6	28	.227	.298	.342
Dave Cash	123	478	79	138	46	33	2	34	.289	.351	.354
Roberto Clemente	132	522	82	178	26	65	13	86	.341	.372	.502
Gene Clines	97	273	52	84	22	36	1	24	.308	.366	.392
Vic Davalillo	99	295	48	84	11	31	1	33	.285	.315	.383
Richie Hebner	112	388	50	105	32	68	17	67	.271	.331	.487
Jackie Hernandez	88	233	30	48	17	45	3	26	.206	.260	.300
Rimp Lanier	6	4	0	0	0	1	0	0	.000	.200	.000
Milt May	49	126	15	35	9	16	6	25	.278	.326	.429
Bill Mazeroski	70	193	17	49	15	8	1	16	.254	.308	.295
Al Oliver	143	529	69	149	27	72	14	64	.282	.323	.446
Jose Pagan	57	158	16	38	16	25	5	15	.241	.314	.342
Bob Robertson	131	469	65	127	60	101	26	72	.271	.358	.484
Charlie Sands	28	25	4	5	7	6	1	5	.200	.375	.400
Manny Sanguillen	138	533	60	170	19	32	7	81	.319	.346	.426
Willie Stargell	141	511	104	151	83	154	48	125	.295	.401	.628
Rennie Stennett	50	153	24	54	7	9	1	15	.353	.381	.458
Frank Taveras	1	0	0	0	0	0	0	0	...	...	...
Carl Taylor	7	12	1	2	0	5	0	0	.167	.167	.333
Richie Zisk	7	15	2	3	4	7	1	2	.200	.368	.467

Pitcher	W	L	PCT.	G	IP	H	BB	SO	ERA	SV
Steve Blass	15	8	.652	33	240	226	68	136	2.85	0
Nelson Briles	8	4	.667	37	136	131	35	76	3.04	1
Franklin Brosseau	0	0	...	1	2	1	0	0	0.00	0
Dock Ellis	19	9	.679	31	226.7	207	63	137	3.06	0
Dave Giusti	5	6	..455	58	86	79	31	55	2.93	30
Jim "Mudcat" Grant	5	3	.625	42	75	79	28	22	3.60	7
Ramon Hernandez	0	1	.000	10	12.3	5	2	7	0.73	4
Bob Johnson	9	10	.474	31	174.7	170	55	101	3.45	0
Bruce Kison	6	5	.545	18	95.3	93	36	60	3.40	0
John Lamb	0	0	.000	2	4.3	3	1	1	0.00	0
Bob Miller	1	2	.333	16	28	20	13	13	1.29	3
Bob Moose	11	7	.611	30	140	169	35	68	4.11	1
Jim Nelson	2	2	.500	17	34.7	27	26	11	2.34	0
Bob Veale	6	0	1.000	37	46.3	59	24	40	6.99	2
Luke Walker	10	8	.556	28	159.7	157	53	86	3.55	0

SOURCES

INTERRVIEWS

Steve Blass, via telephone, Cooperstown, New York, Winter-Spring 1996.

Nelson "Nellie" Briles, via telephone, Cooperstown, New York, Winter-Spring 1996.

Joe L. Brown via telephone, Cooperstown, New York, February 1998.

Dave Cash via telephone, Utica, New York, 1994.

Jim "Mudcat" Grant, Cooperstown, New York, February 2004.

Dave Giusti via telephone, Cooperstown, New York, Winter-Spring 1996.

Richie Hebner via telephone, Cooperstown, New York, Winter-Spring 1996.

Nelson "Nellie" King via telephone, Cooperstown, New York, January 1998.

Al Oliver via telephone, Cooperstown, New York, Winter-Spring 1996.

Bob Robertson via telephone, Cooperstown, New York, Winter-Spring 1996.

Willie Stargell, Cooperstown, New York, January 1998.

ARCHIVES

National Baseball Hall of Fame Library, Cooperstown, New York, player files and questionnaires.

PERIODICALS AND WIRE SERVICES

Associated Press
Baseball Digest

Black Sports Magazine
Boston Record American
Chicago American
Chicago Sun-Times
Christian Science Monitor
Gannett News Service
Houston Chronicle
Newark Star-Ledger
Newsday
Newsweek
New York Daily News
New York Post
New York Times
Pittsburgh Post-Gazette
Pittsburgh Press
Press Wire Service
Retrosheet
Sport
Sport Guide
The Sporting News
Sports Illustrated
Syracuse Herald American
Trenton Evening Times
United Press International

BOOKS

Markusen, Bruce. *Roberto Clemente: The Great One*. Champaign, Ill.: Sports Publishing, 1998.

Pittsburgh Pirates Press Guide: 1972

Street and Smith's Baseball: 1971

Total Baseball: The Ultimate Baseball Encyclopedia (8th edition)

Wagenheim, Kal. *Clemente!* New York: Praeger, 1973.

OTHER

Wayne, Michael. "The Integration of Baseball." Society for American Baseball Research presentation, 2003.

INDEX

ACKNOWLEDGEMENTS

Many people have contributed to the completion of this book, a process that has lasted nearly 10 years. From the National Baseball Hall of Fame Library, Freddy Berowski, Claudette Burke, Bill Francis, and Tim Wiles have all offered assistance. From the Pittsburgh Pirates' 1971 front office, public relations director Bill Guilfoile and Sally O'Leary have been especially helpful, Bill for his overall support of the project and Sally for providing me with contacts and updated information about the 1971 Pirates.

A number of the '71 Pirates have been kind enough to grant me interviews over the years. Thanks to Steve Blass, the late Nellie Briles, Dave Cash, Dave Giusti, Richie Hebner, Bill Mazeroski, Jim "Mudcat" Grant, Al Oliver, Bob Robertson, and the late Willie Stargell. Thanks also to general manager Joe Brown, coach Bill Virdon, and broadcaster Nellie King for their insights.

And special thanks to Maxwell Kates, for his thorough fact-checking of the manuscript and suggestions for improving its quality.